THE NORDIC WELFARE STATE IN THREE ERAS

The Nordic Welfare State in Three Eras
From Emancipation to Discipline

JOHANNES KANANEN
University of Helsinki, Finland

Routledge
Taylor & Francis Group

LONDON AND NEW YORK

First published 2014 by Ashgate Publishing

Published 2016 by Routledge
2 Park Square, Milton Park, Abingdon, Oxfordshire OX14 4RN
711 Third Avenue, New York, NY 10017, USA

First issued in paperback 2016

Routledge is an imprint of the Taylor & Francis Group, an informa business

British Library Cataloguing in Publication Data
A catalogue record for this book is available from the British Library

The Library of Congress has cataloged the printed edition as follows:
Kananen, Johannes.
   The Nordic welfare state in three eras : from emancipation to discipline / by Johannes Kananen.
      pages cm
   Includes bibliographical references and index.
   ISBN 978-1-4094-5773-2 (hardback)
1. Welfare state--Denmark--History. 2. Welfare state--Sweden--History. 3. Welfare state--Finland--History. I. Title.
   JC479.K363 2014
   361.948--dc23

2013023743

ISBN 13: 978-1-138-27073-2 (pbk)
ISBN 13: 978-1-4094-5773-2 (hbk)

Contents

Contents

List of Figures

List of Tables

Preface

This book has grown out of an interest in and concern about the change of course in Nordic welfare policy. In the 1990s, just as scholars such as Gøsta Esping-Andersen had famously indicated the distinctive characteristics of these welfare states, the Nordic governments began to endorse new ideas about national competitiveness, economic productivity and supply-side economics that seemed to compromise fundamental elements of past policies, such as universalism and redistribution. At the same time, scholars debated whether the Nordic model could even in theory be maintained under new conditions of economic globalisation.

I thought a historical perspective might clarify what was happening in Nordic welfare policy. The book at hand thus operates with a threefold periodisation of historical welfare state development in the Nordic countries: first, a period of development is identified until the two World Wars; second, a period of consolidation until the 1970s and 1980s; and third, a period of restructuring and renegotiation from the 1980s until around 2010. I believe this periodisation has helped to create a broad overview of the evolution of Nordic welfare states thus far.

Writing this book would not have been possible without help and support. I have discussed the themes of the book with many people, and I wish to thank particularly Henrik Stenius, Keijo Rahkonen, Hartley Dean, Jane Lewis, Olli Kangas, Peter Abrahamson, Risto Heiskala, Anu Kantola, Helena Blomberg-Kroll, Christian Kroll, Pauli Kettunen, Klaus Petersen, Jørn Henrik Petersen and Jon Kvist for giving important feedback and stimulus for my work. Any errors or shortcomings remain, of course, my own.

While working as a doctoral candidate at the Centre for Nordic Studies (CENS), University of Helsinki, I was able to benefit from a stimulating and intellectual atmosphere. For this, I am grateful to my CENS colleagues. I have also been greatly inspired by the aims of the Nordic Centre of Excellency, NordWel (Nordic Welfare States, Historical Foundations and Future Challenges, funded by NordForsk), a member of which I have had the privilege to be. Directed by professors Pauli Kettunen and Klaus Petersen, the NordWel network has been founded upon the idea that instead of being stable or static entities, Nordic welfare states are multilayered constructions that keep changing over time. Besides the opportunities for many fruitful conversations, the NordWel network granted me a research visit to the Centre for Welfare State Studies at the University of Southern Denmark, for which I am grateful. I have also been able to benefit from the research seminars at the Department of Social Research, University of Helsinki.

The Osk. Huttunen Foundation granted me a scholarship for a research studentship at the London School of Economics, for which I am grateful. I wish to thank the Eino Jutikkala Foundation and the University of Helsinki, for financial support. Most recently, I have been pursuing my research at the Swedish School of Social Science, University of Helsinki in the context of a Finnish Academy project on 'Power Shifts in Agenda Setting: The Making and the Challenging of the Finnish Competition State (POSH)'. I wish to thank the project team for inspiring co-operation, the Finnish Academy for generous funding and the Swedish School of Social Science for providing an excellent research infrastructure. Annika Wickman gave very helpful research assistance in the final stages of writing this book.

Finally, I am most grateful to my family. My parents, Pentti and Ulla-Britta, and my brother Markus have taught me and reminded me about the social value of individual intellectual pursuits. Pentti, my father, continues to be an important source of inspiration. My dear wife Maria has not only inspired me intellectually during our walks in the woods, but also supported and encouraged me much more than I could ever describe. Our son Eelis, who was born during the writing of this book, reminds me of what is important in life.

Johannes Kananen
Helsinki, September 2013

Chapter 1
Introduction

The age of modernity contains a promise of and a belief in increasing human welfare. During medieval and pre-modern times the majority of people lived in conditions in which even hard work could not necessarily guarantee survival. A person born in poor conditions could not be expected to change her/his situation much during the life course. At the same time, a small privileged minority lived their lives under conditions of relative luxury. Since the day the members of this small (often aristocratic) minority were born, they did not have to rely on any external sources in order to maintain comfortable standards through the rest of their lives. To paraphrase Henrik Stenius: 'You could perform your life drama badly or well, but once your hand was dealt, you could not ask for new cards' (Stenius, 2010, p. 36).

Modern Enlightenment brought along emancipation in different ways. The American and French constitutions, along with the slogan *'liberté, egalité, fraternité'*, created a hope that societies could be changed according to new, humane ideals. A modern trust in human reason liberated people from religious dogmas and hierarchies.

Perhaps most importantly, human creative potentials were liberated from previous bonds. Modern techniques of material production and modern ideas of equality allowed each individual to begin to reflect, more consciously than before, on their personal abilities, talents, hopes and aspirations, and on how to put these into use during their life courses. This transformation was associated with the emergence of modern sciences, modern states, modern cities, arts and infrastructure. To a lessening extent societies were structured on the conditions of a small privileged elite.

The transition to modern societies was not smooth or uncomplicated, as exemplified already by the French Revolution. The industrialisation of production was associated with an exploitation of workers, as famously pointed out by scholars, such as Karl Marx. The Christian Church and the more secular elites were not among the engines of change, but instead, sometimes acted as a source of conservatism and resistance. Thus, societal transformations were often associated with a contestation of former authorities.

The modern welfare state is another product of the Great Transformations (Polanyi, 1944) late nineteenth and early twentieth century societies experienced. The term 'welfare state' is often associated with the idea that all citizens are entitled to a minimum standard of living and basic services as a matter of social right (Dwyer, 2003; Dean, 2010; Kuhnle and Sander, 2010). Among modern welfare states, the Nordic ones are particularly interesting. The Nordic countries went through a fairly stable period of modernisation without the emergence of strongly differentiated class societies (as in England) or totalitarian political regimes (as in Germany, Italy or Spain, for instance). Furthermore, modernisation in the Nordic countries was associated with repeated and continuous redistribution of economic resources, coupled with ideals of universalism, solidarity and all humans being worth economic and social investments for the benefit of the future development of society.

Since the emergence of modern political ideologies, the Nordic countries have also been located – both geo-politically and ideologically – between socialism in the east and capitalism in the west (Alapuro, 2004), and have thus in a rather interesting way combined elements of both worlds. Most notably, the combination of the two worlds of socialism and capitalism was manifested in the original type of the modern welfare state that developed in the Nordic countries (for institutional characteristics of Nordic welfare states, see e.g. Esping-Andersen, 1990; Korpi and Palme, 1998; Castles, 2004).

Compared to many other so-called 'Western' countries, the processes of industrialisation began in the Nordic countries quite late and still continued in many ways during the twentieth century. Thus, with regard to economic production and standards of living, the Nordic countries did not before the twentieth century stand out as very special cases compared to other countries that were more advanced in these respects. Comparatively late industrialisation and urbanisation were not, however, the only aspects that distinguished the Nordic countries. Many of the necessary processes associated with the emergence of a modern economic order were in the Nordic countries associated with continuous redistribution of resources in society. The enclosures of common fields and the establishment of private landownership did not result in the kind of concentration of landownership that occured in Britain, where these processes allowed for rapid industrialisation and urbanisation. The timing of the modernisation of agriculture in the Nordic countries coincided, roughly speaking, with the emergence of modern political rights, whereas in Britain there was a long period of time between these processes.

The manifestation of modern societal impulses was disrupted throughout the world in the early twentieth century by two World Wars. As the Nordic countries were not significant military powers they were not major partners in shaping the destinies in Europe, but instead depended on others in the shaping of their own destinies as independent nation states. Although the continued existence of many Nordic nations was uncertain during the first half of the twentieth century, modernisation processes continued under an atmosphere of renewed optimism after the end of World War II. It was under this atmosphere of post-war regeneration that the well-known Nordic institutions of modern welfare policies were established with Sweden at the forefront of implementing policy and creating consensus between the labour market parties (Kettunen, 2011).

Convincing historical evidence about the emergence of comparatively equal social and political structures in the Nordic countries does not, however, imply directly that freedom of individual choice and self-expression have been established once and for all. The emergence of modern political institutions made it possible to formulate general political goals and to create an administrative apparatus in order to implement these goals. Yet, it is possible to remain quite sceptical towards the modern ideals of individual choice and self-expression, and an acquaintance with the social sciences does not necessarily weaken such scepticism. For instance, it is not hard to find evidence that in spite of the existence of modern social structures, people's choices regarding their individual lives tend to reveal quite systematic patterns so that gender, socio-economic background, occupation and geographical place of living tend to correlate strongly with many attitudes and choices that people have or make (Blomberg et al., 2012; Svallfors, 2012). Indeed, many of the social sciences that emerged in association with modern social structures have been preoccupied with analysing and mapping out such connections between these structures and people's behaviour. Findings in these areas legitimise questions about whether choices of economic and social participation can even in theory be thought of as individual by nature, or whether individuals are bound, to some extent, to be products of their social environment. From another perspective it may be asked whether individual choices – if they exist in theory – are bound to be egoistic choices that pay no regard to communal matters, or whether individual choices can contribute to solidarity and community development. Such questions touch the core of what modern societal impulses may be about, and what kind of social development is possible or desirable.

Studying Politics and Modernity

The main interest of this study lies in the unfolding of modernity – the associated international impulses and their manifestations in the evolving Nordic welfare states. In other words, the Nordic welfare states will be placed in the larger context of modern societal change. In order to get a grip on this endeavour, the first aim will not, however, be to present another pre-emptive definition of 'modernity' or to 'apply' any existing ones in 'practice'. Neither will the main focus be on the philosophical question of what distinguishes the modern age from pre-modern ages (for illuminating discussions about these questions, see Taylor, 1975, 1989; Wagner, 2001). Rather, the aim will be to establish a particular perspective (one specific point of view out of many possible ones) on modernity as a process which both emancipates and constrains individual human beings. Existing accounts and perspectives on societal development will be reviewed in Chapter 2. Emancipatory elements of societal development will be discussed in terms of the theories of T.H. Marshall (evolution of modern citizenship rights) and Amartya Sen (societal development and human 'capabilites'). These theories of societal development may be complemented by theories of human agency in the field of sociology. Based on these reflections, emancipatory societal development may be more generally understood as the modern process of liberating and enhancing human creativity – with primary reference to the potential that during the modern age, it has, in principle, become possible for an increasing number of people to begin more consciously than before to reflect upon their positions in society, and to seek to define their various goals in life in an individual manner.

On the other hand there are also many constraining elements associated with societal development. Despite elevated goals of emancipation, modern societies have not in a linear and determined fashion progressed towards this goal, but instead, there have been many previous constraints that modern impulses have been forced to 'penetrate through'. In addition, new constraints have emerged the more societal development has progressed. These constraints can be made subject to conceptualisation and increased understanding with the help of discussion by Karl Marx, Max Weber and Michel Foucault.

Thus, the main question this study seeks to answer is what the relationship between emancipatory and constraining elements has been throughout modern societal development in the Nordic countries. An initial observation is that different aspects of societal development are relevant to this relationship during different periods of time. Thus, there is no single institution or single political process that can be labelled 'emancipatory' or 'constraining'. In the early stages of modernisation it seems that the distribution of landownership has been crucial. In later stages modern welfare state institutions become part of the conscious management of this relationship between emancipation and constraint in societal development.

Although the aim is to complement existing perspectives and possibly open up new ones, this study will obviously draw on many findings presented in the existing body of academic literature on social and political change. In its efforts to contribute to the academic debate, the study will be placed in the juncture between the traditional disciplines of sociology, political science and history. Of these, particularly the discipline of sociology has largely grown out of a concern with how societies change and evolve during the era that has been labelled 'modern'.

Lately, the discipline of sociology has evolved from a dominant concern of societies as organic entities towards efforts to try to understand the further evolution of modern societies. In such efforts, the focus has ranged from accounts of 'information' or 'network' society (Castells, 2004; Kallinikos, 2006) and changes in the organisation of work (Boltanski and Chiapello 2005; Sennett, 2006; Julkunen, 2008) to accounts of 'detraditionalisation' and 'individualisation' (Giddens, 1991; Beck, 1992; Beck et al., 1994; Beck and Beck-Gernsheim, 2002; Touraine, 2002). In addition to these efforts to understand the further evolution of modernity, the idea of 'cosmopolitanism' has also emerged as a critique and reaction against 'methodological nationalism' (Beck, 2000; Chernilo, 2006), which may be interpreted as a reaction against the tradition of associating social issues with one particular nation state.

This study shares with sociological literature the interest in the evolution of modern societies – and the methods of relating particular events to general transformations. However, in sociological literature, there is often a lack of the political dimension of societal development and change in the sense that the study of the contents of state and government policies has usually been left to the discipline of political science. Thus, in an effort to relate political reforms to greater socio-historical transformations, this study will share a field of interest with the discipline of political science as well.

Particularly in Anglo-American political science there is a quite strong and vibrant tradition of comparative historical research about the relationship between the modern state apparatus and economic production according to the (capitalist) logic of supply and demand (for a review, see e.g. Mahoney and Ruschmeyer, 2003). Often aiming at quite holistic research settings, this branch of academic research has dealt with the question how politics and political forces are related to practical solutions in the management of modern nation states and their economies. Starting from the analysis of the emergence of various welfare states in industrialised societies (Wilensky, 1975) this academic tradition with its various sub-traditions has moved towards the study of 'varieties of capitalism' (Hall and Soskice, 2001) and the study of how political forces have reacted to the emergence of a new international economic order since the 1970s (e.g. McNamara, 1998; Scharpf and Schmidt, 2000; Pierson, 2001; Huber and Stephens, 2001; Blyth, 2002). Related to this Anglo-American branch of political science literature is a slightly more specific branch that to some extent can perhaps be regarded as its offspring, namely the branch of comparative welfare state studies. Particularly relevant for this study is the part of this literature that includes the Nordic countries in the analysis. In this respect, it is possible to detect an evolution from pioneering comparisons between West European 'centres' and 'peripheries' (Flora et al., 1983; Rokkan and Urwin, 1983; Flora, 1986) to the study of 'welfare regimes' (Esping-Andersen, 1990, 1999), and more recently, towards the study of the 'continuity of the Nordic model' (Kuhnle, 2000; Kuhnle and Alestalo, 2000; Rothstein, 2000; Kautto et al., 2001; Kangas and Palme, 2005; for a cross disciplinary approach, see Kettunen and Petersen, 2011) and the study of the emergence of the principle of 'reciprocity' or 'workfare' in welfare politics (Gilbert, 1992; Lødemel and Trickey, 2001; Jessop, 2002; Kvist, 2003; Kildahl and Kuhnle, 2005; Dean, 2007; Hvinden and Johansson, 2007; van Aerschot, 2008).

In addition to the aforementioned perspectives borrowed from political science and sociology, there is one more perspective that this study will seek to adopt. By including a historical dimension in the study, the aim here will be to establish a critical distance towards contemporary political reforms and societal transformations. Arguably, this distance is sometimes missing from studies in the field of political science in the sense that conceptualisations related to the present time are taken for granted. Michel Foucault termed the effort to create this critical distance a 'history of the present' (see also Kettunen, 2008, pp. 129–30). It seems that this kind of critical distance is most needed in relation to contemporary conceptualisations of 'globalisation' and the political challenges that are associated with this contested concept.

Methods of Research and Observation

In establishing a critical perspective with regard to contemporary socio-economic transformations, a study of history seems appropriate. But in order to avoid treating history as a linear progression towards the present, it also seems appropriate to try and distinguish between different historical periods and breaking points between these periods. In this study, the Giddensian notion of 'episodic history' will serve as a starting point for such a periodisation (Giddens, 1984, pp. 244–6; for an application, see Broman-Kananen, 2005, p. 33). In short, this understanding of history implies that instead of linear progression, historical change contains important breaking points, after which change assumes a new direction and a new logic. Thus, identifying one particular course of change in a particular historical period does not imply that one can necessarily predict the future course of history. Thus, an episodic understanding of history recognises both the contingency associated with historical change, and the possibility of stable and linear-like progression within a particular period. Chapter 2 will deal with the periodisation adopted in this study with regard to socio-economic change in the Nordic countries.

As the time frame is fairly broad – beginning from the eighteenth century and stretching until the early twenty-first century – the choice of the level of analysis is obviously a crucial choice as well. When previous studies have made efforts to achieve general characterisations of socio-economic change, they have usually sought to include as many countries as possible – for instance the totality of Organisation for Economic Co-operation and Development (OECD) countries or even larger numbers (see e.g. Esping-Andersen, 1990; Huber and Stephens, 2001; Swank, 2002; Iversen, 2005). When the number of countries is increased, although allowing for the identification of general trends, this is inevitably at the cost of precision with regard to the analysis of individual countries (in political science a related dilemma has been termed the 'small N' versus the 'big N' dilemma, see e.g. Blyth, 2002, p. 13; Mahoney and Ruschmeyer, 2003, p. 17). Although the strength of such research settings is the potential level of generality achieved, the weakness is that a great deal of information is lost in the crude quantitative observations that are made about each individual country. Problems regarding the loss of country-specific information may be solved by carrying out studies with international research teams (see e.g. Scharpf and Schmidt, 2000; Taylor-Gooby, 2004, 2005). If, however, findings are not compared along the way of the analysis, it is rather difficult to decide what the most important similarities and differences are, and findings on the general level may remain without the nuance that they could have had.

This study attempts to find a balance with regard to the level of historical analysis of socio-economic change by selecting three Nordic countries as main entities of comparison: i.e. Sweden, Denmark and Finland. The idea is that choosing these three countries will allow one to make observations that are potentially valid for all Nordic countries, even though Norway, Iceland and the Färö Islands are excluded from the study. The selection of countries has been made on the basis of geographical distribution and in an effort to include a representative selection of the Nordic 'Social Democratic' welfare states (cf. Lloyd, 2011). It is interesting to compare developments in these countries, where Social Democratic representation in politics has been strong, trade unions powerful and mutual exchange of ideas frequent (Petersen, 2011). Sweden, historically an old Empire and located geo-politically in the middle of the Nordic countries is usually regarded as a prime example of Scandinavia in international comparisons (Hilson, 2008, p. 179). Although this remains a topic of debate, it appears sensible to include this 'model country' in a comparative study. Including Denmark and Finland is justifiable on the grounds that they are border countries in the Nordic region; Finland sharing a long border with Russia, and Denmark being in a favourable position with regard to overseas trade with the west. Selecting three countries as main entities of comparison will, given the large time frame, allow for a detailed study of historical, cultural and political characteristics of each country.

Despite being interesting cases in modern socio-economic development, the Nordic countries are not similar in all respects. The 'East-Nordic' modern Swedish state is rather all-encompassing, having historically included both landowning peasants and organised workers in the processes of state formation. 'West-Nordic' Denmark has, despite a tradition of absolutism and serfdom, retained more liberal cultural and political traits against a tradition of stronger opposition between political elites and rural groups (see e.g. Knudsen and Rothstein, 1994, p. 218). Thus, including these two countries will provide an opportunity to compare two different historical traditions. Furthermore, including Finland will provide the opportunity to observe how a 'late-comer' follows the historical experiences of other Nordic countries. Norway has been excluded from the study since, in terms of more contemporary developments, it differs slightly from the three selected countries. Sharing features with both Finland and the two Nordic prime examples Sweden and Denmark, Norway was united with Sweden between 1814–1905 (Stråth, 2005), but unlike Sweden, Denmark and Finland, Norway later on adopted a path of socio-economic development outside the European Union (EU). Since the 1970s Norway has also been supported economically by large oil reserves. Sweden, Denmark and Finland thus constitute, perhaps, the most similar cases among the Nordic countries, which should allow for fruitful comparison of societal development.

Historical periodisations are always subject to debate, and by identifying a number of temporal divisions, this study does not wish to imply that the periodisation adopted here has somehow existed independent of historical interpretation (cf. Kettunen, 2008, p. 131). On the contrary, historical periodisation will be posited after a discussion of various perspectives on societal development (Chapter 2), and it will be argued that for the purposes presented here – i.e. given an interest in the emancipatory and the constraining aspects of societal development – the chosen periodisation appears fruitful. Two particularly important breaking points in history will be identified – the first one being the two World Wars during the first part of the twentieth century, and the second one being the socio-economic transformations of the 1970s. Before the two wars three modern impulses in particular 'penetrated through' remnants of pre-modern and medieval constraints. These impulses were:

1. The modernisation of agriculture and the associated shifts in economic production;
2. The establishment of universal education and literacy in particular; and
3. The emergence of the modern polity with modern political rights, e.g. universal suffrage.

These three impulses gave rise to a modern process of liberating and enhancing human creative potential that after the two World Wars was being pursued by means of new rationales and new institutions – in particular, the welfare state institutions that developed in a unique way in the Nordic countries.

It will be argued that the simultaneity of timing of the three key impulses during the nineteenth and early twentieth centuries contributed to enhanced emancipation in Nordic societal development – a development that progressed away from old medieval hierarchies towards a levelling out of socio-economic differences among the population. These two historical periods – the time before and after the two World Wars in the Nordic countries, will constitute the subject matter for chapters 3 and 4.

There are of course other important societal impulses that could, in addition to the aforementioned ones be associated with emancipation and a liberation of human creative potentials. One such impulse is what Therborn has labelled *de-patriarchalization* (Therborn, 2004, p. 73). Patriarchal social relations constituted, particularly for women, one of the strongest medieval constraints by denying women the opportunities to make individual choices concerning their own lives (for a discussion on women and the polity, see Benhabib, 1986, 1992).

In Europe the ideological bonds of patriarchy were challenged by J.S. Mill's treaties on *The Subjection of Women* (1869) and by Norwegian playwright Henrik Ibsen's play *A Doll's House (1879)*, where the heroine leaves a conventional marriage for an uncertain future (Therborn, 2004, p. 25). The Nordic countries were, in fact, together with (although independent from) the Soviet Union, pioneers in breaking the institutional rule of patriarchy: individualist and egalitarian conceptions of marriage were established in legislation in Norway in 1909 and in the following 14 years in the other Nordic countries as well (Therborn 2004, pp. 79–80). According to Therborn, de-patriarchalization progressed with, and allowed for secularization and democratization (Therborn, 2004, pp. 73, 78).

Although relevant to the relationship between emancipation and constraint in societal development, de-patriarchalization is not studied here as a distinct societal impulse. The reason is that out of the institutions mediating between individual and society, the institution of work, rather than the institution of the family will be the focus of this study. Both the institutions of work and family can be regarded as crucial societal institutions, and the Nordic countries certainly constitute interesting cases regarding the development of both (Daly, 2010). But the former institution is different in the sense that the political and public debate concerning its regulation is more explicit and encompassing, whereas changes in the institution of the family tend to be more complex as Therborn's study shows.

Regarding the time period after the 1970s the need for a critical distance from contemporary styles of reasoning becomes increasingly important in order to retain the perspective on the emancipatory and constraining aspects of societal development. A general shift of political and economic focus from the collective to the individual level occurred during the 1970s and 1980s. This is exemplified, for instance, by paradigmatic shifts from Keynesianism towards monetarist ideas (see e.g. McNamara, 1998; Blyth, 2002). Based on this observation, the following period after the historical break of the 1970s will be termed the 'renegotiation of the post-war collectivist social order', and after elaborating this idea in Chapter 5 the study will proceed by analysing this renegotiation process in the three selected Nordic countries in Chapter 6. The focus will be on the one hand on more institutional aspects of change (or policy outcomes), and on the other hand on more ideological aspects (or policy intentions). Analysing institutional and legislative change will be more detailed and context specific – whereas from a more ideological point of view the focus will be on how individual countries seek to adapt international ideological impulses at the local and national level.

Without a critical perspective it would become extremely difficult to decide which political and economic processes contribute to emancipation and which contribute to constraint as concerns socio-economic development. This difficulty becomes obvious when observing, for instance, the language and political rhetoric associated with one of the crucial reforms in this respect, i.e. the so-called 'workfare' reforms. Connecting social security benefits more tightly than before to the taking up of work activity, these policies are referred to as 'activation' policies, seeking to prevent 'passivation' among unemployed benefit recipients. Such policies could be thought of as contributing to emancipation in societal development, as they target individuals with, for instance, 'individual action plans' and other tailor-made measures designed to improve their abilities. On the other hand, these policies are associated with sometimes rather strict and detailed sanctions concerning non-compliance with administrators – which might mean that they could, on the contrary, be interpreted as contributing to constraint in societal development. Indeed, this issue is unsettled in existing research (for a survey of research in the field, see Gilbert, 1992; Torfing, 1999; Lødemel and Trickey, 2001; Jessop, 2002; Kvist, 2003; Kildahl and Kuhnle, 2005; Hvinden and Johansson, 2007; Dean, 2007; Keskitalo, 2007; van Aerschot, 2008; see also *Local Economy* Special Issue 5–6/2012).

Thus, more specifically, taking a critical distance regarding 'workfare' reforms will imply taking a critical distance from administrative concepts such as 'activation', 'passive social security benefits' and 'rehabilitation'. The primary task of the researcher in this area will be to identify the key historical transformations regarding social legislation – and doing this in a comparative manner will be one of the central aims in Chapter 6. In the case of 'workfare' reforms, this will involve the reading of key legislative documents, such as parliamentary acts and government proposals – in cases where such documents significantly reform the existing social policy system. When reading these documents the content will be placed in another context than that created by the original authors. In other words, the documents will be primarily read as key events in the historical process of liberating and enhancing creative potentials, and only secondarily as responses to the social and political challenges that the legislators often talk about in these documents. Creating such a perspective on legislative reform in no way predetermines the results of the analysis. On the contrary, it will allow for a critical contestation of implicit meanings and assumptions made in the texts.

In addition to studying socio-economic transformations after the 1970s and 1980s in the Nordic countries, Chapter 6 will also offer a perspective on ideological change during this period. In this respect key administrative documents stating the current aims, problems and goals of policy will be utilised in a similar critical manner as was adopted with the aforementioned 'workfare' reforms. Drawing on the work of political scientists, such as Hall (1993) and Blyth (2002), it will be assumed that the way policy makers perceive the social world matters with regard to the policies they pursue. It will be argued that political change occurs at the junction of international ideological currents and efforts to adapt them to local and national traditions and cultural characteristics. Regarding this issue, the interplay between international organisations, such as the OECD, and national governments, is highly pertinent.

Interpreting Political and Socio-historical Change

No sharp distinction between an observing subject and an observed object will be made in this study. Thus the method will be distinguished from strict hypothetico-deductive ones, where the observer creates a theoretical hypothesis which is then either falsified or verified (depending on the variant of the method) by empirical observation. Results are often presented in the form of general causal laws (e.g. more social democratic representation in parliament leads to more universal social policies). Instead of proving something positive and definite, the aim of this study will be to open up new perspectives of thinking – perspectives that hopefully stimulate discussion and thought in an open and ongoing manner. In other words, the goal is not to speak the final word on matters of socio-economic change. Rather, the aim will be to complement existing perspectives and possibly open up some new ones for further examination and debate. This method, inspired by hermeneutic and phenomenological thinking[1] implies, for instance,

---

1   Contrary to the hypothetico-deductive method, the phenomenological method proposed by Husserl is not built upon the condition that the individual life world should be excluded from the process of producing knowledge (Husserl, 1931; for a summary of

a certain openness concerning the definition of concepts (on open concepts, see also Wittgenstein, 1981). Instead of treating concepts as carrying one fixed meaning derived from the semantic or grammatical form of the concept, it will be acknowledged that concepts can have different meanings in different contexts – meanings that can be created by individual agents in order to communicate some idea they may have.

In the study of politics, a related methodological choice concerns whether policy outcomes (or structures) or policy aims (or intentions) should receive primary attention. If the former aspect is chosen as the primary focus, studies can for instance look at government spending on certain chosen items, for instance welfare policies (for an example of this method, see Kautto et al., 2001). If the latter aspect is chosen, studies might look at policy discourses (or policy paradigms), which contain definitions of the aims of policy and indeed the definitions of any key concepts that can be associated with politics (for two different ways of studying policy discourses, see Schmidt, 2002 and Alasuutari, 2004). There are risks in both choices. An exclusive focus on structural (or material) aspects may lead to ignorance of important power struggles in relation to central political aims and the meaning of key concepts in politics. An exclusive focus on discursive aspects may result in ignoring important structural transformations (for instance with regard to the distribution of resources and the different living conditions between people) in society and in reducing historical change to changes in intentions. It seems, however, possible to include elements of both policy outcomes and policy aims. Indeed, it may be the case that a sharp distinction between the two perspectives is unnecessary as long as the study does not remain one-dimensional.

This methodological middle way between agency and structure, combined with an episodic, non-linear understanding of history, also appears to allow for a certain degree of flexibility concerning the study of different periods in time. Thus, for instance, the post-war period will not require as much detailed attention as the periods before and after, as the literature about post-war socio-economic developments in the Nordic countries is substantial and the perspectives are many. However, it appears that the period after the Golden Age, i.e. the period after the 1970s will require even more detailed attention than the pre-modern times for at least two reasons. Firstly, a survey of existing academic literature shows that a great many questions remain unanswered regarding politics, agency and socio-economic change after the 1970s. It also appears that there is room for conceptual clarification about how we should study the period after this decade. Secondly, when approaching contemporary times, observations about historical developments acquire a different character compared to earlier times. The criteria according to which relevant events can be distinguished from irrelevant events

---

Husserl's phenomenology, and its relation to Alfred Schutz's ideas, see Heiskala, 1997, pp. 347–51, for a distinction between the 'interpretative' and 'explaining' scientific traditions, see von Wright, 1990).

become increasingly blurred, which must be compensated for by a denser and
more detailed focus of study.

There is one rather crucial and important strand of academic debate that this
study also seeks to contribute to – through combining the variety of perspectives
mentioned in this introductory chapter. This is the debate on the 'continuity of the
Nordic welfare state model' (see e.g. Kosonen, 1998; Kuhnle, 2000, p. 54; Kuhnle
and Alestalo, 2000, p. 15; Rothstein, 2000; Hvinden et al., 2001; Kautto et al., 2001;
Andersen et al., 2007). After the success of identifying various 'welfare regimes'
adding to our understanding of the unique characteristics of the Nordic countries
in post-war socio-economic development, this strand of academic literature has
been concerned with whether the unique characteristics of Nordic welfare states,
such as universalism, inclusion, state provision and redistribution, have persisted
since the transformations of the 1970s and 1980s. This issue, together with other
general observations made during the course of the study, will be addressed in the
concluding Chapter 7.

Chapter 2
Perspectives on Societal Development

Elevated Enlightenment Slogans and Social Reality

Western modernity brought along with it a number of noble and elevated promises for the improvement of general life conditions in human societies. Many of these promises were summarised in the French Revolution slogan 'liberty, equality and fraternity'. Compared to medieval and feudal ideas, they contained an increased trust in the capacities of each human being to shape their own destinies. The first advances of the modern natural sciences transformed the medieval way of viewing the world, and this transformation gave rise to a more general promise of human 'Enlightenment' (for conceptual and philosophical discussions on modernity, see e.g. Taylor, 1975, 1989; Benhabib, 1987, 1992; Wagner, 2001).

Societal development became subject to reflection and assessment – for instance through the birth of the social sciences (e.g. Wagner, 2001, pp. 15–36). In other words, the birth of modern societies was accompanied by efforts to establish a conscious relation to societal development in order to understand it, and perhaps also in order to influence the direction of this development.

One of the first milestones in establishing this consciousness was the observation of a gap between the elevated promises of modernity and the existing social realities in the Western world. Perhaps one of the most influential formulations of such an observation was put forward by Karl Marx. His work has not only influenced classical sociological and economic thinking but also the development of political ideologies around the world. Marx's multidimensional work cannot be considered in any great detail here, but a few central concepts with special significance regarding the key tensions in modern capitalist production are worth mentioning.

In relation to economic modernisation the commodification of land was one of the main conditions for agriculture becoming an economic activity with similar aims to the emerging enterprises of the market economy (Polanyi, 1944). For instance, after agricultural modernisation farms could sell food abroad and produce economic gains. Similarly, the commodification of labour was another condition of differentiated production and economic efficiency. Marx's work focuses, among other things, in great detail on the processes regarding the commodification of labour. He points out that the market relations that are necessary for a capitalist economy, exemplified by the exchange of commodities and money, are not natural relations but in a way, transformations of the social relations in which labour is embedded:

People place in a thing (money) the faith which they do not put in each other ...
that thing is an objectified relation between persons; because it is objectified
exchange value and exchange value is nothing more than a mutual relationship
between people's productive activities. (Marx, 1986, p. 51)

The significance of this is that labour occurs naturally (see also Blyth, 2002) in a
series of social relations without which the commodity form of labour would not
be possible. The commodity form of labour is thus dependent on, for instance,
the health and well-being of the worker, and that she/he is able to sustain a living
outside work as well.

By selling their labour power to someone who privately owns the means of
production, labour is, according to Marx, alienated from what it produces, from
its natural social relations, and ultimately each labourer from her/himself.[1] Marx
foresaw the end of this alienation in the collective or social ownership of the
means of production, something he thought would occur by historical necessity
as a consequence of the internal laws of the capitalist economy. The alienation of
workers is a mere historical phase that is situated between the pre-modern forms
of bonded labour and socialism.

Marx's understanding of labour seems to presuppose a parallel between
the amount of work within the economic sphere and the goods needed for the
subsistence of humans. In a capitalist economic order, all work done in addition to
what is needed for the subsistence of people is, according to Marx surplus labour
that works in favour of the capitalist by accumulating private wealth. In other
words, there are according to Marx two elements in the products of labour in
capitalist societies – the amount of labour that is needed in order to sustain human
societies or 'necessary labour', and the amount of labour which serves to create a
gain for the capital owner or 'surplus labour'.

Arendt has criticised Marx for failing to produce a proper distinction between
labour and work. She distinguishes between the labouring *animal laborans* who is
driven by the needs of its body and between *homo faber* who uses his (sic) hands.
The main division between the two is that the former does not use its body freely,
whereas the latter does (Arendt, 1958, pp. 86–7; 118). In Arendt's view Marx
fails to recognise almost completely the concept of work, and thus the *homo faber*

---

1   In Marx's writings the contrast between 'work' and 'labour' is also of central
importance. It is not, however, immediately clear what Marx means with his concept of
'work'. Rahkonen has noted that on the one hand it appears that 'work' is for Marx a
universal characteristic that can be ascribed to man irrespective of cultural and historical
context. On the other hand, Marx appears to think that 'work' is a historically constructed
phenomenon that takes a quite specific form in modern societies (Rahkonen, 1984,
pp. 16–18). According to Rahkonen this is a contradiction that Marx himself was not
necessarily aware of. On the other hand, Marx's ambiguity regarding the concept of 'work'
can be thought to show that it is a multidimensional concept – perhaps indeed an open
concept (cf. Chapter 1).

element of human action. If Arendt's critique is taken seriously, it could be argued that work in the sense of *homo faber* is not alienating since it involves a sense of freedom quite different compared to labour in the sense of *animal laborans*. Continuing this train of thought, it could be argued that a socialist society is not the necessary outcome of the development of capitalist societies, as Marx suggested. Instead, the main issues for the organisation of capitalist production would be to deal with the exploitation of labour and create conditions in which societies could make the most out of human work.

Nevertheless, Marx's analysis must be understood in the context of early industrialisation when the workers of the time were subject to challenging conditions. From this point of view, Marx's second key concept, exploitation seems rather accurate, illustrated in the following vivid manner:

> ... In its blind unrestrainable passion, its were-wolf hunger for surplus-labour, capital oversteps not only the moral, but even the merely physical maximum bounds of the working-day. It usurps the time for growth, development, and healthy maintenance of the body. It steals the time required for the consumption of fresh air and sunlight. It higgles over a meal-time, incorporating it where possible with the process of production itself, so that food is given to the labourer as to a mere means of production, as coal is supplied to the boiler, grease and oil to the machinery ... Capital cares nothing for the length of life of labour power. All that concerns it is simply and solely the maximum of labour-power, that can be rendered fluent in a working-day. (Marx, 1986, p. 151)

Marx's views contributed to the emergence of an international workers' movement. The workers saw a disparity in power in labour relations in the sense that the worker seemed more dispensable to the employee than the job was to the worker. That is, the worker was more dependent on work than the employer was dependent on a particular individual as an employee, given a sufficient supply of labour. The mobilisation of workers provided the emerging trade unions with concrete means to compensate for the disparity in power relations – they could go on strike. This potentially non-violent weapon was indeed used many times to promote a change in workers' conditions. But perhaps more importantly, in addition to establishing collective bargaining, the political mobilisation of workers allowed for the development of legal regulations of the labour contract. As workers gained representation in parliament, the issues regarding the labour contract could be debated and become subject to legislation and regulation. Thus, the democratic social order also provided means to peaceful resolution of the raised concerns – something that did not seem self-evident given the circumstances of early modern societies.

The Form of Societal Development: T.H. Marshall and Citizenship Rights

As noted above, Marx may be regarded as a thinker who expressed the discrepancy between the elevated promises of modernity and the sometimes harsh realities of the labouring majority of people. The many interpretations of Marx' views of societal development in the form of 'Marxism' or indeed 'socialism' exemplify the extent to which the modernisation of Western societies was a rather unstable process associated with potential conflicts between opposing interests in society. Revolution and violent overthrow of existing political regimes was sometimes the explicit aim of socialist or communist political parties who referred to Marx (and perhaps also Engels) when constructing their political agendas. On the other hand, the so called 'communist threat' forced many non-communist governments to carry out social reforms as part of an effort to contain the spread of radical ideas (see e.g. Korpi, 1981, pp. 167–221; Baldwin, 1990, p. 59; Pierson, 2004, p. 3; Kaspersen, 2005, pp. 64–9).

About a century after the publication of Marx's works we find within the discipline of sociology – the establishment of which Marx influenced a great deal – a view on societal development that takes the class division of society as a starting point, but that at the same time recognises ways of balancing capitalism. This view, which contrasted the establishment of national citizenship rights with the inequalities produced by the class division, was formulated by T.H. Marshall a few years after World War II. Contrary to Marx, Marshall did not focus on the inherent contradictions of capitalist societies, but instead on legislative efforts to alleviate some of the adverse consequences of capitalist production – particularly social inequality.

In his essay *Citizenship and Social Class* (1950) T.H. Marshall associated the establishment of citizenship with societal development.[2] He divided citizenship rights into three categories – civil, political and social – and argued that during pre-modern times these three strands of citizenship were 'wound into a single thread' (Marshall, 1950, p. 11, see also Dwyer, 2010, pp. 39–49). By this he

---

2   In his 1950 essay T.H. Marshall formulated his problem area by referring to late nineteenth and early twentieth century economist Alfred Marshall, who held that societal progress would result in every man being, by occupation at least, a 'gentleman'. Commenting on this view, T.H. Marshall wrote that 'His faith was based on the belief that the distinguishing feature of the working classes was heavy and excessive labour, and that the volume of such labour could be greatly reduced. Looking round he found evidence that the skilled artisans, whose labour was not deadening and soul-destroying, were already rising towards the conditions which he foresaw as the ultimate achievement of all. They are learning, he said, to value education and leisure more than "mere increase of wages and material comforts ... they are steadily becoming gentlemen"' (Marshall, 1950, pp. 4–5). When describing his own aims regarding the conceptualization of citizenship, T.H. Marshall wrote that: '... the modern drive towards social equality is, I believe, the latest phase of an evolution of citizenship which has been in continuous progress for some 250 years' (Marshall, 1950, p. 10).

meant that a single societal institution could possess functions associated with each of these three strands of citizenship. Later each of the three strands became associated with different institutions. Civil rights, e.g. the right to own property, the right to conclude valid contracts, freedom of speech and the economic right to work, became associated with the courts of justice, the task of which was to ensure that these rights were enforced in a fair manner. Political rights, i.e. the right to participate in the exercise of political power for instance by voting, became associated with parliament and the councils of local government – and finally, social rights or 'the range from the right to a modicum of economic welfare and security to the right to share to the full in the social heritage and to live the life of a civilised being according to the standards prevailing in the society' (Marshall, 1950, p. 11) became associated with the educational system and the social services. Especially in Britain, modern citizenship was established in three waves so that civil rights developed in the eighteenth century, political rights in the nineteenth century, and social rights in the twentieth century.

In the essay from 1950 (based on a series of lectures he delivered at Cambridge University) Marshall was particularly interested in ascertaining to what extent the establishment of social rights (in the form of state education, social benefits and social services) was related to the alleviation of social inequalities. He seemed to think, along the lines of Alfred Marshall, that citizenship rights granted a degree of equality between the members of a national community – within the superstructure of economic inequalities (Marshall, 1950, p. 77). In other words, he did not think that social rights would make social inequalities or the class system disappear completely. Instead, he argued that:

> The extension of the social services is not primarily a means of equalising incomes ... What matters is that there is a general enrichment of the concrete substance of civilised life, a general reduction of risk and insecurity, an equalisation between the more and the less fortunate at all levels – between the healthy and the sick, the employed and the unemployed, the old and the active, the bachelor and the father of a large family. Equalisation is not so much between classes as between individuals within a population which is now treated for this purpose as though it were one class. Equality of status is more important than equality of income. (Marshall, 1950, p. 56)

Marshall also pointed out that modern citizenship rights were balanced by a set of duties, such as the duty to pay taxes and insurance contributions and the duty to attain a basic level of education. He also pointed out that each citizen had a duty to work – so that work was in fact simultaneously a right and a duty for a citizen (cf. Kettunen, 2008, p. 156).

Both Marshall's and Marx's works highlight important aspects of societal development in the nineteenth and twentieth centuries. Marx's ideas and his later influence on social and political development suggest that it is worth paying attention to the radicalisation of the workers' movement and the emergence of tensions between different interest groups within society – and to the ways in which these tensions are potentially solved. Marshall's notion of the development of modern citizenship shows that at different periods of time different aspects might be relevant for a single element of societal development. In relating the development of citizenship to history Marshall does not primarily seek to find historical predecessors of modern social rights, but identifies instead a functional differentiation of the three elements of citizenship that develops in three 'waves' during three consecutive centuries.

The Content of Societal Development: Amartya Sen and Human Capability

Marx looked at societal development, the evolution of economic production and some fundamental tensions associated with it. Marshall, for his part, recognised a development towards formal equality between citizens in terms of rights and obligations.

Whereas Marshall can be thought of dealing with the *form* of societal development with an underlying concern of equality, providing another influential perspective, Amartya Sen may be thought of dealing with its *content* with the underlying concern of freedom. Sen's *capabilities* approach identifies a two-way relationship between social arrangements to expand individual freedoms, and the use of individual freedoms not only to improve the respective lives but also to make social arrangements more appropriate and effective (Sen, 1999, p. 31). Thus freedom is viewed as the primary end and principal means of development (Sen, 1999, p. 36).

Sen's view on development is to a great extent that of the individual – as a contrast to Marx who regarded what he called the *economic base* as crucial, and to Marshall, who looked at formal rights. Sen distinguishes between substantive freedoms and instrumental freedoms, the former of which include elementary capabilities like being able to avoid such deprivations as starvation, undernourishment, escapable morbidity and premature mortality, as well as the freedoms that are associated with being literate and numerate (Sen, 1999, p. 36). Instrumental freedoms include political freedoms, economic facilities, social opportunities, transparency guarantees (or trust) and protective security. According to Sen, 'these instrumental freedoms tend to contribute to the general capability of a person to live more freely, but they also serve to complement one another' (Sen, 1999, p. 38). 'Capability' thus becomes a central notion in Sen's approach to development, which can in a slightly simplified manner be seen as the freedom to achieve various lifestyles (Dean, 2010, pp. 82–9).

When giving reasons for expanding the common economic perspective of primarily looking at economic growth as the indicator of development, Sen refers to Aristotle (Sen, 1999, p. 14). Economic wealth or income is not good (in a normative sense) in itself, but only as a means to other ends, such as the opportunities wealth can bring. This point derives from the Aristotelian distinction between 'making' (*techne*) and 'acting' (*praxis*), the former of which may be associated with the generation of wealth. The good that should be valued in itself is to be found in the realm of *praxis*, rather than in the realm of 'making' (see also Guy, 1991). Sen also notes that the development process in many economies has started with 'the replacement of bonded labour or forced work with a system of free labour contract and unrestrained physical movement' (Sen, 1999, p. 28).

Sen's approach to development is highly original and his notion of freedom can be, for instance, clearly distinguished from utilitarian and libertarian conceptions of freedom. The capability approach aims at considering development not only in terms of economic growth, but also in terms of what consequences development may have for human agency. In Sen's view, the arrangements that facilitate development can be both results of capability and means to increased capability.

Martha Nussbaum has presented a rigorous application and extension of the capabilities approach after extensive co-operation with Sen (e.g. Nussbaum, 2000). Both Sen and Nussbaum draw on Rawlsian concepts of freedom, and freedoms, that every rational individual would choose regardless of the situation and plans or goals in life. Even slightly more explicitly than Sen, Nussbaum refers to Aristotelian distinctions between *techne* (making, producing), *poesis* (action as means to something else) and *praxis* (doing, acting that is good in itself) in her definition of 'capability':

> Instead of asking about people's satisfactions, or how much in the way of resources they are able to command, we ask, instead, about what they are actually able to do or to be. (Nussbaum, 2000, p. 12)

Simlarly to Sen, Nussbaum thus distances herself from utilitarian approaches, as well as approaches that equate development with economic growth. In a somewhat Kantian fashion, she insists on a moral philosophy, where every individual should be treated as an end rather than as a means to something else. Nussbaum's stress on doing or being is also reminiscent of Erik Allardt's distinction between 'having' (economic resources), 'loving' (social relations) and 'being' (existential dimension, Allardt, 1996). Nussbaum's focus is global and her special attention is on the position of women who are unable to live a dignified life because they are women (a striking example of this is the 'missing women' figure by Nussbaum and Sen; see Nussbaum, 2000, p. 4).

Both Sen and Nussbaum stress the universality of the capability approach, but the normative message is clearer in Nussbaum's work, as she aims at 'locating injustices in need of urgent attention' (Nussbaum, 2000, p. 71). She also provides a list of 10 explicit 'functional capabilities' that include: life, bodily health, bodily integrity, senses, imagination and thought, emotions, practical reason, affiliation, (respect for) other species, play and control over one's environment (Nussbaum, 2000, pp. 78–80).

Both Nussbaum's and Sen's important characterisations of the capability approach seek to capture and approach many aspects of what it is to be truly human and lead a fully human existence. Nussbaum stresses clearly that her normative focuses are on capabilities and not functionings. The main reason for this is that she assesses what she calls the 'paternalism' argument to be strong enough to restrain her from proposing what people should or should not do. All the capability approach aims to do is to set the scene for everyone, so that people can choose whatever lifestyle they want.

Agency and Structure

The relationship between individual and society appears important because, as both Marx's and Marshall's works suggest, it keeps changing over time. In medieval or feudal times many individuals faced rather radical social constraints, for instance in the form of bonded labour, but Marshall's work shows how the privileges enjoyed during medieval times by a small minority gradually started to expand in the form of modern citizenship rights. Marx's work on the other hand reminds us that the dissolution of social constraints is not an uncomplicated process.

Both Marx and Marshall largely dealt with the relationship between individual and society through the concept of class (Marshall derived his own concept of class largely from Marx's class theory, see e.g. Marshall, 1950, pp. 86–113). Although Marshall argued that citizenship rights alleviated social inequalities in capitalist societies, he held the view that class affected the *Lebenschance*, or social opportunities (a term borrowed from Weber) of an individual. A worker faced significantly different opportunities in her/his life compared to a person belonging to the middle or upper classes – for instance related to career choice, place of living, and so on (Marshall, 1950, p. 92).

This view raises the question of agency: if belonging to a certain social class influences one's life, should we think that individuals are mere 'products' of social circumstances? To what extent is there room for individual choice or individuality if social structures constrain our life choices? Or even more extremely formulated: should all individual characteristics be reduced to the characteristics of social structures such as class?

These are questions that sociologists have preoccupied themselves with since the founding of the discipline. It appears also that the perspective on societal development, to some extent, depends on the perspective on individual agency. After all, societal development is the consequence of human action, but there are many possible ways to understand how human beings interact with one another.

Whereas Sen's perspective on societal development could be labelled individualist, both Marx's and Marshall's views contain elements of 'functionalism' – a strand of thought that stresses the *differentiation* of modern societies (e.g. Joas, 1996, pp. 223–44). Functionalist thought – which for decades dominated the academic understanding of both societal development and individual agency – has, however, a tendency to reduce the behaviour of individual action to the characteristics and functionings of social systems.[3] This tendency may be due to an aspiration to find causal, law-like patterns in societal development – slightly similar to the patterns described in the natural sciences, and evolutionary biology in particular.

There are two theories that provide convincing syntheses of functionalist and individualist understandings of agency – both in original, and thus in slightly different ways. Giddens's theory of the 'structuration' of societies seeks to bridge the gap between functionalism and individualism. Joas's theory of the 'creativity of action' seeks to overcome the rigid abstractions associated with categorising action as either 'rational' or 'normative' or something else. It is worth taking a closer look at these theories, given the connections between agency and societal development.

According to Giddens, social structures are not something external to the individual that impose restrictions on individual behaviour from the outside. Rather, structures are both enabling and restricting at the same time, and they do not exist without a constant production and reproduction over time by individual agents (Giddens, 1984).

Giddens exemplifies this by pointing towards day-to-day routines. These, on the one hand serve as maintaining – or producing and reproducing social structures, but at the same time they are necessary for the individual in order to maintain a continuous sense of self, a sense of autonomy and ontological security. The individual maintaining of the self is done by a constant reflexive monitoring of day to day activities. According to Giddens, this involves both a practical and a discursive consciousness about what is going on in individual action. A reflexive human subject is able to increase and enhance her/his consciousness about the motives of her/his actions.

Thus, according to the Giddensian theory of structuration, structures in spite of involving rules that put limits on individual behaviour also enable the individual to maintain a continuous sense of self. For Giddens, the reflexive monitoring of action may contain the source of motives in individual action, and furthermore, individuals themselves are aware of these motives and are capable of reflecting on the grounds of these motives as well. The main implication of Giddens's theory is thus that through a conscious monitoring of action, the individual may increase her/his capability of defining the goals for her/his own biographical life project. Reflexivity serves simultaneously the purpose of maintaining a sense of self, and placing one's actions in the context of an individually defined life biography.

The Giddensian conception of agency may be backed up by the theory of the 'creativity of action' formulated by Joas. He notes that previous action theories

---

3 The development of functionalist thought in sociology may be traced from Durkheim to Talcott Parsons, and later to such contemporary thinkers as Niklas Luhmann and Jürgen Habermas. However, the two latter scholars provide such complex accounts of both agency and development that it may be too simplistic to label them 'functionalists' (for a discussion and analysis, see Kangas, 2006).

have tended to create types of action, such as rational or normative action, but have been compelled to construct a residual category where all other types of action, e.g. non-rational action have been placed. Thus, these theories have not quite succeeded in providing accounts of the whole spectrum of human activities. According to Joas:

> The alternative ... is to regard creativity as an analytical dimension of all human action. It then becomes possible firstly, to view all action as potentially creative and not only one particular concrete type of action, and, secondly, to ascribe structural features to human action as such which can be summarised under the label of 'creativity'. (Joas, 1996, p. 116)

To treat 'creativity' not as an additional category of human action besides other possible types already points towards aspects of individuality and autonomy vis-à-vis structures, institutions, or indeed social class. Therefore, it is worthwhile to take a closer look at how Joas understands creativity as a dimension of all human action.

According to Joas, intentional goals of action are not constructed in a pre-situational state independently from the world, and then applied to various situations as assumed in the Parsonian means-ends schema. The 'creativity' of action in this sense is that, similarly to pragmatist theories, it is not even necessary to clearly define goals before acting on a particular situation. Instead, goals can be subject to reflective redefinition according to the situation. Another interesting aspect of both Giddens's and Joas's action theories is that they do not seem to operate with a strict distinction between subject and object – i.e. the agent and her/his surroundings. Both Giddens and Joas in overcoming these dualisms refer to childhood development and argue that although a sense of self that is separate from its corporeal surroundings is a condition for action, it is only gradually developed in childhood. Drawing on Winnicott's work, Joas shows that the sense of self emerges through transitional objects and situations, which are not strictly either internal or external, but 'test cases' where the child is able to test their positive and negative emotions and their influences on the external world that gradually becomes perceived as being independent of the child's wishes. Play is according to Winnicott and Joas a transitional situation in which the child is in complete control and able to creatively define the course of events that often contain fragments of perceived external things, and yet it is a situation where the child is interacting with something beyond its inner world. Thus, play represents a prime example of the creativity of action. Setting goals for action may occur in a similar way, creatively, in the situation in which action takes place (Joas, 1996, p. 167).

On the basis of the discussion of various perspectives on modern societal development, it has been possible to establish a few starting points. Firstly, there appears to be a great gap between the elevated promises of modern Enlightenment and the harsh social realities pointed out by Marx. However, it is possible to create a perspective on both the form (Marshall) and the content (Sen) of societal development, so that these to some extent reflect the elevated promises (equality and freedom). In addition, it is possible to ascribe a certain degree of autonomy to individual action (Giddens) and creativity (Joas), so that social structures do not necessarily have to be seen as only constraining, but can also be perceived as enabling individual action. Indeed, Giddens's theory of the structuration of society suggests that it is worth observing how the constraining and enabling aspects of social structures evolve over time.

The Liberation and Enhancement of Human Creative Potentials

Parallell to the way social structures like 'glue' contribute to a moral order keeping society together and integreated, or to put it in Giddensian terms, provide the necessary continuity for maintaining a sense of self, human creativity, as a basis of all material and cultural human activity allows societies to evolve through time. Creativity in this sense is not necessarily associated with creating something completely novel, which might be called an innovation. Although the word creativity is many times used to mean the capacity to innovate, there is a wider meaning of the concept, which corresponds to a fundamental human functioning.

The potential to create something new from an abstract idea is perhaps the main distinguishing feature between human beings and animals. Creativity is present in simple repetitive activity, as well as complex, large-scale innovations with vast consequences. For instance, laying bricks on top of each other in order to build a house is creative action in so far as the builder has an idea of the complete house and the process of accomplishing the completion through different stages of development.

We may imagine the first immediate needs for which human beings must use their creativity. These are, of course, the needs to have food and shelter as humans live as physical beings on earth. As long as these needs persist, human beings must use a certain amount of creativity to meet them. This point has been formulated by Aristotle in his distinction between 'making' (*techne*) and 'acting' (*praxis*) and it is referred to frequently by scholars such as Sen and Benhabib. In Aristotle's terminology, 'making' belongs to the realm of necessities which must be organised somehow so that societies may develop.

Apart from being a theoretical and conceptual issue, the social organisation of creativity is also a historical issue. Understanding the ways in which creativity is organised is fundamental to understanding the development and evolution of societies. Associated with the transition to modernity there appears to have been a historical shift in the relationship between 'making' and 'acting'. Whereas formerly the majorities of the populations were preoccupied with producing the material necessities for sustaining human life (nutrition and shelter), after this shift the share of such population groups has tended to decline. In principle, this allowed people to start reflecting upon their positions in society, on their inclinations, talents, preferences and goals in life – in other words, to focus more on 'doing' or 'acting' rather than 'making'.

From this perspective modern societal development may be understood as the *process of liberating and enhancing human creative potentials*. Modern societies appear to have been subject to three impulses of key importance. First, there appears to be a *temporal* impulse in the liberation and enhancement of creative potentials. This occurred when medieval ways of agricultural production transformed into more modern forms – a process which was much influenced by the progress of the natural sciences and the development of new techniques of production. Agricultural modernisation allowed for another key development, namely industrialisation, but it was also accompanied by an important change in the conception of landownership – something that Marx and Polanyi (1944) have discussed extensively – namely the establishment of private landownership and the 'commodification' of land. What was formerly perceived as natural environment or the king's property could gradually become private property. Polanyi has noted that the commodity form of land is a fiction, but nonetheless a fiction that modern capitalist production is founded upon – similarly to the commodity form of labour.

The temporal impulse related to the modernisation of agriculture consists of liberating a great deal of biographical time previously tied to the production of necessities. This liberated biographical time could, in principle, be used for goals determined more individually – goals that might relate more to individual inclinations, talents, preferences and so on. Marx has, of course, shown that liberated biographical time frequently became subject to exploitation by factory owners, but this does not prevent one from recognising this temporal liberation in principle.

Two other key impulses that are part of the liberation and enhancement of creative potentials may be derived more directly from the works of Marshall and Sen. The second one may be thought of as a *reorientative* impulse, by which individuals gain the capacity to reflect upon their position in society and to act in accordance with societal arrangements. In practice, this occurs in modern societies through the educational system, which is a social service that Marshall recognised as a key element of social rights (cf. Buchardt et al., 2013). More specifically, literacy may be thought of as a condition to think and act in accordance with existing societal arrangements – a condition which Sen and Nussbaum recognised as a basic condition for human capability (see also Freire, 1974 for a discussion of literacy and 'critical consciousness'). Thus, whereas the temporal impulse liberates biographical time from the production of basic needs, this second impulse contributes to the reorientation of this liberated biographical time towards goals defined more individually.

The third impulse of the liberation and enhancement of human creative potentials may be thought of as concerning *the relationship between the individual and society*. A condition for modern emancipation was that feudal arrangements of hereditary privilege were removed. As discussed above, T.H. Marshall recognised this as crucial for the development of civil and political rights. The medieval relationship between individual and society was transformed. Gradually, the formal privileges enjoyed by a small elite during medieval times were extended so that all citizens were able to vote, express their opinions, influence the management of political affairs and apply for public offices. In other words, the emergence of the modern polity may be thought of as the third impulse associated with the liberation and emancipation of human creative potentials – an impulse that could also be termed *the societal management of human creative potentials.*

Thus, three impulses seem crucial from the point of view of the modern process of liberating and enhancing human creative potentials:

1. The modernisation of agriculture and the 'commodification' of land (temporal impulse);
2. The emergence of universal education (reorientative impulse); and
3. The emergence of the modern polity (impulse related to the societal management of creative potentials).

As noted above, this threefold perspective on modern societal development is neither self-evident nor uncomplicated, and it is worth discussing the more constraining and oppressing aspects of societal development as well, in order to complement the picture.

Techniques of Normalisation, Latent Power and the Constraints of Action

As far as the basic democratic political rights are concerned, e.g. universal suffrage, freedom to express one's opinions and form parties etc., one only needs to consider the number of authoritarian regimes in Europe since the nineteenth century (e.g. Spain, Italy, Germany) and the picture of a smooth transition from a pre-modern social order to modern democracy is distorted. The rise of fascism in particular is an issue that historians have yet to come to terms with.

A great deal of social research and social theory has been dedicated to the critique of modernity with an effort to doubt the emancipatory aspects of modern societal development referred to above. This research usually does not, however, take its starting points from the rise of fascism, but rather from issues of power and ethics. One quite influential critic is Foucault, whose thinking has influenced several disciplines, including philosophy, sociology and history. Foucault is a highly original thinker who escapes categorisations. His work has many dimensions and levels and as it provides an influential position in the central issues regarding the transformations of modern societies, some aspects of Foucaultian thinking are worth exploring from the point of view of societal development. Foucault seems to take a categorically opposite position to everything that was said above about the modern process of liberating and enhancing creativity.

Contrary to, for example, Marshall, Foucault does not see the emergence of modern political rights primarily as a shift in the distribution of power from the few to the many. Rather, he points towards a radical qualitative shift in the sense that power, along with the establishment of modern democracies and modern societies, is transformed from being manifest to being latent, from operating physically on human beings to influencing the subconscious. Power is, according to Foucault, distributed more evenly within society, but instead of liberating people, it puts people under constant surveillance by being present everywhere and at all times. Here the emergence of clinical knowledge, such as medicine and psychology has played a key role in Foucault's view.

When assessed against the background of the promises of modern democracies – embedded in a language of freedom, justice and rights, Foucault's position may seem as either far-fetched, radical or overly pessimistic. The careful way by which he aims to illustrate power contains, however, several insights that can hardly be overlooked in any political research. In his work, Foucault chooses to operate with metaphors and not with conceptual abstractions – a method he masters in a most powerful and persuasive manner.

Foucault's metaphors often aim at describing processes of normalisation, which can be regarded as one of the central themes in his work. The reader is given the opportunity to extend these metaphors and in this way gain an increased understanding of history. However, it must be pointed out that history in the traditional sense of chronological events is not the main topic of Foucault's work. Rather, his main interest can perhaps best be characterised as thought systems (Rabinow, 1984). Of Foucault's many influences, perhaps the concept of governance (Miller and Rose, 2008) and the method of discourse analysis are the most central.

According to Foucault, the external orders imposed upon man by the church or the sovereign ruler during pre-modernity were replaced by *normalisation* i.e. the imposing of norms that are derived from the social body. These norms are not normative in the moral or ethical sense, but norms that can be derived from scientific measurements – for instance of means and averages. According to Foucault, the main task of modern societies was to generate a social order in which normalisation was carried out most efficiently and economically. To Foucault, however, normalisation primarily served the function of maintaining certain power relations. In terms of power relations, modern societies were largely characterised by the rise of the bourgeoisie into power.

Among Foucault's main metaphors for normalisation are the prison, the army, the police, the hospital and the school, the evolution of which he describes in great detail. The prison and the penal system, for instance, underwent a significant change in the face of modernity. During modernity, legal punishment was transformed to serve the function of normalisation. Punishment was no longer concerned with redemption, but became more of an effort to change the behaviour of the criminal so that she/he would fit into mainstream society. In prison, each inmate was kept under surveillance, and a diverse range of methods was applied to record and examine their behaviour, for instance from a medical or psychological point of view.

An often-quoted illustration of surveillance that Foucault uses in his *Discipline and Punish* (Foucault, 1977) is the Panopticon designed by the British utilitarian, Jeremy Bentham. The Panopticon is an ideal architectural design that could, for instance, be used in prisons in order to make surveillance as effective as possible. The genius of the Panopticon is that each prisoner can be observed without them having the possibility of being sure whether at any given point in time they are being observed or not. Therefore, in a sense, they become their own guards, as, in principle, the central tower would not even have to be manned to achieve the same result.

The metaphor of the Panopticon, which was never applied in reality as such, but which served as a model for many actual prisons, can be extended to represent a technique, or technology of normalisation – panopticism. Foucault argues that techniques of making individuals and people visible for observation are a central characteristic of modern societies. Military barracks, hospitals, schools and even working class housing estates have, according to Foucault, been built in order to govern the space in which individuals move (Foucault, 1977, pp. 170–76). The mechanical eye, the camera, can also easily be made to serve the purposes of observation, and can also be seen as a technology of normalisation. Observation (or panopticism) and surveillance would thus appear to have at least two dimensions. First, it may detect deviation from the norm, and second, it encourages individuals to correct their own behaviour in the knowledge of being observed.

Other technologies of normalisation include discipline and examination. Discipline is a central feature of many modern institutions, the army being probably a prime example. Discipline has of course existed long before modernity, but not as a means of normalisation. The examination, on the other hand is an effective technology in recognising deviance from the norm. Examination is present most notably in schools but also in medical or psychological treatment where patients are examined by a doctor. Therefore, Foucault treats knowledge and power as largely inseparable. Power is associated with the capacity to define truth and falsity.

Foucault's notion of the modern polity presents a clear challenge to the perspective according to which modern societal development is primarily about emancipation or liberation of human creative potentials. Foucault's work could indeed be interpreted as suggesting the contrary. This does not, however, render the perspective on the more emancipatory aspects of modernity obsolete. Rather than simply denying all potentially enabling or emancipating characteristics of modern societal development on the grounds that Foucault has presented one could, for instance, interpret Foucault's work as an invitation to form a balanced view. Hence, both emancipatory and constraining elements of societal development could be acknowledged, or indeed the question whether either element dominates could be left open for research on particular circumstances during particular historical periods.

When relating the Giddensian and Joasian views on the human subject to the Foucaultian notion of normalisation, one could perhaps say that in principle, it is possible for individuals to become conscious of the various normalisation techniques they encounter, and take them into consideration when defining the goals of their individual life courses. This might even be seen as an ethical choice since it may often seem more advantageous for an individual not to consider any possible normalisation techniques, as it would imply the questioning of authority and existing power relations.

Periodisation of Societal Development

Instead of progressing teleologically towards a predestined goal, history is associated with breaking points that mark a qualitative change in the development (cf. Giddens, 1986). In other words, after such a breaking point historical and societal change takes a completely different shape and proceeds according to a quite different logic compared to the time before the breaking point.

In the following analysis of the Nordic countries before the World Wars, the emphasis will be placed on the historical manifestation of the three impulses that emancipatory societal development consists of (i.e. the modernisation of agriculture, the establishment of universal education and the emergence of the modern polity), and on the question whether there is something uniquely Nordic with regard to these developments in Sweden, Denmark and Finland. It also seems rather obvious that the two World Wars should be regarded as a breaking point in the histories of these countries. The two World Wars were decisive for the fates of two out of the three nation states selected for this study. Denmark was for a period of time occupied by Germany, and Finland, after having experienced a brutal civil war, struggled to maintain its independence between German and Soviet influences (Hentilä et al., 2002, pp. 241, 263–70; Kaspersen, 2005, p. 64). The post-war developments in these countries to some extent reflected efforts to deal with the fateful experiences of the wars.

Thus, we may anticipate that after the two World Wars the logic of societal development has been somewhat different compared to the period before the wars. In the Nordic countries, the wars were followed by the institutionalisation of the modern welfare state – something the organised labour movement and Social Democratic parties pursued with remarkable success in all Nordic countries (see e.g. Baldwin, 1990; Esping-Andersen, 1990, 1999; Karisto et al., 1998; Kettunen, 2006; Pierson, 2006). This was, of course, to some extent a development shared by the entire Western world, and the post-war period was characterised by both tensions and balance-seeking between the Western super power, i.e. the US and its Eastern counterpart, the USSR.

As the interest of this study lies in the emancipating and the constraining aspects of societal development on the one hand, and on uniquely Nordic characteristics on the other hand, the institutionalisation of the modern welfare state should be considered important. However, there is another associated aspect that appears particularly crucial regarding the period after the two World Wars. As this aspect is not entirely obvious on the basis of the discussion of societal development so far, it is worth pointing to the theories of another influential figure in social theory, namely Max Weber.

According to Weber, 'bureaucracy inevitably accompanies mass democracy' (Weber, 1968, p. 983). This is quite easy to see as the management of a polity with its differentiated institutions and functions – in the context of modernity, for instance schools, hospitals, the police, the army, and, depending on the role of the state in the economy, the development and maintenance of means of transportation, supply of energy and water, and so forth – require a rationalised structure in order to be administered efficiently. The simultaneous processes of democratisation, modernisation and economic growth contained the opportunity, in principle, for all people to be part of this administration in the modern society, as opposed to pre-modern and feudal times when public offices were typically restricted to particular groups of people in society.

Not only was the bureaucratic form of organising work relevant for state agencies and institutions, but, as Sennett (2006) has pointed out, it was a significant structuring principle for private enterprises as well. This was because not only was bureaucracy an efficient and rational form of organising work, it was also an inclusive one as well: when each and every one was given a place within the organisation, they felt part of a greater whole with a purpose which could potentially give meaning to peoples' lives. Each office of the organisation defined the talents and skills a person needed for inclusion, and the obligations he or she had to fulfil (Sennett, 2006, p. 30). Bureaucracy thus had a wider social significance as well.

The separation between the person who holds the office in a bureaucratic organisation and the actual office – the personal qualities of the office holder, his emotions, passions and desires and the purposes of the single office as a part of the whole organisation, represents an important and crucial point in the bureaucratic form of organising work. According to Weber, a successful bureaucracy depends on the 'dehumanisation' of the office (Weber, 1968, p. 975) so that it functions rationally and predictably like a part of a machine. The 'office' may thus, in a sense, categorically exist independently from the office holder, and the qualities and skills needed for the fulfilment of the duty implied by the office can be defined without regard to any person in particular, but instead, they can (and must) be derived from the purposes and functions of the whole organisation. In practice, this is exemplified in the fact that the qualifications needed for an office can be made subject to legal specification – they are not subject to circumstantial or contextual definition but can be made timeless and universal by stating them in the law.

It may be justifiably asked where creativity can exist in this kind of bureaucratic organisation. Weber indeed invented a much-used analogy of the 'iron cage' when describing the inhumane characteristics of bureaucracy. Sennett has used an analogy of 'living in a house you have not designed' (Sennett, 2006, p. 31), where the office holder of a fixed-function organisation slowly crawls up (or down) the hierarchy, step by step as if living someone else's design. These characteristics may be regarded as constraining.

Sennett makes a few more important points about the Weberian bureaucracy. First of all, and not without significance to creativity, the bureaucratic form of organising work contains an interpretative modulation of orders as they pass down the hierarchical pyramid (Sennett, 2006, p. 34). Therefore, at the different levels of the chain of command, there is always some 'room for manoeuvre', interpretation and discretion when passing down, or executing tasks. This interpretation occurs, however, without questioning the general rationale of the bureaucracy. For Sennett, this was the main reason why Taylor's scientific analyses of the factory never seemed to resemble reality. Secondly, the bureaucratic pyramid has been an important condition for the welfare state. Benefit recipients were obliged to behave like officeholders in the Weberian sense rather than as individuals with distinctive life histories (Sennett, 2006, p. 33).

The points made by Weber and Sennett have at least two implications for the study of the post-war period in the following chapters. Firstly, the collectivism of modern bureaucracies appears to evolve after World War II. Secondly, changes in the organisation of work during the same period should be paid attention to.

Regarding the first point, it is necessary to think of the differences between modern and medieval bureaucracies in order to see how the collectivism has evolved,. As noted already, prior to the establishment of modern bureaucracy, offices in the management of political affairs were not open to all, but instead, were allocated on the basis of birth status. Modern bureaucracy with its collectivist structures contributed to establishing a kind of meritocracy in which birth status no longer mattered when selecting people for public offices. Instead, it was thought that the desirable qualities of an officeholder could be defined at the collective level, and the extent to which an individual fulfilled these qualities could be assessed at the individual level.

One of the main arguments that will be developed in chapters 4 and 5 is that this collectivist aspect of modern bureaucracy did not remain in a stable manner the source of meritocracy throughout the period after World War II. Indeed, it appears that after having contributed to emancipation, collectivism turned into a source of constraint, and gave rise to a new societal impulse. In chapters 4 and 5 it will be argued that this new impulse may be characterised as a *renegotiation of the post-war collectivist social order* that began to take shape after the 1970s. This renegotiation process involved the questioning of the foundations of the post-war order, and efforts to find new directions for societal development, and it may therefore be regarded as a breaking point in historical change similar in scale to the two World Wars.

Thus, on the basis of the discussion so far, three distinct historical periods emerge. In the following chapters, each of these three periods will be studied with a particular interest in the Nordic countries. The study will be concerned with the emancipatory and the constraining aspects of societal development – by looking at the manifestation of impulses relevant in each particular historical period.

Chapter 3 will be concerned with the period up to World War II, and the focus will be on the manifestation of three modern societal impulses, and on whether there was anything uniquely Nordic in these developments. Chapters 4 and 5 deal with the period until the breaking point of the 1970s and 1980s with a view to the characteristics of the Nordic welfare states and in relation to earlier historical developments. In addition, these chapters seek to describe the evolution of the collectivist character of societal institutions. Chapter 6 deals with the period after the breaking point of the 1970s and 1980s until around 2010, with a focus on the outcomes of the renegotiation of the post-war collectivist social order.

Regarding the third historical period, i.e. the period after the 1970s and 1980s, it will be argued – and this will become more evident once the study of the preceding historical periods has been carried out – that the renegotiation of the post-war collectivist social order has resulted in two interesting developments in particular.The first element will be arrived at when considering what kinds of reform processes the post-war Nordic welfare states have been subject to since the 1980s and the 1990s. One characteristic of the post-war Nordic welfare states has been that rights to social security (public insurance against e.g. ill health, old age, unemployment and disability) have been based on the principles of universalism and citizenship (see e.g. Kildal and Kuhnle, 2000). In the Marshallian sense, one could argue that social rights were rather extensively developed during the post-war period in the Nordic countries. These social rights were, however, subject to considerable reforms after the 1980s, and the balance between rights and duties was altered by a series what may be termed'workfare' reforms (workfare = work-for-your-welfare, Lødemel and Trickey, 2001; Kvist, 2003; Hvinden and Johansson, 2007).[4] These reforms implied that basic income support benefits were more closely tied to the take up of work. It can be argued that these reforms constitute the foundation of a new social order that has gradually emerged in the Nordic countries since the 1980s – particularly if one thinks of income support legislation as the minimum terms and conditions of the social contract.

The second interesting element in the renegotiation of the post-war collectivist order will be arrived at when considering that post-1980 workfare reforms have not been a phenomenon unique to the Nordic countries. In fact, the term 'workfare' is of American origin (Lødemel and Trickey, 2001, p. xi), suggesting that the ideas underlying the reforms have travelled to the Nordic countries from abroad. Put simply, the logic is that the more generous a social security system is, the less incentives it contains for the take up of work which, in turn is a disadvantage to economic growth. This type of argument is a part of a new set of international ideas that challenged post-war Keynesian thinking at the end of the 1970s and early 1980s. It will be argued in Chapter 5 that this new set of international ideas constitutes a policy paradigm that has dominated the renegotiation of the post-war

---

4　Nordic governments do not use the term 'workfare' about legislation that redefines the rights and obligations of social security benefit recipients. Instead, they use terms such as 'activation' and 'rehabilitation'.

collectivist social order. For individual countries there has been a choice between being part of the international political order (and adapting to these new ideas) or becoming isolated. The study of the two preceding historical periods will show what kinds of national characteristics and traditions are at stake in these efforts to balance international ideas and local traditions after the 1980s.

We are able to summarise the perspectives on each historical period this study will adopt. The focus will be on the evolution of the emancipating and the constraining aspects of societal development in the sense discussed above. This will, among other things, allow us to ask how the modern process of liberating and enhancing human creative potentials has progressed during these three periods. It must be emphasised, that the study in no way assumes in advance that all actual historical developments have, as a matter of course, contributed to the liberation and enhancement of creative potentials throughout all three historical periods. On the contrary, this is an issue that will be returned to in the concluding part of the study.

Table 2.1   Periodisation of modern historical and contemporary societal development

	Key ideological transformations	Key structural/ institutional transformations	Indicators of key transformations
Period of modernisation (up to World War II)	Replacement of medieval notions of individual and society with the ideals of the Enlightenment, establishing the idea of a nation state	Modernisation of agriculture, industrialisation/ urbanisation, establishment of universal education, establishment of a modern polity	Literacy rates, suffrage, percentage of workers in agricultural work
Post-war period (up to the 1970s)	Establishment and application of Keynesian economic ideas and Beveridgean social policy ideas, balancing socialism and capitalism	Institutionalisa– tion of the welfare state, evolution of the collectivist character of social structures	Social security legislation, social service legislation, legal tradition (e.g. common law vs civil law)
Renegotiation of post-war social order (up to 2010)	Replacement of old Keynesian ideas with new ideas about national competitiveness in a global world economy	Reformulating previous collectivist structures, finding new sources of social order	'Workfare' reforms, finding a balance between international ideas and local traditions, organisation of work

Table 2.1 summarises the aspects of the three historical periods that this study is concerned with. The three historical periods are separated, in accordance with the episodic understanding of historical change, by the two breaking points identified above. The two World Wars constitute the first breaking point, and the discontinuities of the 1970s constitute the second breaking point. It must be noted, however, that these periodisations are somewhat tentative at this stage. The study of the individual countries will show that the breaking points vary to some extent in time depending on the circumstances in each individual country. For instance, the World Wars did not constitute such a significant breaking point in Sweden as they did in Denmark and Finland, where a greater degree of instability was experienced at the time. Furthermore, as we shall see in the following chapters, the various modernisation processes associated with the first historical period in the table occurred much later in Finland than in the other Nordic countries.

Therefore, at this stage the identification of breaking points and central elements will only serve as a guideline, directing the research towards aspects that will hopefully illuminate the proceeding of the liberation and enhancement of human creative potentials – as well as the constraining aspects associated with it.

Chapter 3
The Emergence of a Modern Social Order

The analysis will now turn to the Nordic countries with the aim of demonstrating the manifestations of three emancipatory societal impulses recognised in the previous chapter. These are:

1. The modernisation of agriculture (the temporal impulse);
2. Establishment of universal education (the reorientative impulse); and
3. The establishment of the modern polity (the relationship between individual and community).

Together these emancipatory impulses can be regarded as the modern process of 'liberating and enhancing human creative potentials' which gradually replaced the constraints associated with the medieval social order – constraints that kept the majority of the population occupied with producing the necessities for maintaining social life. In practice these constraints included forms of bonded labour and perceptions of the determining nature of birth status.

In the following, Sweden will be presented first, followed by the presentation of Denmark and Finland. This is because (with or without justification) Sweden is often thought of as the 'model' Nordic country (see e.g. Hilson, 2008). Therefore, it seems justified that Sweden is presented first so that the country then constitutes a basis for further comparisons with the other Nordic countries.

As indicated in Table 2.1 specific 'indicators' will be followed when assessing the manifestations of the three selected emancipatory impulses. It will not, however, be claimed that these indicators are exclusive or objective criteria for the manifestation of each impulse in time (statistics of these and other indicators can be found in Flora et al., 1983). Each of the three impulses has been fruitfully studied from a variety of perspectives. Henrik Stenius has, for instance, studied the emergence of the modern polity from the point of view of voluntary associations – a perspective that also involves considerations for emancipating and constraining aspects of societal development (Stenius, 1980, 2010).

The aim here will be to illustrate how the three chosen historical processes (modernisation of agriculture, establishment of universal education, emergence of modern polity) have occurred – involving many interesting features that constitute potentially something uniquely Nordic. Establishing certain common criteria will constitute a comparative ground, against the background of which these potentially uniquely Nordic features may become apparent.

Regarding the modernisation of agriculture, the common indicator for deciding when this occurred in the history of a specific country will in the following analysis be the point in time when less than half of the workforce was occupied with agricultural production. Thus, the historical processes contributing to the decline in the share of the agricultural workforce will be reviewed in each selected country. In the sections concerning the modernisation of agriculture, some statistical data illustrating the distribution of landownership, demographic development and employment patterns will be presented. The data presented are not directly comparable across countries. However, the statistics will hopefully help readers to create a more comprehensive picture of the particular historical processes in each country – e.g. the pace of modernisation and changes in the distribution of landownership.

Regarding the establishment of universal education, the criterion for its realisation will not be when it was established in legislation, but instead, when the educated generation may have been considered literate. Admittedly, this is a rather basic criterion of education, but as we shall see, the point when all children were literate has typically been much later in time compared to when state provided education was established in legislation. Literacy also corresponds with the requirements of capability in Sen's and Nussbaum's sense, and with the requirements of 'critical consciousness' in Freire's sense (Freire, 1974).

Regarding the establishment of a modern polity, the chosen criterion will be the point in time when suffrage was universal. This may be regarded as a criterion, according to which all adult citizens are considered equal members of the polity. Again, the processes leading up to this point will be reviewed, as many interesting ideological and institutional changes have accompanied the establishment of universal suffrage in the three countries analysed here.

Sweden

Modernisation of Agriculture: Enclosures and Redistribution of Landownership

Two partly simultaneous historical processes were associated with the early modernisation of Swedish agriculture. There was firstly a change in the *conception* of landownership and secondly, the establishment of private landownership *in practice*. The enclosure of common fields was associated with both processes. Here the main interest will be in reviewing the contours of these historical processes in order to establish a comparative basis for the review of the Danish and the Finnish cases.

Table 3.1 shows the approximate development of the distribution of landownership in Sweden during the eighteenth and the beginning of the nineteenth century. Before 1680, the nobility had possessed about two thirds of the land but as the table shows, the establishment of modern conceptions of landownership implied some significant redistribution wealth (Østerud, 1978, p. 88).

Associated with the pre-modern and semi-feudal conceptions of landownership was a type of rural settlement that consisted of a nuclear village surrounded by

Table 3.1   The distribution of the types of Swedish farms (%)

	1700	1772	1815	1825
Crown lands	35.6	20.2	14.5	12.7
Noble lands	32.9	32.9	32.9	32.9
Peasant lands	31.5	46.9	52.6	54.4
Total	100	100	100	100

Sources: Østerud, 1976, p. 131; Heckscher, 1949, p. 271; 1957, p. 188.

land stripped into furlongs, in accordance with the medieval farming practices that were common throughout Europe. The practical establishment of private landownership implied first and foremost a change in this type of settlement. As a consequence of the lengthy process of the enclosure of common fields, the estates of a nuclear village were in most cases physically moved to a separate place connected with the newly established consolidated piece of land. In Sweden the enclosure of common fields occurred in three phases between the mid eighteenth century and the mid nineteenth century. The first phase (storskifte, i.e. repartition into large pieces) started in 1757 and involved a consolidation of the furlong strips into large single pieces of land. It was conducted by a public land surveyor, and the plan was to be ratified by the local courts (Østerud, 1978, p. 144). Enclosures were organised in a top-down manner (Alapuro, 1988, p. 21; Saarenheimo, 2003, p. 350) and they were strongly encouraged by the authorities although never officially mandatory if no peasant farmer supported them (Østerud, 1978, p. 146). In some cases peasants opposed enclosures and rather preferred the former organisation of farming.

The storskifte was succeeded by two further phases of enclosure – the enskifte, which aimed to make the process of enclosure more efficient, and the laga skifte (legal partitioning) whereby it was no longer obligatory for all farms to move out of the village cluster (Østerud, 1978, p. 145). In many ways, the enclosures that were completed by 1870 were a continuation of the strengthening position of the peasantry since the Union and Security Act of 1789. It would be wrong, however, to suggest that the Swedish enclosures did not result in social differentiation – the establishment of peasant freeholding resulted in a division between landowning peasants and a non-landowning rural proletariat. But nonetheless, although the population was growing more rapidly than during any previous time in history, there was not a significant concentration of landownership. Although market principles slowly entered Swedish agriculture in the nineteenth century, the commodification of land was never associated with significant speculation or profit seeking.

The right to partition of estates resulted in an increase of crofters, and their number continued to grow until 1860. At the same time, the population continued to grow, and so did the share of the landless population. Between 1861–1930 about 1.4 million people emigrated from Sweden to North America (Morell, 2001,

p. 76). The economic depression of the 1860s also contributed to emigration abroad (Morell, 2001, p. 76). The depression resulted in shortage of food, but only the Northern parts of Sweden were hit by famine.

More generally, the late nineteenth century was a decisive period regarding the modernisation of Swedish agriculture in many ways. During this modernisation, non-landowning groups were not presented with immediately obvious employment opportunities. Different industries started to develop during this period, but their demand for labour was not yet comparable to the agricultural sector. Among other things, the repeal of Corn Laws in Britain and other reforms contributing to more liberal foreign trade increased the demand of Swedish raw materials, such as wood and iron.

The establishment of a forest industry was an important step, although other forms of industry also started to emerge. The last formal obstacles to establishing and operating sawmills in Sweden were removed in 1842, and the 1850s has been characterised as the 'breakthrough' period of the Swedish sawmill industry. Initially, sawmills were water driven, but from the 1870s onwards the steam engine replaced other sources of power (Magnusson, 2000, p. 117). In addition to these changes, trade and crafts were liberalised and urban privileges were removed gradually between 1846–1863 (Østerud, 1978, p. 176).

The transformation of Swedish society was much debated in political fora, and particularly the issues of the increase in the value of forests and the employment opportunities of landless people received much attention. The Norrland issue (*norrlandsfrågan*) and on the other hand the home ownership issue (*egnahemsfrågan*) were the most pressing issues relating to the landless population and the rise of forest value (Morell, 2001, pp. 121–41). Industrial firms sought to buy forestland from anyone able to sell. The existing policies that aimed to expand the colonisation of previously uninhabited northern parts of Sweden were ultimately seen to benefit the industrialists who made a profit out of the forests they had bought from subsidised colonial farmers. Therefore, a political counter movement emerged demanding a stop on the transfer of the ownership of forests from individuals to firms in the north. This initiative eventually became law in 1906, but at that time industrial corporations already owned 29 per cent of the land area in Northern Sweden (Morell, 2001, p. 126).

Parallel and related to the *norrlandsfrågan* was the debate regarding the employment opportunities of non-landowning people and the appropriate government housing policy. At the end of the nineteenth century and at the beginning of the twentieth century strong support was given to subsidise small-scale farming which was seen to solve both the problems of limited employment opportunities and the demand of seasonal labour in the countryside. In 1904 a foundation worth 10 million Swedish crowns providing subsidised mortgages for new homeowners was established. Sixty-five per cent of the mortgages provided by this foundation was used to finance new farms and the rest for the improvement of old ones (Morell, 2001, p. 132). Only 19,000 new farms were established through the government scheme, which is a modest share of the total number of about 300,000 farmers at the time. However, the fact that these kinds of housing policies were in place shows that the general political attitude at the turn of the century was in favour of small-scale farming. This in turn maintained the comparatively equal distribution of landownership and wealth, as the political aim was to increase the number of landowners. This is a notable feature of the modernisation of Swedish agriculture in spite of increasing social differences at the time.

In the beginning of the twentieth century it was often argued in political debate that small-scale farming was economically more efficient than large-scale farming (Morell, 2001, p. 129). These notions were eventually to shift in the 1930s when none of the previous reasons to promote small-scale farming seemed to exist anymore. Small farms did not prosper as expected and there was less demand for seasonal labour, although there was increasing demand of labour in the industries and services. Government subsidies to small-scale farming were eventually abolished during the 1940s (Morell, 2001, p. 141).

When the awareness that the share of the agricultural workforce in Sweden decreased below 50 per cent of all workers during the interwar period (Alestalo and Kuhnle, 1984, p. 21) is added to the discussion above, the only remaining issue here is to establish an interpretation of the time sequence of the modernisation of Swedish agriculture. It is fairly evident that the modernisation did not coincide with the enclosure of common fields, although sometimes in historical literature this period of time has been labelled the *agricultural revolution*. At the beginning of the eighteenth century the share of the agricultural workforce was, however, still very high. The decline of the share of the agricultural workforce started in the 1880s and reached its most rapid phase between 1940 and 1965 (Isacson and Morell, 2006, p. 201). The period between the 1880s and 1940s is also the period during which Swedish agriculture can be said to have been modernised.

Universal Education: A Folk School for All Children

Publicly provided elementary education was established by legislation in 1842 (Isling, 1980; Nordström, 1987; Richardson, 2004; Sjögren, 2008, p. 26). It is difficult, however, to talk about a reorientation of creativity at this point in time as the first impulse associated with the liberation and enhancement of creativity (modernisation of agriculture) was manifested only decades later. Thus, understandably, the Swedish educational system contained many divisions during the latter part of the nineteenth century, but these divisions gradually developed towards more universal provision of education.

During the nineteenth century there was a marked distinction between education in urban and rural areas, and even within the rural education system itself. Furthermore, there was a distinction between those attending full time and part time education; between those attending a touring school and those attending a school with a fixed location; and between those taught at home and those in schools. Also, girls and boys received a rather different kind of education for the most part of the latter nineteenth century.

The ideological background to the 1842 reform represented a division between liberal and conservative ideas (Richardson, 2004, pp. 55–6). Liberal ideas associated with the French Revolution of 1789 had gained varying degrees of attention in Sweden ever since the constitutional reform of 1809 (Isling, 1980, p. 62). Universal education featured among these liberal ideas as a means towards abolishing social distinctions and promoting liberty and democracy. Slightly paradoxically, a member of the clergy, Carl Adolf Agardh, represented the liberal thinking minority in an educational committee set up in 1825. He held, against the views of the conservative majority in the committee, that the provision of universal education was indeed the state's responsibility, just as it was providing basic religious education for everyone. The conservatives, however, held that the responsibility of the state was only to educate civil servants and clergymen, and education for the purposes of trade and business, not to mention the education of deprived groups in society, was a private interest (Isling, 1980, p. 71). The 1825 committee decided not to propose any reforms to the existing system in which the Church provided for basic theological education with limited resources and where the state provided education for a small minority in order to train future civil servants or clergymen.

The scarcity of the population and long geographical distances between habitations proved to be an issue which complicated the early implementation of the 1842 reform in Sweden. The initial five-year transition period in the Act turned out to be rather unrealistic concerning the establishment of Folk School education for all children. Long travelling distances and lack of material resources are given as the main reasons behind low attendance in the late nineteenth century (Isling, 1980, p. 120). In the 1850s about 50 per cent of all school-aged children were registered at Folk Schools, but according to some estimates only half of the registered children actually attended school (Isling, 1980, p. 120).

Educational historians refer to cultural clashes in the sense that especially in rural areas parents were reluctant to let their children go to school for various reasons, for instance because they were needed as a domestic labour force. It is difficult to estimate exactly the share of children attending schools at different periods of time precisely because of the variety of educational institutions. The publicly provided education system was parallel in the sense that most children either went to Folk School or to secondary schools via private preparatory schools or preparatory education provided at home. In addition, in rural areas – mainly in order to increase attendance – different types of Folk Schools were established and some exemptions were created. So called *minor Folk Schools* were established in the 1850s that were smaller in scale compared to the rest of the Folk Schools, and they began to represent the early grades of the entire Folk School. As mentioned, some children – for instance those who were seen as poor, those with 'poor understanding', and interestingly enough girls (Nordström, 1987) – could be exempted from the higher grades of Folk School education, in which cases their educational career was restricted to only a few years (Richardson, 2004, p. 60). The exemption for children with disadvantaged backgrounds was in place in the legislation until 1936 (Nordström, 1987, p. 25).

The distinction between rural and urban areas is highlighted by the fact that in 1880 about 15 per cent of school-aged children living in cities attended secondary education, whereas the corresponding figure in rural areas was 1–2 per cent. The publicly provided *läroverket* schools did not charge tuition fees, but admission required the passing of an entrance examination and the schools were often located in cities and were also administered by the Church (Rothstein, 1986, p. 122). The distinction between Folk Schools as primary education and *läroverket* as secondary education began to manifest itself after 1894 when it was formally recognised that the *läroverket* entrance examination required the level of knowledge and skills corresponding to grade three in Folk Schools (Richardson, 2004, p. 107). Thus a distinction between primary and secondary education began to take shape, although, the two systems remained in principle and in practice parallel and comprised partly the same age groups. In practice, private education remained the only route to *läroverket* schools (Egidius, 2001, p. 53). The *läroverket* schools were finally freed from Church influence in 1904 when the state gained control of teacher appointments (Rothstein, 1986, p. 122).

As mentioned above, the 1842 act granted access to primary education in principle to both boys and girls – although there were exemptions in place for girls. In accordance with the existing social order, women had few opportunities to create a role other than within the domestic sphere. Secondary schools admitted boys only for the reason that they were seen as potential future civil servants and clergy – vocations that at the time were only open to men. The public sphere was thus limited in the sense that it was seen as the role of the state only to educate men for these vocations and for these vocations only (Nordström, 1987, p. 26; Richardson, 2004). For the most part of the nineteenth century it was not seen as the responsibility of the state to educate children to better succeed in business either. Therefore, the only available secondary schools for girls were private girls-only schools that were established in the 1860s. The state began to support these schools gradually from 1874 onwards (Nordström, 1987, p. 27) and in 1886 7,176 girls received some kind of secondary education, whereas the corresponding figure for boys was 12,981. These figures were presented in a committee report, which found the share of girls in secondary education surprisingly high (Nordström, 1987, p. 29). Girls were admitted to university after 1870 (Nordström, 1987, p. 29).

The first publicly provided mixed secondary schools came in 1904 (the so-called *samrealskola*). These were established in connection with the reform of the *läroverket*, which still retained its elite status. It now became possible for girls to obtain the same formal qualifications as boys on a level higher than the Folk School (the *realexamen*) (Nordström, 1987, p. 28). From 1905 onwards the *läroverket* schools were divided into *realskola* (five plus one years) and *gymnasium* (three years). From the point of view of establishing universal education, the most significant reform occurred, however, in 1909 when publicly provided *mellanskolor* (middle schools) were established. These were accessible in principle for anyone with a Folk School background and were maintained by the municipality (Sjöstrand, 1965, pp. 335–6; Egidius, 2001, p. 53). In the reform of 1927 a kind of double connection was established between the Folk Schools and the middle schools. A four-year middle school could be entered after six years of Folk School, or a five-year middle school could be entered after four years of Folk School (Richardson, 2004, p. 112). Along with this reform the position of the Folk School as a gateway to middle school was finally consolidated as state support for private preparatory schools ceased. Thus, the Folk School typically no longer remained the only education for its pupils.

The many divisions in the provision of primary or elementary education make it difficult to see a complete reorientation of creative potentials in Sweden during the nineteenth century. Provision varied greatly between cities and rural areas, boys and girls, well-off people and worse-off people and so on. However, the first steps towards universal education were certainly taken during the nineteenth century through the establishment of Folk Schools and the introduction of compulsory attendance for children aged 7–13 in 1882 (Isling, 1980). School attendance increased at the end of the nineteenth century, and by the early twentieth century literacy rates reached 100 per cent (Isling, 1980, p. 96). Certain exemptions concerning attendance (e.g. for 'poor people') remained in place until the 1930s. The period between 1909–1927 can be regarded as the beginning of the reorientation of creative potentials. The generation educated around this period was the first to benefit from universal opportunities for primary education. Nevertheless, the education system still remained parallel even after 1927 in the sense that there was some overlapping between the Folk School and middle school.

The Modern Polity: Emergence of a Harmonious and Strong State

When considering the history of eighteenth and nineteenth century Sweden three periods are usually distinguished between. The year 1712 marked the end of an absolutist regime and started the 'Age of Liberty' during which popular representation in politics balanced the power of the King. The Age of Liberty lasted until 1772 when tendencies towards absolute monarchy reappeared under the rule of Gustav III (Jutikkala, 1965, p. 80; Knudsen and Rothstein, 1994, pp. 209–10). Accordingly, the era under his succession has been labelled 'Gustavian', and it was ended by a constitutional reform in 1809 when Sweden became a constitutional monarchy after a few eventful years involving wars, coups d'état and competition for power (Hadenius, 1997, pp. 109–25). A French officer, Jean Baptiste Bernadotte was appointed Crown Prince and successor to the throne, and a new constitution was drafted containing aspects of Montesquieuian separation of powers. In the aftermath of the Napoleonian wars, Sweden's former eastern province, Finland, became a Russian Grand Duchy in 1809, and Norway was unified with Sweden in 1814.

During the Gustavian era the Diet consisting of four Estates (Nobles, Clergy, Burghers and Peasants) was only to be summoned at the King's will. The new constitution of 1809 established regularity in this matter (Jutikkala, 1965, p. 147) and the Estates were to meet once every five years. In 1844 the interval was reduced to once every three years (Kurunmäki, 2000, p. 51). Ever since the new constitution, after which the Swedish National Day has been celebrated every year, there was a debate on national representation in politics for the most part of the nineteenth century. According to Jutikkala, the dominant idea at the time, especially among the powerful and influential groups, was that only a person of sufficient material wealth was able to pursue political issues free from all self-interest. Political matters, i.e. matters regarding the state, were conceived of as something completely different from private matters (Jutikkala, 1965, p. 148).

Small adjustments to estate-based representation had been made in 1823 when university teachers were included in the political system, and in 1830 when men of considerable wealth were included in the electorate (Jutikkala, 1965, p. 148). The crucial issue of the nature of representation had remained unsolved and under debate, but did not lead to any reform until the 1860s when an 'innovating ideologist', Baron De Geer presented his Reform Bill containing a proposal for the establishment of a bicameral parliament (Kurunmäki, 2000, p. 222). De Geer was Minister of Justice (the office of Prime Minister was established in 1874) at the time when he presented the Bill, and led the campaign for the reform. In the Bill, De Geer referred to the principle of persons, which according to Kurunmäki had become a leading idea since the 1830s. Geier had begun to speak of free and individual persons who would organise themselves in free associations in order to break loose from existing corporate ties (Kurunmäki, 2000, p. 154). The Reform Bill had to defeat conservative opposition before its proponents could hope to implement it. J.J. Nordström was one of the most prominent opponents of the reform. His view was that society as a whole, not individuals, ought to be represented in politics, and that the four Estates best mirrored society the way it existed at the time (Kurunmäki, 2000, p. 156). Another leader of the conservative campaign was J.A. Södergren, who defended the existing notion of representation on the grounds that for him it gave in a fair manner representation and legitimacy to those who were competent and qualified for it (Södergren 1865, cited in Kurunmäki, 2000, pp. 160–61). More generally, the opponents of the Bill argued that it was based on foreign theories rather than domestic tradition. The supporters in turn tried to refer to the existing systems in Norway and Denmark in order to avoid the label of 'theorist' (Kurunmäki, 2000, p. 224).

The opponents of De Geer's Reform Bill failed to provide a convincing alternative solution, and pressured by the public, the Nobles voted for the reform in December 1866. Three days earlier the Bill was passed by the Burghers and the Peasants (Kurunmäki, 2000, p. 39) and the support of the Nobles thus decided the success of the Bill. The outcome seems to have been a rather modest change in representation, though. In the 1870s about 20 per cent of adult men were entitled to vote. The electorate of the First (upper) Chamber was larger than that of the

Second (lower) Chamber but the voting scale was constructed so that men of more wealth also had more influence in the elections. Members of the Second Chamber were elected with equal votes, but eligibility criteria were quite strict and based on real property. Thus, the outcome of the first elections resembled remarkably the representation structure of the estate-based system (Kurunmäki, 2000, p. 50). Jutikkala has interpreted that the new structure was actually more favourable for the Nobles than the old one (Jutikkala, 1965, pp. 151–2). Nevertheless, representation was no longer automatically determined at birth. Thus, Kurunmäki has emphasised the conceptual and ideological shifts that emerged in the rhetoric in the campaign for the reform.

The constitutional reform of 1866 almost coincided with the liberalisation of trade, which occurred, as mentioned above, in 1864. At the same time the unionisation and organisation of workers became legal. According to Hentilä (1980), the liberalisation of trades was followed by widespread exploitation of workers, and employers and capital owners used every possible means to profit from the worsening of workers' conditions. The position of workers deteriorated also partly because of the removal of old patriarchal relations. It is, however, noteworthy that the legal symbol of patriarchal relations, the requirement of legal protection, was not removed until 1885 (Hentilä, 1980, p. 104).

As the conditions of workers deteriorated the number of strikes and power of workers' organisations began to grow. One of the best-known and most widespread strikes of the time occurred in Sundsvall in 1879, and affected the sawmill industry. With 5–6,000 participants, the strike was a consequence of an agreement between employers in the sawmill industry to reduce wages by up to 20 per cent in spite of the industry having been granted a major government loan. Hentilä has noted that the government ignored the demands of the workers by referring to the existing requirement for legal protection, i.e. that all citizens should be employed, and that the strike was thus illegal (Hentilä, 1980, p. 104).

Trade unions grew in number fairly rapidly between 1880–1885 – from nine to 105 (Hentilä, 1980, p. 105). The degree of organisation increased as well, beginning at the local level and later involving the national level. A Social Democratic workers' party (SAP) was founded in 1889, and after a slow start the number of its members started to grow rapidly so that in 1906 the members of the party were more than 100,000 in number (Hentilä, 1980, p. 149). With the restrictions of suffrage – only a small proportion of people had the right to vote in parliamentary elections – the SAP had, however, few concrete ways to influence social reform. Hentilä has argued that the question of the extension of suffrage became a cornerstone around which the aims of the Social Democrats culminated. Hentilä has analysed the ideological shift of the early SAP and the workers and characterises it as a shift from socialism to reformism (Hentilä, 1980, pp. 101–303).

Notwithstanding differing ideological aims, the SAP and the workers (a top trade union named LO was established in 1898) pursued the extension of suffrage and constitutional reform. Compared to Britain, the extension of suffrage was thus less of a liberal agenda, and compared to Finland it was an issue for the whole nation. An initial extension of suffrage was achieved in the period between 1907–1909 with universal male suffrage for the second chamber. In 1918 universal suffrage was established for both men and women in both chambers. This paved way for the long Social Democratic hegemony in the twentieth century.

The emergence of the modern polity, and thus the manifestation of the third impulse associated with the modern process of liberating and enhancing human creative potentials in Sweden, occurred between 1866–1918. The first constitutional shifts in 1866 indicate some change although suffrage was not in effect extended. As Kurunmäki has pointed out, this reform implied an ideological shift towards the liberal 'principle of persons', as it was conceptualised in Sweden. The extension of the polity during the late nineteenth century is indicated by the growing number and organisation of trade unions and by the Social Democratic Party. The estate-based society was gradually replaced by corporatist organisation both at the local and the state level: organised business and organised labour were given responsibilities in *implementing* state policies in addition to representing members' interests (Kudsen and Rothstein, 1994, pp. 212–13). At the time of the establishment of universal suffrage in 1918 one can think of the modern polity being in place in Sweden. We are now in a position to evaluate the temporal sequences of the three elements of the modern process of liberating and enhancing creative potentials in Sweden:

As Figure 3.1 indicates, it is possible roughly to outline the contours of the time period relevant to each manifestation. Thus, although it was established that the criterion for the emergence of the modern polity is universal suffrage, the emergence of the modern polity was a complex process that began in Sweden around the 1860s, as explained above. After both legislative and ideological change which took several decades, there was a system which granted suffrage for all adult citizens and within which hereditary privileges mattered significantly less than before.

In theory, the modern process of liberating and enhancing human creative potentials is difficult to imagine without the modernisation of agriculture. As long as the majority of the population was working to provide necessities, biographical time was still subject to its medieval bonds, as explained in Chapter 2. What is interesting in the Swedish case is, however, that instead of being a linear process starting with the modernisation of agriculture, the manifestations of the three impulses associated with the modern process of liberating and enhancing creative potentials appear roughly to coincide with one another in time. Thus, when the first manifestation could be observed (modernisation of agriculture), the two others were in place as well. Furthermore, it was possible to observe a number of processes that contributed to the redistribution of wealth, particularly in the form of landownership throughout the crucial time periods reviewed above. These observations may be relevant from the point of view of the development of the emancipating aspects of modern Swedish society, but at this stage, before further

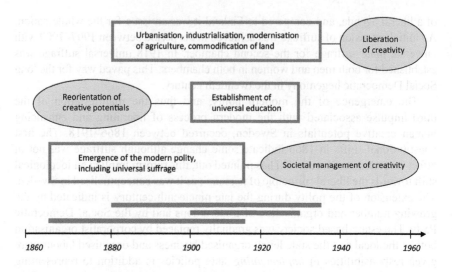

Figure 3.1   The manifestations of three modern societal impulses in Sweden

reflections on this general question, it is first worth turning to the other Nordic countries in the analysis at hand in order to gain some more comparative ground.

Denmark

Modernisation of Agriculture: From Serfdom to Co-operatives

The transformation of conceptions and practices of landownership in the sense discussed above with reference to Sweden, occurred in Denmark between the late eighteenth and the early nineteenth century. Compulsive labour duties were restricted and could be replaced by a monetary rent (Østerud, 1978, p. 105). Privileges for large estates were also restricted and parcelling and partitioning of large farms into smaller ones also gradually became possible. These transformations occurred simultaneously with the upheaval of old village clusters and the switch to individual farming – i.e. enclosures of common fields and the practical consolidation of private landownership. The first public statutes about enclosure were issued in 1758–1760 and the pace of enclosure reached its peak at around the turn of the century (Dombernowsky, 1988, p. 330). According to Hentilä, the enclosures in Denmark were, unlike in Sweden, initiated from below, i.e. not by the state (Hentilä et al., 2002, p. 135).

Enclosures were practically completed by 1810 (Bjørn, 1988, p. 13), which indicates a more rapid pace compared to Sweden. The land area in Denmark at the time was (and still is) of course smaller, which may account for part of the more rapid pace of enclosure. By this time ownership conceptions had also changed dramatically and all of these transformations occurred more rapidly than anywhere else in Europe. During the lifetime of one generation the ownership of land was practically transformed from a feudal system to independent peasants (Hentilä et al., 2002, p. 135).

Associated with the change in conceptions and practices of landownership in Denmark was an increase in peasant freeholding. This change also implied a change in ownership structures. Whereas in Sweden roughly a third of taxable land was used primarily by peasants according to the semi-feudal conceptions and practices of ownership, peasant freeholding in any form was virtually nonexistent in early eighteenth century Denmark. The acquiring of smallholdings by peasants was stimulated by the state – some of the purchases of smallholdings were supported by capital from the new royal credit bank, especially during the period between 1790–1810 (Østerud, 1978, p. 127). Also, the first land to be acquired by peasants was crown land (Hentilä et al., 2002, p. 135). State bankruptcy in 1813 temporarily slowed down the acquiring of smallholdings, but another wave occurred between 1830–60 (Bjørn, 1988, pp. 94–123).

The relative structure of farm size remained more or less constant throughout the period of ownership restructuring and increase of freehold. Between 1835–60 the share of large and small farms increased only slightly while the share of middle-sized farms decreased (Bjørn, 1988, p. 95), indicating that no large-scale concentration of ownership took place during the transformations of conception and practices. In Denmark smallholders were still dependent on the work large estates could offer, especially during the earlier part of the nineteenth century. But this work was carried out in return for a wage and not as an obligation. In the mid nineteenth century the last privileges of large estates were abolished (Bjørn, 1988, p. 96) together with a series of significant reforms relating to the establishment of the polity – for instance the constitutional reform of 1849 (to be discussed later). During the same wave of reform free trade was also established in 1857 (Østerud, 1978, p. 176) – slightly earlier in comparison with the other Nordic countries.

As mentioned already, forestry and mining became the first main industries in nineteenth century Sweden resulting in increasing prices of land and a gradually increasing foreign export of products in these sectors. In Denmark agriculture itself became subject to industrialisation along with the switch from the production of grain to animal husbandry (Henriksen, 1993, p. 159). Grain was imported from abroad in increasing amounts towards the end of the nineteenth century, and animal products were in turn exported mainly to Britain. In this respect Denmark was able to benefit from its favourable geopolitical position together with the establishment of free foreign trade in Britain in the mid nineteenth century. The main export products were butter and bacon.

Table 3.2 indicates that the expansion of agricultural export coincided with demographic transitions. The period between 1870–1914 is usually regarded as

Table 3.2   Demographic development in Denmark 1840–1901

	1840	1860	1880	1901
Total population (in thousands)	1,289	1,608	1,969	2,450
Urban pop. (%)	21	23	28	39
Rural pop. (%)	79	77	72	61
Agr. workforce (%)	56	53	51	41

Source: Christensen, 1983, pp. 56, 93. Table reproduced with the permission of the copyright holder.

the period during which the composition of the agricultural labour force changed (Henriksen, 1993, p. 164; Petersen and Petersen, 2010, p. 125). This change occurred fairly simultaneously with the corresponding shift in Sweden, but the size of the urban population had been initially considerably higher in Denmark even before the modernisation of agriculture – about 20 per cent of the total population. The information about the share of the agricultural workforce given above is not directly comparable to the information cited with regard to the Swedish case, as the numbers in the above case are calculated as a share of the total population, not the total workforce. According to Henriksen (1993, p. 163) the share of the agricultural work force declined from 52 per cent in 1870 to about 39 per cent in 1914. Population growth was also remarkably rapid at the turn of the century – from about 2 million to 2.9 million during the period 1880–1911 (Christensen, 1983, p. 93).

This period of structural change (between 1870–1914) was crucial for the distribution of wealth as well. Table 3.3 below shows the distribution of farms by size according to a Danish measure of unit of land based on estimated productivity.

The numbers indicate that the middle-sized farm (1–8 *tønder hartkorn*) retained its share of total land, while there was a definite restructuring within the middle-sized group in favour of the smaller farms. Large farms (8–12 *tdr. hk.*) decreased both in size and number while the number and size of estates (12+) increased (Henriksen, 1993, p. 167).

As noted in Table 3.3, about 700 estates owned 65 per cent of Danish land in 1720 (Hentilä et al., 2002, p. 132). This was before the emergence of peasant ownership and the enclosure of common fields. A hundred and forty years later, in 1860, the 824 largest estates owned slightly more than 10 per cent of all *hartkorn*. The measurements of land area and *hartkorn* are of course not directly comparable. Different types of land produce different yields, and the measurement of *hartkorn* was developed in order to simplify taxation. Nonetheless, the largest estates' share of total *hartkorn* at the end of the nineteenth century indicates that considerable restructuring of landownership took place in association with the processes of enclosure and the establishment of private landownership. The Danish ownership structure emerged gradually as a consequence of the enclosures and the

Table 3.3   Danish farms by size according to *hartkorn*

With a hk. of:	1860		1885		1905	
	Number	Total hk.	Number	Total hk.	Number	Total hk.
< 1	139,286	–	188,526	–	212,520	43,128
1–2	17,600	25,557	20,979	30,150	23,060	33,123
2–4	20,793	61,274	23,397	67,876	24,365	70,457
4–8	27,474	157,498	24,636	139,887	23,327	132,005
8–12	4,284	39,988	3,953	37,152	3,765	35,525
12–20	1,054	15,592	1,145	17,092	1,174	17,635
20–	824	36,471	896	39,517	919	40,547

Note: Hartkorn is a Danish unit of land valuation based on estimated productivity.
Source: Henriksen, 1993, p. 168; Rasmussen et al., 1988, pp. 223, 225

establishment of private ownership, before the actual modernisation of agriculture, which took place during the decades around the turn of the twentieth century.

Towards the end of the nineteenth century, and during the first few years of the twentieth century, a number of political land reforms were carried out in Denmark in a somewhat similar fashion to Sweden. As indicated above, there had been a steady increase in smallholding since the 1830s but smallholders and cottagers were usually still dependent on work opportunities outside their own holding. There was also a considerable number of landless agricultural workers and due to restructuring and modernisation towards the end of the century, work opportunities in agriculture were evolving. In an effort to manage the transitions, and among other things, in order to prevent excessive emigration abroad, a law was passed in 1899 granting the right for every farm worker to a small piece of land (2.7–10.9 acres). According to the reform, the state was to subsidise the mortgages of those concerned up to a maximum value of nine tenths of the value of the property. The conditions of the state-subsidised mortgage were quite favourable for those acquiring the land as repayments were not required until after the first five years of taking the mortgage (Christensen, 1983, p. 96).

After a new government took over in 1901, the 1899 law was revised but still remained very favourable for smallholders. Indeed, 9,000 new smallholdings were established within the first 20 years after the introduction of the law (Christensen, 1983, p. 96). Later it also became possible for smallholders to acquire subsidised loans for the construction of buildings.

The Danish ownership structure in effect prevented the accumulation of large capital in the hands of a small elite, which resulted in a rather unique kind of agricultural modernisation (and industrialisation). In this respect, Danish producer co-operatives played a crucial role, as many historians have noted (e.g. Iversen and Andersen, 2008). Agricultural producers in Denmark found a way of organising production, so that small producers could benefit from the same scale advantages as large producers.

The first producer co-operative in dairy farming was established in 1882 and 595 new ones emerged between 1885–1895. The alternative form of organisation was the private enterprise, which in many other Western European countries was the most common mode of organisation. At the end of the nineteenth century private dairy enterprises existed in Denmark as well, but they soon found themselves unable to compete with the co-operatives, which acquired the largest market share. By 1914 there were 1,168 co-operative dairies in Denmark with 175,000 individual members (Christensen, 1983, p. 103) and only a couple of hundred private dairies (Rasmussen et al., 1988, p. 370; Henriksen, 1993, p. 172). Often the capital invested by the co-operatives came from savings banks established by the peasants themselves (Henriksen, 1993, p. 170). Later, in 1914 the successful Co-operative Bank (*Andelsbanken*) was established.

In addition to dairy farming, another area of agricultural production to be dominated by the co-operative form of production was pig farming and butchery. Within this area co-operatives were established slightly later than dairies and to some extent as a reaction against private bacon factories. Since the establishment of the first co-operative bacon factory in 1887 there was some intense competition between private and co-operative factories but by the beginning of World War I the co-operative was clearly the dominant mode of production. Producer co-operatives were also established within the fields of egg export (1885), live cattle export (1898/1916), feeding stuffs (1898) and fertilising (1906) (Christensen, 1983, pp. 108–9). They were a significant cultural phenomenon as well and they have been largely held as a significant chain in the political self-emancipation of peasants (Henriksen, 1993, p. 170). In addition to producer co-operatives, consumer co-operatives were also established (Christensen, 1983, pp. 111–12) and they had a significant influence on cultural life. Christensen has concluded that by 1914 Danish farming had become more or less fully organised through farmers' unions and the co-operative movement (Christensen, 1983, p. 114).

As noted in the literature concerning the modernisation of Danish agriculture, the period between 1870–1914 was crucial in several respects. During this period the focus of production was shifted from vegetable to animal production in order to better adapt to the world market (Iversen and Andersen, 2008, p. 279). Butter and bacon became the two main agricultural export products, the production of which was organised according to the co-operative form. At the same time, the share of the agricultural work force declined below 40 per cent of the total labour force before 1914. Therefore, this period can be regarded as the period during which agriculture was modernised in Denmark and creative potentials liberated from the production of basic needs. There are a few interesting contrasts to be noted in comparison to the case of Sweden.

Universal Education: Compulsory Education without Compulsory
School Attendance

The history of education in Denmark resembles in many ways that in Sweden, except for a slightly earlier timing of reforms. The Danish Education Act of 1814 was fairly similar in content compared to the Swedish 1842 Education Act with regard to the establishment of Folk Schools and compulsory education. Due to the costs of the Napoleonic wars and the state bankruptcy in 1813 economic prospects for establishing a countrywide school network were poor (Hakaste, 1992, p. 303). For the most part of the nineteenth century education in Denmark, as in Sweden, remained strongly differentiated. Urban and rural conditions varied greatly, the affluent and the disadvantaged as well as boys and girls had very different educational opportunities.

In towns, a common route to education for the elite was through private education in the home to one of the so-called 'Latin schools' (*Lærde skolor*), which resembled the Swedish *läroverket* with their classical curriculum which prepared pupils for university studies. The Latin schools accepted pupils from the age of 9 and for most of the nineteenth century they provided an eight-year classical curriculum (Dybdahl, 1982, pp. 113–14). The Folk Schools in the countryside and in towns (so called *borgerskole*) were intended for children between 7 and 13 years of age and remained in most cases the only education they would ever receive (Dybdahl, 1982, p. 110). In addition to these schools, there were 'pauper schools' (*fattigskole*) especially in towns, for those who could not afford to pay the school tax upon which entrance to the 'burgher schools' was conditional (Hakaste, 1992, p. 307). They were free of charge and were, as a consequence, aimed at the most disadvantaged children. There were also private girls' schools providing various types of curricula, for instance oriented towards house-keeping (Hakaste, 1992, p. 308). Girls had in principle access to folk schools, although they were taught separately from the boys. The Latin schools were for boys only and universities did not admit women until 1875 (University of Copenhagen) (Hakaste, 1992, p. 309). It was not, however, possible until 1900 for girls to obtain the same formal educational qualifications above primary school level as boys.

For children (or boys in most cases) older than 13 there was an alternative to the Latin schools. These were the practically oriented *realskolor* that had originally been established for the needs of the bourgeoisie (Larsen, 1984, pp. 99–118). The *realskolor* dated back to the eighteenth century and their position varied throughout the nineteenth century according to various educational reforms.

In principle, school attendance in Denmark was never compulsory (the same applies to Sweden) – only the attainment of a certain degree of education corresponding to the education provided at Folk Schools. This principle was inherent in the Education Act of 1814 and was further consolidated in 1855 (Sjöstrand, 1965, p. 387). There are few records showing how this principle was checked or controlled, and it can be seen more as an ideological principle indicating ideas about individual autonomy and independence from formal institutions. This principle turned out to be rather important as it could easily be incorporated with ideologies such as Grundtvigianism and the free school movement of the late nineteenth century.

Despite not being compulsory, school attendance can be regarded as a useful indicator of the differentiation within the formal educational system. From the point of view of the reorientation of creative potentials what matters are the formal educational *opportunities*. According to a rough estimate, in the mid nineteenth century, a quarter of Danish children attended publicly provided education, whereas half of the children attended some kind of private school and a quarter of children were outside formal education (Hakaste, 1992, p. 308). Attendance within different schools also varied greatly during the nineteenth century. In 1867 attendance in rural Folk Schools amounted to 94 days a year, whereas attendance in urban schools was twice as much per annum (Dybdahl, 1982, p. 115). This reflects, of course, in addition to varying demands in urban and rural schools, the fact that children in the countryside were needed as a labour force (Henriksen, 1993, p. 165).

In theory, and without knowing the historical conditions in Denmark in detail, one could argue that although a quarter of school-aged children were outside the formal education system in the mid nineteenth century, they could have received education of a similar standard at home. Therefore, to continue this train of thought, one could think that creative potentials were reoriented even before the establishment of universal statutory educational opportunities. After all, the law explicitly stated that school attendance was not compulsory, only the attainment of a certain level of education. There is, however, one piece of evidence that contradicts this kind of suggestion. The earliest reliable assessments of literacy of Danish recruits from 1881 reports severe problems of writing among 43 per cent of army recruits (Dybdahl, 1982, p. 107; Henriksen, 1993, p. 162). If this result were to be generalised to the whole (male) population it would certainly be positively biased as it may be assumed that literacy on the whole increased in the nineteenth century. Thus, according to the criterion for the realisation of universal education used here, i.e. 100 per cent literacy rates, Denmark did not yet qualify in the 1880s.

The ideological principle establishing compulsory education without compulsory school attendance gave some room for alternative, private, educational institutions in addition to those established by the state. One such institution was the free school movement in the late nineteenth century having its origin in Grundtvigian ideology. The free schools were privately established and operated a free policy concerning their curriculum being ideologically rather close to Freirean pedagogics – although from a much earlier period, of course (Sjöstrand, 1965, p. 387). The emphasis in Grundtvigian free schools was on storytelling, the 'living word' and discussion among peers (Østergard, 1992, pp. 14–15). This resembles the Freirean principle of not considering the teacher as the active distributor of knowledge and the pupil as a passive recipient, but rather seeing both of them in a mutual effort of establishing a relationship with the world. The Grundtvigian ideology was also an important influence on the co-operative movement discussed in the previous section.

What was also notable regarding the early stages of Danish education was that the church never played such a prominent role as in the early stages of Swedish education (Johansen, 1979, pp. 247–66). The Education Act of 1814 had stated that it was the duty of parents to organise the education of their children between the ages of 7–13 in one way or another according to specified criteria. State schools had existed earlier, but the 1849 Act consolidated the right to receive state provided education, and financial exemptions could be considered if parents did not have the necessary means to send their children to school.

During the latter part of the nineteenth century, the political scene was dominated by a distinction between *Højre* (right wing conservatives) and *Venstre* (representing peasant interests). With education the conservatives pursued policies of increased state control whereas the *Venstre* were in favour of local autonomy (Kruchov, 1985, p. 134). The disagreement between the two parties blocked all educational reforms until 1899, when a new education act was passed. This law did not radically change the existing educational system but made a few specifications regarding the central issues of the degree of local autonomy and teacher qualifications, the appointment of teachers and the contents of curricula. A legislative reform four years later, in 1903 was more directed towards the structures of the Danish education system.

In summary, education in nineteenth century Denmark was in many ways similarly differentiated as in Sweden. But the project of establishing a nation-wide Folk School system had begun a few decades earlier. The schools that were later to become secondary schools in an integrated education system, i.e. *realskoler* and Latin schools, were also adapted to later reforms slightly earlier than in Sweden (Sjöstrand, 1965, p. 392). This development paved the way for the 1903 reform that was carried out in accordance with social democratic ideals. The Education Act of 1903 established a unified education system where the first five years were common for everyone – a system that resembled the one introduced in Sweden in 1927 (Sjöstrand, 1965, p. 392). The initial five-year Folk School was to be followed by either two years of complementary studies or by four to five years at the *realskole* or the newly established 'middle school' (*mellemskole*). The *realskole* would lead on to vocational training and the middle school to upper secondary education (*gymnasium*), opening up the possibility of university studies (Dybdahl, 1982, p. 117).

The 1903 reform can be regarded as decisive for the reorientation of creative potentials in Danish society. This was a first step towards unified education for all, especially for children both in the countryside and in cities. From this reform onwards the various routes to differentiated schooling started to disappear, and a clear distinction between primary and secondary education started to emerge. It is not, however, possible to conclude that creative potentials were reoriented instantly by the introduction of this particular legislative reform. Rather, this was the first step after which future generations faced fairly similar educational opportunities at least with regard to primary education and very early stages of learning, such as reading and writing. Therefore, it is fairly safe to say that creative potentials were reoriented somewhere between 1903 and about 20 to 30 years later.

The Modern Polity: From Absolutism and War to Democracy

As mentioned above, Denmark lost Norway to Sweden as a consequence of the Napoleonic wars. The Duchies of Schleswig and Holstein were under Danish rule but the latter belonged at the same time to the German empire (Hentilä et al., 2002, pp. 156–8). The period until the 1830s was politically rather stable in Denmark and an absolutist regime had a firm grip on the country. A liberalist and nationalistic awakening was, however, to come during the first half of the nineteenth century.

A bourgeois liberalist opposition on the one hand and an agrarian movement on the other began to emerge with figures such as Orla Lehmann having a strong impact on the former. Bishop Grundtvig, as mentioned earlier, was one of the main figures of the agrarian movement. He inspired spokespersons, such as Rasmus Sørensen in the countryside (Friisberg, 1998, pp. 164–7).

Orla Lehmann's view was that the state apparatus should not be static and everlasting as the absolutist ideology assumed. Rather, the form of government should first and foremost be subject to debate and also subject to reform. As public discussion and public gatherings were controlled within the absolutist regime, the first step for the liberalist opposition was to create a public realm for discussion about the existing order. This was not an easy task to do as especially all debate on the legislative process and form of government was strictly banned. The ban was enforced by literary censorship maintained by the government (Friisberg, 1998, pp. 41–56).

One important step towards popular representation was taken in the 1830s through the establishment of provincial Estate Assemblies (Kolstrup, 2010, p. 210; Friisberg, 1998, pp. 41–5). These assemblies only had a consultative role towards the King and their opinions were not decisive in any legislative issue. Nonetheless, as they represented the Estates through elections, their emergence also resulted in a debate about the election system, which in many ways anticipated the debates about a national representative body (Friisberg, 1998, p. 79). Another event in the early 1830s also triggered debate and stirred liberalist opinions, namely the Polish uprising in Russia. Sympathies in favour of the Poles were expressed and at the same time implicitly directed against the existing regime in Denmark. After all, the Poles were seen to fight for freedom against an autocratic Russian regime that in many ways resembled that in Denmark.

Concerning liberalist ideas there were various emphases ranging from Lockean formulations of an Anglo-Saxon character to continental Hegelian and Kantian notions (Friisberg, 1998, pp. 83–5). The notions of freedom and autonomy varied accordingly so that those resembling British and American thinking emphasised the negative freedoms of absence of government (or freedom from the intrusion of the state) and those resembling continental thinking emphasised more the nation as an organic entity consisting of free and autonomous citizens fulfilling their duty towards the state of their own free will. Political rights, such as freedom of speech and gathering, and personal rights such as religious freedom and individual ownership were among the most debated. The Danish liberals believed that economic freedom would strengthen the country as a whole as potentials would be unleashed that were restrained under the absolutist order (Friisberg, 1998, p. 88).

In the largest cities the liberalists consisted of academics and other bourgeoisie who desired more political influence than was possible under an absolutist regime. An organisation that was an important forum for these people was the *trykkefrihedsselskabet* (society for the freedom of the press) established in 1835 with Orla Lehmann among one of its leading figures. The society sought to expand the freedom of printing and press but it also served as a forum for debate of the constitution. As this was banned, the government intervened in the society's activities (Friisberg, 1998, pp. 98–9). In the 1840s nationalistic undertones became manifest in the liberalist movement and they were added to claims of popular representation (Hentilä et al., 2002, p. 199).

The peasants added to the political pressure created by the bourgeoisie. Whereas the *trykkesfrihedsselskabet* provided a forum for the liberalists in towns, the *Bondevenneselskabet* played a corresponding role for the peasants and the agricultural population in the countryside. One journal in particular, the *Almuevennen* (founded in 1842) voiced the political concerns of peasants. Whereas Orla Lehmann was one of the leading figures of the bourgeoisie liberalists, Peter Hansen and Rasmus Sørensen were the two main spokespersons for the peasants. Their aim was to unite the political voice of the peasants and make sure that political issues of concern for the peasants were included in the debate over the constitution. These issues included equal taxation of land and the abolition of the crofting system (*fæstevæsende*) (Friisberg, 1998, p. 160).

Political pressure to reform the absolutist regime increased in 1848 in association with the revolution in France and an uprising in Schlesvig. In the same year King Christian VIII died and his successor found himself under serious pressure from the liberalist opposition. The liberalists wanted a new government with their own representatives, and demanded that the new government start to plan the introduction of a constitution that would secure popular representation in decision making at the national level. This was expressed to the King in a petition in 1848 and given the difficult situation the King had no choice but to accept (Friisberg, 1999, p. 7). In June 1849 Denmark was presented with a new constitution implying a separation of powers and popular representation in the legislative organ, the parliament. There were two chambers in the parliament and fairly strict eligibility criteria both for voters and candidates, but no voting scales, i.e. each vote had equal weight. Furthermore, the constitution guaranteed basic rights, such as freedom of expression, religious freedom, freedom of the press (and abolishing of censorship) and freedom to form and join organisations (Iversen and Andersen, 2008, p. 269).

Eligibility criteria for voting for the two chambers were as follows: all heads of households (in practice husbands and fathers) of more than 30 years of age were eligible to vote for the first chamber (*folketinget*) whereas the second chamber (*landstinget*) was elected by proxy. In order to participate in the election of the second chamber one had to pass fairly stringent age and means tests (Hentilä et al., 2002, p. 200). Although the principle of parliamentarism was not fulfilled in this constitution – the King still had rather sovereign executive power – the constitution of 1848 was nonetheless a significant initial step towards the emergence of the Danish polity. What was perhaps most exceptional was that no voting scales were applied in the election of the two chambers.

After a war against Prussia the constitution was, however, slightly revised. Denmark had lost the two Duchies of Schlesvig and Holstein and conservatives accused the nationalistically minded liberals of the war. Before their victory over the constitution, the liberalists had pursued a tighter connection between the Duchies and the Monarch, but these efforts backfired a few decades later. The conservatives utilised the weak situation of the liberals after the war and made a few revisions to the constitution in 1866, one of them being that the king appointed 12 lifetime members out of 66 members of the second chamber (*landstinget*) (Jutikkala, 1965, p. 155; Dybdahl, 1982, p. 141). As a consequence, the dominance of wealthy landowners and other financially well-off individuals in the second chamber was further consolidated. This widened the political gap between the two chambers. Compared to Sweden at that time, the first chamber had a wider representation but the second a more exclusive.

From the 1870s onwards, political parties began to take shape in Denmark revolving around the ideologies of conservatism, liberalism and social democracy. The first chamber was dominated by the *Venstre* party, which later split into two parties (*Venstre* and *det radikale Venstre*) (Hentilä et al., 2002, p. 229). The present day party structure still resembles in many ways the one that began to take shape in the 1870s.

The principle of parliamentarism was established in 1901, whereby the government had to be supported by the parliament. Resembling the developments in other European countries, the unionisation of workers began in the late nineteenth century and a top trade union (*De samvirkende fagforbund*, DsF) was established in 1898 – the same year as in Sweden. Left wing parties pursued extensions of suffrage and the constitution was finally revised in 1915 in order to include all citizens, both men and women, in the electorate (Hentilä et al., 2002, p. 232). The two chambers still remained in place and the members of the second chamber (*landstinget*) could only be elected by those over 35 years of age. The second chamber was finally abolished in 1953. Thus the modern polity gradually emerged in Denmark between 1848, when the absolutist regime ended and 1915 when universal suffrage was finally introduced. The manifestation of the third impulse associated with the modern process of liberating and enhancing creativity to a large extent thus resembles that in Sweden – although there was a stronger heritage of individualism and popular self-reliance drawn from the struggle against the strong state in Denmark (Knudsen and Rothstein, 1994, p. 218).

Figure 3.2 illustrates the manifestation of the three societal impulses associated with the modern process of liberating and enhancing creative potentials in both Sweden and Denmark. First, it is of course possible to observe that the relevant historical processes which contributed to the manifestation of these impulses occurred rather simultaneously in the two countries. Accordingly, the same kind of overlapping that was found in Sweden could also be detected in the case of Denmark. As noted in the Swedish case, this feature is not consistent with a linear progression of the liberation and enhancement of creative potentials, starting with the modernisation of agriculture – something that could have perhaps been anticipated on the basis of the theoretical discussion. In addition, the modernisation of agriculture appears to have been associated with a redistribution of wealth in both Sweden and Denmark. In other words, the liberation of creative potentials did not result in significant social differentiation in terms of wealth and status – although some differentiation inevitably occurred. These observations invite a few questions

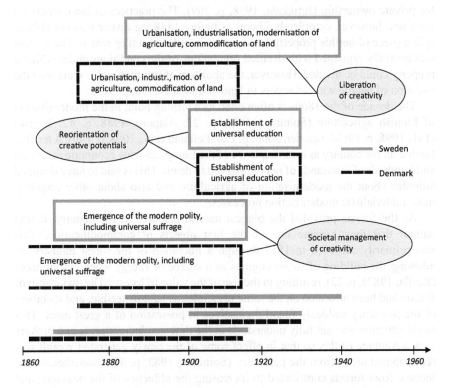

Figure 3.2   The manifestations of three modern societal impulses in Sweden and Denmark

for further analysis. Could the overlapping of the three relevant time periods be a uniquely Nordic feature in the liberation and enhancement of human creative potentials? What consequences does the simultaneous timing have for future emancipatory elements of societal development? Before tackling these questions, it will be useful to gain even more comparative ground by examining another Nordic country, namely Finland.

Finland

Modernisation of Agriculture: A Rural Nation Forever?

In 1809 Finland's political status changed as a consequence of the Napoleonic wars from being part of Sweden to being an autonomous Grand Duchy of the Russian Empire. The enclosures were carried out according to the principles established under Swedish rule. The peak of the enclosures in Finland was between 1801–1848, during which a quarter of the country's land area was enclosed for private ownership (Jutikkala, 1958, p. 309). The practices of landownership were not, however, completely liberal as before 1848 the owner was not able to split a piece of her/his property for instance in order to sell or rent it. The system was centrally regulated with detailed regulations of the conditions under which a property could be divided. However, the abolition of common rights worsened the situation of people without access to land (Jutikkala, 1958, p. 311).

The decade of the 1860s is often cited as a turning point in the modernisation of Finnish agriculture (Soininen, 1982, p. 27; Alapuro, 1988, p. 42; Karisto et al., 1998, p. 19; Meinander, 2006, p. 128; Fellman et al., 2008, p. 140). A terrible famine hit the country as a consequence of the European-wide economic recession and hundreds of thousands of people starved to death. This is said to have changed attitudes about the modernisation of agriculture and also about other ongoing, more materialistic modernisation processes.

As the forests provided the biggest natural resource in the country, it was natural that they became one of the first objects of commodification. This was primarily achieved in 1857 through a liberation of the forest industry by allowing the building of steam engines as a source of energy when cutting trees (Rasila, 1982a, p. 22), resulting in the rise of the value of forests. The ownership of forests had been allocated on the same principles as landownership, and members of the peasantry suddenly found themselves in possession of a great asset. This novel situation was not fully understood at the time and industrialists and brokers took advantage of this so that in effect some of the newly generated wealth was redistributed away from the peasantry (Soininen, 1982, p. 48). Nonetheless, the income from forests contributed to increasing the affluence of the peasants, and thus contributed to the modernisation of agriculture making investments in more modern methods possible.

The start of the process of modernisation of agriculture did not immediately result in a rapid decline in the agricultural workforce. There was a group of people in late nineteenth-century Finland who sought subsistence by any means possible. Neither agriculture nor the slowly emerging industry could absorb this group of non-property owning people, whose size is varyingly estimated to have been somewhere between 20–40 per cent of the population (Karisto et al., 1998). At the time people with neither access to land nor any employment opportunities were perceived as 'excess population' (Rasila, 1982b, p. 136). An anachronistic label for them would be the unemployed, but this term does not have much meaning in the context of the late nineteenth century (cf. Rasila, 1982b, p. 136). What probably also slowed the process of modernisation of agriculture was the fact that not all of the land area that could have been cultivated was being used. Therefore, one of the most central aims of agricultural policy at the time was to increase the total amount of arable land to increase returns (Jutikkala, 1982, p. 211).

Finland did not adopt economic competition as the route to the modernisation of agriculture. On the contrary, land did not become a market commodity until the mid twentieth century, and the housing policies of the early twentieth century contributed, again, to a redistribution of wealth away from the peasantry in favour of the non-landowning groups. The political focus of the early twentieth century was centred not on the non-property owning, a fairly large group, but on crofters, who rented their farms from the peasants under rather unfavourable conditions. This situation contributed to a political conflict, resulting in a bloody civil war in the aftermath of the Russian Revolution in 1917, when the socialists in Finland – supported by the crofters – attempted to take over the government. Jutikkala (1962) has argued that one of the reasons for this conflict was that the peasantry and the crofters were essentially in a similar position in society, and the exploitation of the latter by the former was thus harder to accept. Nevertheless, in 1918 a law concerning the right to buy out rented farms was passed, and as inflation was not a well-known phenomenon, the conditions under which crofters were able to buy their farms turned out to be rather favourable. The payment period could extend up to 37 years (Rasila, 1982b, p. 144; Jutikkala, 1982, p. 209). Thus, the real price the crofters paid for their farms was relatively low, which implied a transfer of wealth away from the peasantry.

As the social problems of the crofters were solved by what essentially involved a redistribution of wealth from peasants to crofters, the political leaders of the time saw no reason why the issues of the non-property-owning groups could not be resolved in the same manner. Although there was much debate, legislation was passed in 1922 (the so-called Lex Kallio named after Prime Minister Kyösti Kallio who made the initiative in the Parliament) that granted all those not owning an estate or a farm, or any land or assets, but who had some knowledge of the art of farming and some tools, the right to a small piece of land. The only way this right could be secured, according to the government, was by confiscation of private land. Although in practice confiscations are said not to have been large scale, this policy contributed to the growth of small-scale farming, and, as the table below shows, was not associated with a rapid decline in the agricultural workforce. On the contrary, this policy can be seen as further slowing down the pace at which the share of the agricultural workforce declined. On the other hand, it contributed to a comparatively equal distribution of landownership.

As Table 3.4 shows, the share of the agricultural workforce began to decline in Finland only between the 1930s and 1950s. The ultimate modernisation of Finnish agriculture took place in the 1950s. During this decade manual farming methods were finally replaced by mechanised methods and the urban population began to grow in size. The share of the agricultural workforce then fell very rapidly from more than 60 to less than 40 per cent in a period of 20 years. Thus, regarding the manifestation of the first impulse associated with the modern process of liberating and enhancing human creative potentials – the modernisation of agriculture – it may be concluded that this was achieved in Finland between the 1930s and the 1950s. This is slightly later than in Sweden and significantly later compared to Denmark.

Table 3.4   Employment patterns in Finland (%)

	1860	1880	1900	1920	1940	1960
Agriculture and forestry	82	79	73	70*	54	35
Industry, handicraft	5	6	11	14	18	31
Services and trade	4	6	8	10	16	34**
Other	9	9	8	6	12	0

Note: *Depending on the source either 70 or 66. **Includes transport industry, communications, retail and finance.
Sources: Rasila, 1982, p. 140; Pitkänen, 1982, p. 200; Wiman, 1982, p. 494.

Universal Education: The Ideals of Cygnaeus and Snellman

To some extent, in theory, the realisation of universal education is conditional upon the modernisation of agriculture. In other words, creative potentials in society may not be completely reoriented before they are liberated from the production of basic needs. Therefore, when examining the case of Finland in detail, it is important to keep in mind that at the turn of the twentieth century, more than 70 per cent of the work force still gained their livelihood from agriculture. This does not imply, however, that it is uninteresting to consider the processes regarding the manifestation of the second impulse before the manifestation of the first.

Finland was, of course, not an independent nation during the nineteenth century, but a Grand Duchy of Russia and thus under the rule of the Russian emperor, the Tsar. There was a national Finnish assembly, the Diet, and a governing body –

the Senate. But these were subsumed under the Russian emperor so that each legislative act had to be confirmed by the Tsar before it could be enforced. As the country had not been completely sovereign before, the emergence of a national Finnish education policy presupposed a national self-understanding of Finland as a political subject and entity. This kind of self-understanding emerged gradually during the nineteenth century.

Inherited from the period under Swedish rule, Latin schools in various Finnish cities had during the eighteenth century educated children for forthcoming services in government or in the Church. The first legislative step towards universal education in Finland was taken in 1866, when all cities were required to establish a public Folk School (*kansakoulu*) (Ahonen, 2003, p. 67; Fellman et al., 2008, pp. 147–8, for an overview of education in Finland up to this decade, see Hanska and Vainio-Korhonen, 2010). This first step occurred in other words decades later than in Sweden and Denmark. This legislative act was preceded by a report drafted by one of the leading figures of Finnish educational policy of the time, Uno Cygnaeus, who drew from Rousseau and other Enlightenment thinkers (Ahonen, 2003, p. 44). The philosophy behind Cygnaeus' report was to a great extent based on education as a right of the individual, in a similar fashion to many continental European countries.

Although drawing to a great extent on continental thinking, the political debate around the establishment of statutory-provided education was by no means homogenous in mid nineteenth century Finland. In addition to Cygnaeus, another prime figure in the educational debate was J.V. Snellman, who was a member of the Senate and a prominent and respected intellectual of his time. Snellman was very much a Hegelian with ideas about the state, citizenship and civil society that corresponded to Hegel's idealistic worldview. According to this worldview the ennobling or civilising of citizens was a key to the formation of a strong, flourishing state and education was, according to Snellman, of crucial importance in becoming civilised and ennobled. Snellman was thus a supporter of the neo-humanistic *Bildung* project (Ahonen, 2003, pp. 23–33). This project was not only about building a strong state, but also contained the idea of individual emancipation and freedom that would result from civilising and ennobling oneself.

The Education Act of 1866 establishing state-provided education has been described as a compromise between the liberalist education philosophy of Cygnaeus and the Hegelian philosophy of Snellman (Ahonen, 2003). The act contained a hope that by establishing the folk schools, they would start attracting an increasing number of pupils, which would lead to increased prosperity and 'civilisation' (Halila, 1949, p. 40). In reality, the Lutheran church schools (*kiertokoulut*) that toured from town to town and village to village continued to provide education for the majority of pupils. In addition, access to education was still far from universal for several decades after the 1866 act (Isosaari, 1973; Ahonen, 2003, p. 55). The church schools were less strictly organised than the folk schools and their curriculum was less demanding, more limited, and fairly theologically oriented (Ahonen, 2003, p. 55). Their duration was also fairly modest – only two terms, three months each (Halila, 1949, p. 132). Still, children attending both church schools and folk schools were expected to know the basics of reading even before they started, although no formal entrance examinations were in place.

Both the church schools and folk schools grew at the end of the nineteenth century, but in the beginning of the twentieth century the church schools still had twice as many pupils (Isosaari, 1973). This was not quite the situation that the legislators of 1866 had hoped for. The latter part of the nineteenth century also saw the establishment of many secondary educational institutions (the so-called *oppikoulut* or *lyseot*) (Salminen, 2003, pp. 78–94). These were in most cases established on private initiative, particularly in the countryside. The state founded a number of secondary schools in the largest cities after the 1860s, schools that required the passing of an admissions test.

Thus, a rather differentiated and partly overlapping educational system was in place in late nineteenth century Finland. Tuomaala (2004, p. 68) has noted that especially in rural areas, church schools were sometimes used as a route to folk schools – the latter tending to provide slightly less elementary education than the former. In urban areas, children typically went from private preparatory schools straight to a secondary school that would allow them to carry on to university. The urban population represented, however, a small minority of the entire population, and in 1930 still only 12 per cent of children went on to secondary schools (Ahonen, 2003, p. 102). In theory, it was of course possible to continue from a folk school to secondary schools, but in practice, and particularly in distant rural areas this was quite rare. At the turn of the century the absolute number of pupils attending secondary education was slightly less than 15,000 and the number of secondary educational institutions in the same year was 96 (Isosaari, 1973). In rural areas the financial burden of establishing a folk school was in many cases too large to bear in the late nineteenth century. Another practical obstacle in increasing school attendance in rural areas was the scarcity of the population, which created impractical travelling distances for children wishing to attend school.

A legislative act in 1898 sought to increase school attendance by dividing the country into schooling districts and also by requiring rural municipalities to establish folk schools, so that no child would have to travel further than 5 km (Kuikka, 1992, p. 69). The act was formulated as a right to education though attendance was not made compulsory. Folk schools at the time were mainly funded by the state and the municipalities, but in most cases they also charged fees according to parental means. First, separate schools (with similar curricula) for boys and girls were also in place, but as joint schools proved to be more cost efficient, they gradually became more and more common (Halila, 1949, p. 86). The number of pupils in folk schools grew quite rapidly between 1890–1910 – from 54,000 to 181,000 (Isosaari, 1973).

The beginning of the twentieth century was characterised by major social and political unrest in Finland. There was a major strike in 1905 and a traumatic civil war in 1918. Before the civil war there had been a parliamentary reform in 1906 establishing universal suffrage, and the country was declared independent in 1917 in connection with the Russian revolutions and the overthrow of the Tsar's regime. A committee report on educational policy was published in 1907 which recommended compulsory attendance in schools. The committee had members such as Mikael Soininen and Santeri Alkio and its legislative motion was already approved in parliament in 1910 but rejected by the Russian-minded Senate (Tuomaala, 2004, pp. 69–70). After the civil war a similar motion was presented and finally approved in 1921 under the rule of the Finnish Agrarian Party. The law that was passed did not strictly speaking require school attendance, but required all school-aged children aged between 7–15 to attain a certain level of knowledge and skills. In practice, school attendance became the most popular way of achieving this. As universal school attendance was far from a practical reality in 1921, a transition period of 16 years was allowed in rural areas and 5 years in urban areas. This transition period was later extended by 10 and 5 years respectively. Thus, universal provision of education was attained in practice in the 1940s in Finland.

The education system that the 1921 act sought to establish consisted of two levels – the elementary folk school and secondary schools (Ahonen, 2003, p. 68). There were in effect two routes to secondary schooling – through an entrance examination taken at age 11 in folk schools or through a preparatory school, the latter of which remained the typical route for people in urban areas. Those not qualifying for a secondary school at age 11 continued in folk school for a few more years and had after that the opportunity to carry on to a 'folk institute' or technical schools. Secondary education led to the qualifications necessary for attending university. This system was established throughout the country by the 1940s but it was not, however, to remain in place for very long. A major schooling reform in the 1960s abolished the two-level system into a single comprehensive school without any selection whatsoever for children between 9–15 years of age.

The reorienting of creative potentials in Finland can be recognised from approximately the 1940s onwards. There was a vague aim to level social distinctions with the help of schooling in the late nineteenth century in Finland. The brutal civil war of 1918 indicates that this effort was not successful. The first steps towards reorienting creative potentials were thus taken in the beginning of the 1920s and universal schooling was finally established in the 1940s. As creative potentials were not liberated from providing for basic needs until the 1960s, the effective reorientation could not take place much before this. Therefore, the educational reforms of the 1960s are highly interesting and relevant in terms of the modern process of liberating and enhancing creative potentials in Finland.

The Modern Polity: Struggle for Independence and Peace

In the last decades of the nineteenth century Finland became a modern state in the Weberian sense, characterised by a legal order, bureaucracy, binding authority over a territory and monopolisation of the legitimate use of coercion (Alapuro, 1988, p. 39). However, it must be noted that none of the three impulses associated with the modern process of liberating and enhancing creativity had yet been manifested at that time. Liberation of creative potentials had begun and progressed slowly. Furthermore, in addition to domestic issues and processes, the emergence of the Finnish polity was firstly tied to the emergence of a national self-understanding, and secondly, to the political situation in the Russian empire. This was especially the case in the early decades of the twentieth century that saw some major unrest in the Finnish domestic political scene. Compared to Sweden and Denmark, the emergence of the Finnish polity was a slightly more precarious and eventful process involving one civil war and participation in World War II.

The origins of parliamentary democracy in Finland can be traced to 1863 when the Russian emperor decided to reengage the four-chamber Diet in political decision-making (Alapuro, 1988, p. 36; Virrankoski, 2001, p. 505; Pesonen and Riihinen, 2002, p. 23). In 1809 when Finland became part of the Russian Empire the local administration of the time continued to operate in a similar way to what it had been doing under Swedish rule. From 1816 onwards, the highest domestic authority had been the Senate, which was chaired by a Russian Governor General, who was the highest official in Finland and also the Commander-in-Chief of the Russian troops in Finland (Alapuro, 1988, p. 23). After 1863 the Diet began to convene regularly and the Senate's influence over domenstic affairs was balanced to some extent. The Diet consisted of four Estates that represented the different (property owning) groups of people in society. The nobility, the most influential group, gained their position in the Diet by inheritance. The second group, the clergy, gained their access to the Diet by virtue of their profession. The third group consisted of the burghers, who elected their representatives. As in many other countries, eligibility criteria were rather restricted concerning who could stand as candidate and vote in the elections, and were linked to income and wealth. The fourth group in the Diet was – rather exceptionally in a comparative sense – the peasantry.

Reengaging the Diet in 1863 can be seen as an increase in the political influence of the peasantry, as the state bureaucracy before 1863 had tended to be more closely linked with the three other groups. According to the prevailing views at the time only those men wealthy enough to be free from concerns related to self-interest could participate in politics, which was seen as the business of society as a whole (Jutikkala, 1965, p. 150). As the prevailing economic view was, in addition, that the wealth of the nation was fixed, it seemed natural to engage only those people in politics that had a privileged position with regard to property. In 1890 the share of this privileged group was around a third of the entire population (Alapuro, 1988, Table 2).

In the mid nineteenth century two main ideologies featured in Finnish politics – fennomania and liberalism. One of the main figures behind the former set of ideas was J.V. Snellman, whose role in Finnish politics was discussed earlier. One of the aims of the Fennomans was to make Finnish the main administrative language instead of Swedish, which had predominated thus far. Interestingly enough, the patriotic and nationalistic ideology had originated within the Swedish-speaking elite and in their plans 'a Finland united in language and culture was to establish itself not by dismantling the traditional structure of power, but by subjecting it to guidance by a patriotic intelligentsia' (Alapuro, 1988, p. 95). The Fennomans' and in particular Snellman's Hegelian ideas were rather different from the liberalist ideas of his British counterpart, J.S. Mill, who saw politics as a way of development requiring the inclusion of the non-property-owning groups in society. There was, of course a liberalist movement in nineteenth century Finland supported by bourgeois groups stressing Finland's position as a politically separate unit (Alapuro, 1988, p. 97).

The emergence of the Finnish modern polity turned out, however, to be quite different from the idealistic picture the Fennomans had envisaged, and the processes whereby it was achieved were anything but smooth and predictable. At first, of course, the Finnish modern polity was more about creating a social order where the place of the individual would not be determined at birth, and where the individual would be regarded as a sovereign agent with regard to the rule of law. A number of factors and processes contributing towards this development can be outlined. The emergence of voluntary organisations on a large scale, such as the Finnish revivalist movement, the temperance movement, and the voluntary fire brigades, contributed to the creation of the modern nation state (Stenius, 1980; Alapuro, 1988, p. 102). They included active individuals as their members creating a sense of solidarity that disregarded the traditional intermediaries of corporate society, and they also transcended narrow local boundaries (Alapuro, 1988, p. 102). The temperance movement and youth organisations were in the beginning of the twentieth century larger in number than the Social Democratic Party and the trade unions, and for a few decades they continued to be a source of solidarity and national integration. The right to organise into associations was formally acknowledged in 1906, but organisations were formed relatively freely even before that.

In addition to the organisation of voluntary associations, the establishment of certain individual liberties was crucial to the early foundations of the Finnish polity. Until the end of the nineteenth century each person living in the country was obliged to seek 'legal protection', which meant effectively that each individual, if not an owner of property themselves, would have to become involved in a patriarchal wage relationship. The spirit of this obligation was to ensure that individuals made themselves 'useful' in a social order that was based on fixed roles determined at each individual's birth, and not lead a 'bad and lazy lifestyle' (Rasila, 1982a, p. 20). A legislative act in 1879 established individual rights to choose one's place of work and habitation and the obligation to seek legal protection was abolished in 1883 (Rasila, 1982a, p. 20). Thus the patriarchal employment relationships were replaced by a liberal order in which each individual was free to engage in a mutual contract.

From a formal point of view, an important process in the emergence of the modern Finnish polity was also the establishment of municipal self-governance in the countryside in 1865 and in towns in 1873. This development created a counterbalance to national politics that was initially firmly based on personal wealth rather than corporatism, and that increased the political influence of freeholding peasants (Alapuro, 1988, p. 103). Local government became eventually accessible to everyone in 1917 (Hjerppe, 1989, p. 123).

The early history of the Finnish Social Democratic Party is linked with the temperance movement in the sense that the party was founded in 1899, a year after the so-called 'temperance strike' that had attracted wide attention also for the workers' movement (Alapuro, 1988, p. 109). Thus the early political aims of the Social Democrats, which adopted the social democratic label in 1903, included not only universal suffrage but also total prohibition of the sale and distribution of alcohol. Eventually both aims were achieved – although the prohibition law was first vetoed by the Russian emperor. Universal suffrage was achieved through a series of multidimensional processes of both domestic and external character. The turn of the century was marked by a conflict with the empire that was mainly due to efforts aiming to tie Finland culturally more strongly to Russia. These efforts did not please the nationalistic-minded dominant groups such as the Fennomans, and they were therefore more keen on seeking support from the popular groups, such as the workers' movement.

Nationalistic concerns contributed to the widespread support of parliamentary reform in 1906 (Jutikkala, 1965). The Diet approved of a proposal to establish a one-chamber parliament elected in universal and equal elections, and to ensure stability, the Russian emperor Nikolai II confirmed the proposal (Mylly, 2006, p. 249). The ultimate veto power remained, however, with the Russian emperor, so the establishment of universal suffrage cannot be regarded as the landmark of the establishment of the modern polity in Finland. In any case, the Social Democrats emerged as the largest party after the first general elections in 1907 with 38 per cent of the votes and 80 seats out of 200 in the new parliament (Alapuro, 1988, p. 117).

What was characteristic of Finnish Social Democracy of the early twentieth century was that the movement enjoyed widespread support among the less privileged agrarian population groups. In fact, as the country was mainly rural at the time, large-scale political organisation could not have been achieved without support from the countryside. The support of reform can be linked to the limits of creativity that the landless population was experiencing at the time. Although agriculture was not modernising, the prospects of the non-landowning groups in society were not very good at the time. The crofters were subject to rather unfavourable leasing conditions and the population without access to any land at all continued to grow. Discontent with the political situation was widespread (Alapuro, 1988, p. 117). Consequently, hopes and expectations were great when the Social Democrats finally established a position in the polity. But naturally, both local government and the state bureaucracy remained unchanged by the first general elections creating widespread frustration.

National stability had also become a major political issue after the dissolution of the domestic troops in Finland between 1901–1905 (Alapuro, 1988, p. 152). Before that, Finns were not obliged to serve in the Russian imperial army but possessed an army of their own. After 1905 the only armed forces in the country that were linked with statutory authority were the Russian imperial troops but they were effectively paralysed by the February Revolution in Russia. As both worker and bourgeois militias had been founded throughout the country in both cities and on the countryside, the distinction between public and private maintenance of order was not entirely clear. After the Russian autocracy collapsed in February 1917, government and the implementation of the rule of law became volatile. The Social Democrats failed to gain full internal Finnish autonomy during the time of the provisional government in Russia before the Bolshevist Revolution in October 1917. The provisional government dissolved the Finnish parliament in summer 1917. The new parliamentary elections worked against the Social Democrats and increased frustration among workers and a coup d'état was finally carried out. The bourgeois government declared the country independent in late 1917, and the Social Democrats and their allies declared the sole right of government belonged to themselves in early 1918. This led to the outbreak of a violent civil war that lasted until May, and was followed by a number of terrorist acts. As a consequence tens of thousands of lives were lost and a national trauma that was to last for several decades was caused (Virrankoski, 2001, pp. 709–53).

The workers' uprising – the 'Reds' – was defeated by the 'Whites' (the bourgeoisie) with the support of German troops in late spring 1918. Immediately after the civil war there were plans to create a monarchy dependent on Germany and led by a German-born king, but the German defeat in the First World War altered this course. The Entente required Finland to organise democratic elections in 1919 as a condition of international recognition, and this condition was fulfilled. Once again the Social Democrats emerged as the strongest party with 80 seats out of 200 and the Agrarian Union gained 42 seats (Alapuro, 1988, p. 206). The two main legislative reforms that were approved of during the unstable situation of 1917, the eight-hour working day law and the local government act, remained in force. A number of legislative acts concerning employment relations were passed in the 1920s – an act concerning the minimum conditions of work in 1922 and an act on collective bargaining in 1924 (Siipi, 1967, p. 44).

In Finland, the modern polity began to emerge as a series of incidents and conflicts some of which were internal and domestic and some of which were external and out of control. Socialist ideas started to reach Finland at the end of the nineteenth century, but they were received mainly within an intellectual elite as theoretical issues regarding the relationship between liberalist and socialist political projects (Eräsaari and Rahkonen, 2001, pp. 11–148) as the country was predominantly rural and agricultural. Thus, the modern polity can be said to have emerged by the time of the first democratic elections in independent Finland, i.e. by 1919. This conclusion along with the observations made about the manifestation of the two other impulses allows us to present a summary of observations so far.

The first impression when looking at Figure 3.3 where Finland is added is that this third country follows the other two in the modern process of liberating and enhancing creative potentials. In other words, the modernisation of agriculture,

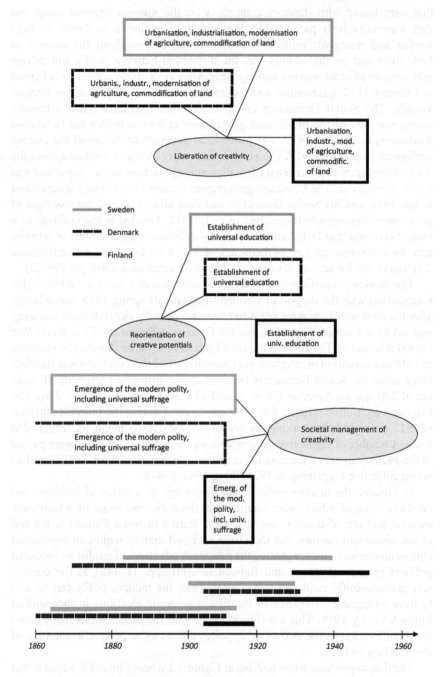

Figure 3.3   **The manifestations of three modern societal impulses in Sweden, Denmark and Finland**

the establishment of universal education and the emergence of the modern polity all occurred slightly later in Finland than in Sweden and Denmark. The second impression is that although occurring later in time, the three relevant time periods are shorter in Finland than in Sweden and Denmark. Thus, for instance, the modernisation of Finnish agriculture (in the sense discussed above) occurred during a period of twenty years, whereas in Sweden the corresponding process took more than half a century. Similarly, the volatile Finnish situation of the early twentieth century affected the length of the two other relevant time periods. Reorientation of creative potentials cannot be said to have been significant before the civil war, and the establishment of the modern polity was subject to challenges under Russian rule. Otherwise, it appears that Finland was subject to similar patterns as Sweden and Denmark.

In all countries studied above, the three impulses are rather simultaneous. Thus, modernisation of agriculture does not precede the other two processes, as one could have perhaps initially expected. In addition, regarding the two other countries, the establishment of private landownership and the enclosure of common fields occurred long before the modernisation of agriculture, and was associated with a redistribution of wealth that continued into the early twentieth century in the form of e.g. policies for the landless (see also Alestalo and Kuhnle, 1984, p. 12).

On the basis of the comparison of three Nordic countries, it appears that the simultaneity of the three impulses associated with the modern process of liberating and enhancing creative potentials might be something which is characteristic to the Nordic countries. Its significance for the emancipating aspects of societal development becomes clearer when considering the corresponding developments of a non-Nordic country, such as Britain. Often considered the pioneer of Western industrialisation, Britain was among the first countries where agriculture was modernised in the sense discussed above. But unlike the Nordic countries, this modernisation occurred quite simultaneously with the enclosures of common fields, i.e. during the eighteenth century (see e.g. Slater, 1907; Hammond and Hammond, 1911; Thompson, 1966; Turner, 1980, 1986; Berg, 1994). In addition, contrary to the Nordic development, the enclosures of common fields and the modernisation of agriculture appear to have been associated with a *concentration* of wealth, primarily landownership, rather than redistribution (Thompson, 1966; Beckett, 1986). In Britain, a three tiered ownership structure was consolidated after the modernisation of agriculture: wealthy landowners rented their land to tenant farmers, who in turn managed the farm by employing labourers (Turner et al., 2001, p. 9). In other words, landowning peasants were not found to the same extent as in the Nordic countries.

In Britain relatively early modernisation of agriculture ensured an increase in productivity, which in turn speeded the industrial revolution. Labourers moved from agriculture to factories, and so in principle, creative potentials were liberated from their previous temporal bonds. What is notable in the case of British societal development is, however, that at the time when creative potentials were liberated, there were no processes contributing to the *reorientation* of creative potentials.

Thus, during the nineteenth century when it was in principle no longer necessary to tie the majority of the labour force to the production of necessities, educational opportunities were rather segregated – and political rights were rather limited. After the liberation of creative potentials it took quite a long time before universal education and the modern polity were established in practice in Britain around the twentieth century (Held, 1996; Stephens, 1998; McCull, 2002).

Now, it is often assumed that the particular landownership structure in nineteenth century Britain was a necessary condition for increased agricultural productivity, and therefore also a condition for self-sustained economic growth and world economic leadership. Thus, it is also suggested that the accompanying social inequalities were necessary in this sense. But such an assumption fails to recognise the contingency of societal development. A comparison with the Nordic countries shows that societal development characterised by the same three impulses may result in a rather different outcome. In the Nordic countries, particularly the modernisation of agriculture was a process that seemed to have progressed much slower than in Britain, but as noted, this process in the Nordic countries was associated with continuous redistribution of resources. In addition, once agriculture was modernised and creative potentials liberated from previous bonds, educational opportunities and political rights were already in place. In other words, as soon as biographical time was liberated from its medieval bonds, a large proportion of the population was potentially able to use this time in more self-directed ways.

One particular conclusion may be drawn from the difference between Nordic and British societal development. The emancipatory effects of the three impulses appear to be stronger when they occur simultaneously, as in the Nordic countries. In Britain, all three impulses contributed to the liberation and enhancement of human creative potentials, but during the twentieth century many social and economic constraints remained in place for large groups of people. Wealth and social opportunities were rather unevenly distributed in British society compared to the Nordic countries, where the three modern impulses occurred rather simultaneously. In the Nordic countries a proportionally larger share of the population was subject to a similar kind of liberation and enhancement of creative potentials.

Thus, the simultaneity of the three modern societal impulses, and as a consequence, a strengthened emancipatory effect, may be seen as a uniquely Nordic characteristic with regard to modern societal development. In the following chapter we shall see how this societal development continues after the two World Wars in terms of its emancipatory and constraining aspects. But regarding the effects of the uniquely Nordic characteristics of societal development, it may also be noted that a certain kind of local government structure emerged where local municipalities were subject to democratic elections and notable administrative responsibilities (Kröger, 1997). It seems likely that without the relatively equal distribution of landownership, this type of local government could not have developed. In Britain, where landownership remained concentrated, the role of local government remained smaller in comparison with the Nordic countries.

Chapter 4
Welfare States and the Wave of Post-war Emancipation

Once the three modern impulses discussed in the previous chapter (education, suffrage, modernisation of agriculture) were manifested in the Nordic countries, the two World Wars disrupted societal development with known consequences (Stenius et al., 2011). In Giddensian terms, the post-war period starts a new episode, but at the same time, some elements are carried over, so to speak, from the preceding period. In other words, societal development does not begin anew; it merely enters a new phase. Among the general discontinuities was that whereas the pre-war period was characterised by the replacement of medieval notions of the relationship between individual and society, new societal and economic ideas began to emerge and spread after the end of the two World Wars. In the Nordic countries a major task during the post-war era was to find a balance between socialist ideas coming from the East and capitalist ideas coming from the West – and, of course, to manage this ideological balance against any domestic tensions between different interest groups.

If one looks at the emancipating and the constraining aspects of societal development during the post-war period, it seems that some continuity from previous time periods can be detected. Emancipatory societal development was associated with the redistribution of resources, and a local government structure that in accordance with the landownership structure allowed for a significant role for the local municipalities in administering local political affairs. During the post-war period, it appears that these emancipatory elements of previous times are carried forward by the welfare state institutions. Institutionalised social security programmes (unemployment benefit, pensions, sickness insurance) carried on the function of redistributing resources between population groups, and local welfare services (schools, hospitals, health care etc.) administered by the local municipalities were available on equal grounds for all citizens (Pierson, 2004, p. 5, 2006, p. 115). These welfare state institutions sought to ensure an inclusive societal development, and to the extent that they succeeded in doing so, they may be regarded as contributing to the further liberation and emancipation of human creative potentials during the post-war period. In principle, to the extent that social and economic opportunities were equalised during the post-war period, each new generation was to an increasing extent able to direct their biographical time towards self-chosen ends.

Thus, it seems that from the point of view of the emancipatory and the constraining aspects of societal development, post-war welfare state institutions and their development are worth a closer look. Although these institutions have origins in earlier periods, it is only after the two World Wars that they start carrying forward the emancipatory aspects that different processes contributed to during the pre-war period. In this sense, they may be regarded as 'new' institutions from the point of view of the emancipating and the constraining aspects of societal development. There were, of course, constraining aspects in societal development during the post-war period in the Nordic countries, and these will be returned to in Chapter 5. In the sense of 'old' and 'new' aspects of societal development, there were some 'old' constraints reminiscent of a past social order with hereditary privileges, but in accordance with the new logic of societal development, new constraints also developed during this post-war period. These new constraints will be the subject of Chapter 5, after reviewing the 'new' emancipating institutions of the post-war era, i.e. the Nordic welfare state institutions. It must also be remembered that these institutions were not automatically emancipating for all citizens. Laws of forced sterilisation were passed on grounds of racial refinery in accordance with prevailing understandings of eugenics. Thus, it is perhaps more accurate to say that the new welfare state institutions were associated with some emancipating elements – and that emancipation societal development was not new as such but had a background in nineteenth-century developments.

It is, of course, recognised in the existing literature on comparative welfare state research that there are many unique features of post-war welfare state institutions in the Nordic countries, and these familiar traits will be briefly outlined in what follows. But what is perhaps less acknowledged is the dynamic character of these features, and the fact that they have 'inherited' some emancipatory aspects from previous times.

Modernism, the Natural Sciences and Twentieth-century Society

A main portion of the uncertainty and instability of the early-twentieth-century Nordic countries was due to international affairs – two World Wars and a worldwide economic recession in the interwar period. Totalitarian regimes emerged throughout Europe and east of Europe as well, while the Nordic countries built and developed their political *Sonderweg* (Sejersted, 2005, pp. 57–111) in the form of democratic institutions without fascist or socialist coups. Therefore, in retrospect, the early twentieth century appears as a period of uncertainty during which the continued development of democratic institutions was not that self-evident in the Nordic countries.

The uncertainty and instability was perhaps most evident in Finland and Denmark – the destinies of which to a large extent depended on the outcome of World War II, upon which these two small countries had no influence. In Sweden, on the other hand, many of the foundations of the post-war period of stability were already laid during the first half of the century – for instance during the 1930s when the two famous agreements between labourers and industrialists (1933) and urban and rural groups (1938) were made (Hentilä et al., 2002, p. 254). These agreements reflected a commitment to co-operation by groups in society with quite different perspectives on social and economic life. In addition, the Social Democratic rule in Sweden that came to last for more than 40 years began already in the beginning of the twentieth century. It was under the rule of the Swedish SAP (*Socialdemokratiska arbetarpartiet*) that many of the institutions of the post-war welfare state were established.

As seen in the previous chapter, the modernisation of agriculture was among the first processes whereby the fruits of modern technology were utilised. The modern scientific attitude gave rise to a future optimism and a belief in the rational capacities of human beings also during the twentieth century (von Wright, 1993, p. 140). In a similar manner with natural science and technology, a belief arose that general social laws could be detected using methods reminiscent of natural science, and society could be steered accordingly towards chosen ends. In other words, there seemed to be no limits to the possible achievements of the rational human mind. Furthermore, all moral issues were excluded from the investigation of natural laws (von Wright, 1993, p. 175), so in order to remain cohesive, moral issues had to be excluded from social scientific research as well. It was also during this period that the spread of disciplines such as economics and demographical statistics occurred.

To paraphrase Peter Wagner, post-Enlightenment human beings no longer accepted any external guarantors to the continuity of their selves, to the certainty of their knowledge, and to the capacity of constructing their own laws (Wagner, 2001, p. 4). One aspect of this 'modernism' was the notion of the unity of science – or to be more precise the claim that all academic disciplines ought to follow the methods of Galilean/Newtonian natural science. Based on this notion a hierarchy between different disciplines was seen with mathematics on the top, followed by (theoretical and practical) physics, chemistry, biology, medicine, psychology and the human sciences including economics, sociology, social psychology and political science. The academic arguments for this kind of unity of science are perhaps not that relevant, but as a cultural trend the belief in the all-round superiority in Galileian/Newtonian natural sciences had some notable implications for societies in the early twentieth century.

In the efforts to maintain methodological consistency, the links between natural science and society were sometimes pushed to the extreme. The medical branch of eugenics is an example of such an effort. Eugenics in its early-twentieth-century form contained the notion of the possibility to refine the human race in order to conquer aspects that might make its survival more difficult, such as mental and physical illnesses, particularly if they were seen to be inherited. These medical conditions were seen as challenges that could be overcome by racial refinery. Once these observations were combined with a totalitarian social order, the consequences were drastic to say the least. This happened, as is well known, when Germany was under the rule of National Socialism (Burleigh, 2000).

In the Nordic countries eugenic ideas were combined, not with a totalitarian social order, but with a collectivist one. We shall later go into the details why this social order may be called collectivist, but under all circumstances the consequences of the adoption of the ideas of eugenics in post-war social engineering were drastic. The extinction of people thought to be of an inferior kind did not occur in the Nordic countries, but based on the prophylactic principles of the time, laws regarding forced sterilisation of women were passed. Interestingly enough, the prophylactic principle contains many of the elements that characterise Nordic social policy during the post-war period, but, as Sejersted (2005, p. 129) has pointed out, when combined with eugenics, this principle was pushed to its extreme. It was observed that poor people had significantly more children compared to more affluent people, and that poverty tended to persist from one generation to another. Therefore, the obvious solution seemed to be that women subject to the perceived challenges should be sterilised, because they presented challenges not primarily to the individual in question, but to the future evolution of society (the links to Social Darwinism seem obvious in this respect). Laws concerning forced sterilisation were established in Sweden in 1934. Later in 1975 this law was modified so that sterilisation without consent was no longer possible. During the time when the law was in place 44,000 sterilisations were carried out in Sweden, half of which were forced (Sejersted, 2005, p. 129).

In the same year as the law on forced sterilisations in Sweden was passed, an influential figure in Swedish academia and politics, Gunnar Myrdal, published together with his wife Alva a pamphlet dealing with demographic planning (Myrdal and Myrdal, 1934). This pamphlet contained an outline of the prophylactic principle that would become an influential ingredient in the social policies of all Nordic countries. The principle stated that social problems should not be only reacted against, but with careful planning they could be foreseen and prevented in a way that simultaneously was beneficial for economic growth. In the 1934 pamphlet the Myrdals also linked the prophylactic principle with demographic planning, eugenics and forced sterilisations (Therborn, 2004, p. 254).

Besides sharing the contemporary trust in social engineering based on the methods of natural science, Myrdal developed some highly original and fruitful thoughts within the field of economics that also earned him the Nobel memorial prize in 1974. He did not conform to the ideas of mainstream classical liberal economics, but having his intellectual origins in the Stockholm school of the 1930s with Knut Wicksell as teacher, his ideas came to resemble more those of institutionalists such as J.K. Galbraith. Myrdal's contributions in the field of political economy may be understood from his rejection of the distinction between production and distribution made in classical economics. According to Myrdal, this distinction leads economists to focus on issues related to production at the expense of distribution, which they think is a matter of money incomes. By rejecting this distinction, and by adopting a more holistic view of the economy, Myrdal focused his attention on issues he termed 'equality of distribution' in the economy allowing for the design of extensive social policy reforms (Myrdal, 1973, pp. 8–10).

Perhaps more in line with J.K. Galbraith and Robert Heilbroner than J.M. Keynes, Myrdal argued that well-planned egalitarian policy reforms would be preventive, prophylactic and thus productive. He firmly believed that the expansion of social policy could spare individuals and society from future costs and/or increase future productivity (Myrdal, 1973, p. 41). He developed this view in contrast with mainstream economists, who would argue that egalitarian reforms are a burden on the economy and slow down economic growth. In other words, Myrdal's economic ideas allowed for an investment in the individual person as a resource for economic growth. This was translated in politics into a positive form of providing incentives for economic participation, as a contrast to the negative form proposed by classical liberalism, where incentives sometimes involved a struggle for existence. This kind of thinking, in addition to the prophylactic principle, provided a fruitful background for Swedish Social Democrats to carry on with the redistributive tendencies associated with earlier modernisation, thus enforcing the inclusive and emancipatory aspects of Swedish society.

Finding a Nordic Application of Keynesian and Beveridgean Ideas

Despite the differences in socio-economic structure and the timing of social reform, and sometimes also the administration of benefits, a number of common features in the emerging Nordic welfare states distinguish these countries from other contemporary nations. The main engine that put in practice the prophylactic principles formulated by Gunnar Myrdal in Sweden and Pekka Kuusi in Finland (see e.g. Kuusi, 1964) was the social security system that provided income maintenance during times of lost income due to sickness, unemployment, disability and old age. There were at least three distinctive aspects to the way this social security system served as a mechanism of redistribution and also as a means of preventing social problems by investing in human beings. First, income distribution was kept narrow both due to the high income replacement rates of the benefits themselves and due to the funding mechanisms (e.g. progressive income tax). Secondly, the benefit structure was designed to stimulate economic growth by distributing the income of high earners to low earners with the consequence that the former group's consumption decreased less than the latter group's consumption increased. Thus, total consumption was thought to increase as a consequence of the redistribution of income, which would contribute to economic growth. Thirdly, and partly following from the two previous points, economic growth was not based on creating income differences as economic incentives, but on creating opportunities for economic participation for all citizens, including married women (Åmark, 2006, pp. 299–335). This kind of positive incentive structure was aimed to encourage each individual to develop their own individual potential instead of creating negative incentives that would involve a threat of hunger and misery.

The social security system that in addition to public welfare services became one of the distinctive characteristics of the Nordic welfare states was established in several waves, each of which was accompanied by extensive planning and deliberation regarding benefit coverage, funding, benefit levels and administration (Kangas, 1988; Baldwin, 1990, pp. 55–157; Karisto et al., 1998; Huber and Stephens, 2001, pp. 115–44; Hentilä et al., 2002, pp. 293–311; Sejersted, 2005, pp. 118–26; Edling, 2006; Petersen and Åmark, 2006, pp. 145–89; Pierson, 2006, pp. 105–42). A first wave around the turn of the twentieth century had brought basic worker protection legislation, health insurance and pensions although coverage and levels of benefit remained rather low. Generally speaking, among the three countries considered, Denmark was the first to introduce social security reforms, followed by Sweden and Finland. A second wave occurred after World War II when there was a strong sense of redevelopment throughout Europe. In the UK, where the renowned Beveridge plan was realised, containing for instance the establishment of universally provided public health care (Baldwin, 1990, pp. 116–46), extensive social reforms had been promised by leading politicians during the war. In Finland, despite the atrocities the war served to unite the people and alleviate the cleavages and oppositions originating in the civil war a few decades earlier, and contributing to a post-war consensus, thus paving the way for social reform.

The sense of nation building was associated with a 'baby boom' and many cohorts of children that were particularly large in number. Many social policy reforms tended to follow the needs of the 'baby boom' generation. Child allowances, primary and secondary schools, the expansion of higher education, housing policies and public day care facilities can be seen in this light (Hentilä et al., 2002, p. 303).

The origins of government pension schemes in the Nordic countries date back to 1891 in Denmark where special provision for 'deserving' elderly was established (Petersen et al., 2010). Sweden followed after careful planning and deliberation with a provisional pension reform in 1913. In Finland, a corresponding reform was carried out in the late 1930s, but wartime inflation rapidly decreased the real value of the benefits that were not high in the first place. These pension allowances introduced before World War II were not high enough to constitute a sole source of income for recipients. After the second wave of pension reform after World War II pensioners could, however, avoid having to rely on social assistance in the Nordic countries (Hentilä et al., 2002, p. 299; Petersen and Åmark, 2006, pp. 145–89).

Although the timing of social security reform was different in the Nordic countries, a quite distinctive tax-benefit system was developed during the post-war period. At the same time, the social security system interacted with other central institutions, such as the taxation system and the wage setting system and the social services system in general (schools, hospitals, care services). When compared directly with the systems in other Western countries, benefit levels and coverage during the post-war period appear much more comprehensive in the Nordic countries. There is more emphasis on the principle of universalism and less emphasis on targeting and status. When viewed from the point of view of the division between the economic and the social, the state seems to play a bigger role in the Nordic countries compared to other Western European countries particularly when it comes to intervening in the market.

Esping-Andersen (1990, 1999) has systematically analysed the main characteristics of the Nordic welfare states in comparison with other Western countries. His analysis rests on a Polanyian understanding of labour as a 'fictitious commodity' (Esping-Andersen, 1990, p. 36). He then concludes that the Nordic countries' social security system contributes to the *decommodification* of labour to a larger extent than any other welfare state model (Esping-Andersen operates with three ideal types). In other words, it allows for greater independence from the market from the point of view of the labourer (Esping-Andersen, 1990, pp. 221–30).

Esping-Andersen's analysis cannot be overestimated concerning the impulse it has given to comparative welfare state research. However, the concept of 'welfare model' that has remained influential is rather static with its fixed degrees of decommodification (either low, medium or high). A static understanding of decommodification does not, ultimately, increase our understanding of the dynamic processes regarding the evolution of labour markets. Thus, although Esping-Andersen's analysis is valuable in distinguishing some of the central characteristics of the Nordic welfare states in relation to other welfare states, comparative researchers are left with the task of developing a dynamic understanding of welfare state change including conceptions of change over time (cf. Kettunen and Petersen, 2011).

Pauli Kettunen has highlighted two ideas that were to a large extent the outcome of the historic compromises of the 1930s, and that would since then constitute the cornerstones of post-war Nordic societies. These ideas were firstly, parity between workers and industrialists, and secondly, a virtuous circle between efficiency, solidarity and equality:

The first idea was a parity between the labour market parties, organized symmetrically at various levels of national society. This parity between employers and workers was not just a formal juridical construction, nor just an ideological disguise of the factual asymmetry between labour and capital. It became included in the future-oriented principles of democracy. The strong trade unions were supposed to extend democracy in two senses, both as a "popular movement" and as one of the two "parties" making parity-based agreements on the labour market. The second idea was a virtuous circle between efficiency, solidarity and equality. This was supposed to be achieved through compromises between different collective interests of capitalists, workers and farmers. As part of the Scandinavian class compromises of the 1930s, the labour movement accepted that economic growth and thus rationalisation were necessary in order to create resources for social welfare and equality. At the same time, bourgeois groups and employers accepted that the collective organisation of labour and the widening of workers' rights could bring about positive economic results. Thus, the needs and interests of capital, or employers, gained a moral and political legitimisation as the needs and interests of the working class gained an economic legitimisation. (Kettunen, 2006, pp. 59–60)

According to Kettunen, the 'virtuous circle' between efficiency, solidarity and equality was based on three ideological strains: the spirit of capitalism, the utopia of socialism and the idealised heritage of the free independent peasant. In the later development of the welfare state, this background contributed to the parallel reinforcing of two principles: the Universalist idea of social rights based on citizenship, and the normalcy of wage work (Kettunen, 2006, p. 60). Contrasted with Esping-Andersen, Kettunen's understanding of work and social rights cannot, thus be reduced to a polarity between commodification and decommodification as opposing principles. On the contrary, the normalcy of wage work and social rights based on citizenship are seen as mutually reinforcing principles (Kettunen, 2008, p. 156). Moreover, in the absence of one, the other would not work.

It may be noted that the state is seen as a benevolent actor and source of solidarity in the political language and culture of the Nordic countries. Thus, the state is not, for instance, seen as a threat to individual sovereignty. This becomes evident in the linguistic assimilation of 'state' and 'society' that is common to all Nordic languages including Finnish (Kettunen, 2003, p. 170). This assimilation is not a product of the modern welfare state, but has occurred much earlier, as exemplified by the way the conservative historian and statesman Yrjö-Sakari Yrjö-Koskinen in Finland used the term 'society' in the political debate of the late nineteenth century (Eräsaari and Rahkonen, 2001, pp. 56–101). In his rhetoric four different meanings to the term 'society' appear – first, it is used as synonymous with the 'state' or 'government', secondly, it is used as the practices that the state should regulate, thirdly, as the order that emerges as a result of this regulation, and fourthly, as the totality of which the state is a part (Kettunen, 2003, p. 184). Later, the social security system became part of this 'society' and the failure of the social security system is almost without exception generally experienced as the failure of 'society'.[1]

Managing Social Opportunities: Education and the Labour Market

When looked at together, the features mentioned above – prophylactic social policy, state involvement, decommodification and 'virtuous circles' – certainly capture a great deal of the distinctive characteristics of the welfare arrangements in the Nordic countries. In addition to these, there are, however, two aspects or points of view that deserve some attention – especially regarding the emancipatory aspects of societal development. These two aspects may be found when the life-

---

1   This is frequently evident in the letters to the editor pages of major Finnish newpapers, where citizens demand 'society' to intervene if serious problems arise – problems that affect the well-being of citizens (see e.g. HS 8 April 2010).

course and agency of the individual is examined more closely. One of these aspects is, again, education.

As mentioned in the preceding discussion regarding the basic features of the reorientation of creative potentials by establishing the right to equal basic education for all children, a strong '*Bildung*'[2] ideal was eminent during the nineteenth century. Central proponents of this ideal were Snellman in Finland, Geier in Sweden and Gruntvig in Denmark, all of whom were key figures in the cultural and political life of the time (Stenius, 2010). Although the 'Bildung' ideal contained many aspirations towards better educational opportunities, education was, however, organised according to social background. This began to change in the early twentieth century when educational opportunities increased, and the parallel school system was finally abolished in the 1960s by a thorough educational reform in Sweden (1962), Finland (1968) and Denmark (1972) (Hentilä et al., 2002, p. 303). An expansion of higher education also took place and free university education was made more available for people living in different regions.

As a consequence of the educational reform, which took a fairly similar form in all Nordic countries, all children between 7 and 15 years of age could receive a similar kind of education provided by the local municipality. This system replaced the partially parallel previous system, where some children continued from primary education (the folk school) to secondary education, and others remained in a kind of extended primary school. In effect, the folk school was replaced by a single school for all children until the age of 15. Thereafter, children could either go on to upper secondary schools or vocational training. The educational reforms of the 1960s were quite similar in content in all the Nordic countries, although some traces of the parallel system were left in Denmark (Hentilä et al., 2002, p. 303). The aim was to provide children with equal, high standard education regardless of social background, gender or place of birth. No one was supposed to be left out, and no one was supposed to be singled out.

This education system – together with all other aspects of the 'Nordic society' contributed to the inclusiveness of these societies. As all children received the same education until the age of 15, they all possessed the same educational capacities to reorient their creative abilities onwards from that point of their life cycles. This system was quite unique, as education (including school meals) was free of charge and educational systems other than the one provided by the state were quite exceptional. Nordic educational systems have received high scores in comparisons among OECD countires. A key reason for the success may be the equality of access to high quality public education (for systematic comparisons of educational systems in OECD countries, see OECD, 2009a; OECD, 2010ab).

After education, an important stage in an individual's life course is often employment. This is even more so in the Nordic countries that, as Kettunen points out, are founded to a large extent on the pillar of wage work. Naturally,

---

2   The *Bildung* ideal is an understanding of education that contains a notion of personal development.

not all people enter into an employment relation. Some people are self-employed, some stay at home with a family, and some others may have a disability or illness preventing them from fulfilling the expectations usually involved in employment. Nonetheless, a high employment rate has been an explicit target in Nordic labour market policy during the first episode of the modern process. As work and employment relate closely with the realisation of individual creative potentials, the management of the employment relationship in the Nordic countries during the post-war period deserves some attention.

Full employment in addition to a maximal employment participation rate has been the explicit target of Nordic labour market policy (Hentilä et al., 2002, p. 311). This implies that those who want to work should have the opportunity to do so. Furthermore, the conditions of employment relationship in the Nordic countries – wage, working hours, holidays, health and safety – have not only been the concern of the individual employee, but the concern of centralised interest organisations. Ever since the historic compromises of the 1930s, the trade unions have been fairly influential in national politics, not only in Sweden but also in Finland and Denmark as well. Trade union membership has increased since then and exceeded 90 per cent in Sweden and Finland in the 1980s (Hentilä et al., 2002, pp. 294–5). The *corporatist* model of labour market policy implied that both labour market parties, i.e. workers' and employees' representatives, were mostly consulted in an effort to seek consensus over significant reforms concerning the economy and the labour market – for instance social security policies. Trade unions also had a role in implementing policy, as Knudsen and Rothstein (1994) have noted.

It is worthwhile taking a slightly closer look at the post-war employment policy model that developed in Sweden. This is not only because it has received a fair share of international academic attention, but because it demonstrates the way in which all aspects and parts of economic, labour market and social policy were interrelated and part of a carefully planned system run by the state and the labour market parties. Regarding employment and labour market policy, the design of a unique Swedish model culminated in 1951, when the LO (*Landsorganisationen*, the Swedish top trade union) accepted a 200-page document entitled *The Labour Movement and Full Employment* as its key strategic paper (Sihto, 1994, pp. 43–7). Much of the economic and employment policy model designed by Gösta Rehn and Rudolf Meidner was contained in this document. The rest of the chapter will deal with Nordic labour market policy and associated interesting issues, such as the role of the state in the economy and notions of justice and fairness. These issues are, in turn, linked with the social opportunities people are presented with, and with the ways in which they are able to use their creative potentials (cf. Chapter 2).

Looking a few decades back from the passing of the key document of 1951, an interesting development of the aims and ideas of the labour movement in Sweden can be detected. Among the first goals of the labour movement had been, as noted in the discussion regarding the emergence of the modern polity, the establishment of universal suffrage, which was accomplished in 1918. Universal suffrage as a policy goal can be seen as an initial step towards reformism, rather than revolution, from the point of view of the labour movement. The next step involved a debate regarding private ownership (Blyth, 2002, pp. 97–101), which occurred during a time of economic struggle. Unemployment had been on the increase during the 1920s and the recession at the beginning of the 1930s fuelled pessimistic (or optimistic, depending on one's point of view) voices regarding the collapse of the capitalist order and a subsequent socialisation of the means of production. Once in power, the Social Democrats in Sweden never quite aspired towards the practical realisation of Marxist/Leninist ideas. First, having gained access to government, they even governed according to the ideas of classical economics in the lack of any original new ideas (Blyth, 2002, pp. 101–4). But the historic compromises of the 1930s paved the way for an original solution in social and economic policy, a solution that carried on the traditions of inclusion and redistribution described in Chapter 3.

The three components of the Rehn–Meidner model of economic and employment policy were not entirely novel when presented to the LO in 1951 (Sihto, 1994, pp. 43–7). They had been either in use or recognised before, but what the LO document of 1951 did was to present a new connection between the three components, creating a new kind of justification for the system that they would form. What was also new was that such a comprehensive national strategy was presented by a trade union. The three components consisted of:

1. A restrictive fiscal policy;
2. Active labour market policies; and
3. A solidaristic wage policy.

The overarching goal of the model was to achieve economic stability and full employment. Swedish economic policy makers at the time had a gut feeling about what was later to be articulated as the Phillips curve regarding the non-linear relationship between inflation and unemployment (Sihto, 1994, p. 88). The post-war economy grew more rapidly than economic experts had anticipated, and high demand and tight labour markets created inflationary pressures (Blyth, 2002, p. 119). In a booming economy, workers found themselves in a good negotiating position, and as firms were in need of labour, inflation was a real threat. The Rehn–Meidner model responded to this threat by including a restrictive fiscal policy as the cornerstone of the model. This measure included, among other measures, profit capping so that industries were unable to respond to inflationary wage demands (Blyth, 2002, p. 120). In practice, this profit capping was executed by taxes, which were compensated by subsidised loans by the state, especially during times when increase in demand was again needed. Private consumption was also restricted.

The downside of restrictive fiscal policy was a tendency towards local unemployment, which was compensated for by the second pillar of the Rehn–Meidner model, i.e. active labour market policies. These measures included the establishment of government employment agencies, government relocation and retraining measures in order to increase worker mobility. Thus, Rehn and Meidner did not trust the classical economists' assumptions about perfect information, mobility and competition. In an article from 1952 Gösta Rehn expressed the aims of employment policy in the following manner:

> The cause of the tendency towards excessive wage increases does not lie solely in the strong bargaining position of the trade unions, which is the result of the elimination of unemployment. Full employment, and the certainty that it will be permanently maintained, must also tend to result in high profits and thereby give rise to fierce competition for the labour with the help of which the profits are gained ... Therefore, we must see to it that profits in general are so small that any exaggerated wage competition between firms is checked. But smaller profits imply that, in some fields, private initiative tends to make umployment insufficient, so that special State efforts are called for to prevent the unemployment that threatens to appear. (Rehn, 1952, pp. 32–3)

Manageable profits could, according to Rehn be achieved through indirect taxes on investment goods (Rehn, 1952, p. 51). State efforts to alleviate local unemployment were to include active labour market policies. The third pillar of the model, a solidaristic wage policy, was justified by its contribution to structural adjustment. A solidarity wage in this respect meant similar pay for similar work across sectors. The aim was to harmonise wages according to the level of skills that were expected by the workers, thus creating a fair income distribution but also creating incentives to training (Sihto, 1994, p. 42). The solidarity wage was also supposed to prevent sectoral wage competition that might again increase inflationary pressures. It also contributed, however, to structural adjustment by forcing inefficient firms either to rationalise or to go bankrupt, as wage dumping was no longer possible (Blyth, 2002, p. 121). Together with the active labour market measures, this policy helped make workers available in areas where efficient business operated, whilst creating pressures to rationalise production in inefficient areas (cf. Rehn, 1952, pp. 40–41, 43–4).

Two aspects must be kept in mind when assessing the Swedish post-war model of employment policy. First, it was created during times of rapid economic expansion. Unemployment did not cause problems unless demand restriction went too far, or if it was not compensated for by other measures, such as the ones in the Rehn–Meidner model. Secondly, the model must be seen against the background of the evolving goals of the Swedish labour movement and the strong positions of both the political party SAP and the trade union LO in Swedish politics ever since the extension of suffrage and the historic compromises of the 1930s. On the one hand, private ownership was not contested, nor was the fact that the aims of economic policy were to create the best possible conditions for businesses to operate in. But on the other hand, nor was the necessity of state intervention contested either.

According to the principles laid out in Saltsjöbaden in 1938, the trade unions were supposed to be 'independent' of both political parties and the state. When proposing a comprehensive economic policy, the LO kept in mind not only the interests of its own members, but also perceived its role as carrying the responsibility for the functioning of the entire Swedish economy. Thus, the goals of the labour movement had evolved from Marxist/Leninist aspirations towards an understanding that sustainable economic growth would in the long run benefit the entire society. This was the basis of the consensus between workers, industrialists and agriculture, which was in any case needed despite the strong position of the Social Democrats and the trade union.

A year after the publication of the crucial LO document, the Finnish Prime Minister (later President) Urho Kekkonen published a pamphlet entitled *Do We Have the Patience to Prosper?* (Kekkonen, 1952). The post-war economic scene was rather different in Finland compared to Sweden after a lost war, which had to be compensated for economically. Politicians maintained that the only way forward for Finland was to catch up economically with the rest of the Western world. This would require 'patience' in the form of investments in business and industry, and restrictions on private consumption. Thus, an expansion of the economy was not built in the post-war Finnish economy in the way it was in Sweden (or so it was perceived). Instead, growth would require heavy public investments in areas where private capital was not sufficient to generate growth. Later, this Finnish model of investment-led growth was criticised as inefficient with too few returns on investments and too many restrictions on consumption (Pohjola, 1996, p. 33; Böckerman and Kiander, 2006, p. 139).

Twentieth-century societal development appears to have been most stable and continuous in Sweden. The country was under Social Democratic rule for 40 years continuously, and experienced stable socio-economic development which was not disrupted by the war as in Denmark and Finland. Many discontinuities accompanied the early years of Finnish independence, but there were other features as well which made Finnish post-war development different from that found in both Sweden and Denmark.

The Finnish post-war period of economic and social development is usually divided into two periods: the period up to the end of the 1960s, and the period thereafter (Andersson et al., 1993; Alasuutari, 1996, pp. 104–23; Huber and Stevens, 2001, pp. 134–40). The period after World War II until the 1960s was politically characterised by agrarian dominance and a divided trade union movement, and a language of moral concern about nation building and resettlement of war refugees. The second period, on the other hand, was characterised by tripartite corporatism and a more united trade union movement and a language of rational social planning (Alasuutari, 1996, pp. 104–15; Huber and Stevens, 2001, pp. 134–5; Rainio-Niemi, 2009, pp. 77–8, 94). Increasing state centrism was, however, common to both of these periods, a feature that also united Finland and Sweden. In other words, the state began to take an increasing responsibility of economic and social development during the post-war period (Kosonen, 1998, p. 83; Rainio-Niemi, 2009, p. 93).

Two policy goals in particular were of considerable importance to Finland during the post-war period, i.e. growth (or structural transformation), and the international competitiveness of the export sector. All other short-term policy goals were subordinated to these two main ones (Kosonen, 1998, p. 89) and the main goals were pursued by strong state leadership. This policy has been characterised as an alliance between heavy industry (forest and steel) and the government (Pohjola, 1996, p. 33), but underlying this strategy was a concern about the social and economic development of the entire nation. Alasuutari has called the country at that time a single, large corporation managed by its political leaders aiming at the best possible yield in international trade, given the raw materials provided by the land and the effort of its people. In return this 'Finland inc.' aimed to distribute the economic yields without creating severe income differences between different groups of people (Alasuutari, 2004).

Another feature of the state-centred growth strategy in Finland was a heavy reliance on investments and restrictions on private consumption – a strategy that was, as noted above, promoted by Prime Minister Urho Kekkonen at the beginning of the 1950s. This strategy, which was not only a personal opinion of the Prime Minister, but also expressed in a government committee report (Pohjola, 1996, p. 34), acknowledged that private capital had not accumulated in such a way that market forces alone would bring about a rapid structural transformation in a country that structurally resembled Poland and Hungary more than Sweden and Denmark (Huber and Stevens, 2001, pp. 134–40). Thus, the state had to acquire an active role in capital formation, investment and also in the running of businesses. In addition, it was perceived necessary to limit private consumption in order to facilitate heavy investments.

Fiscal policy was procyclical in the sense that contractionary policies were applied during recessions and expansionary policies during periods of growth. Currency devaluations also played a key role in securing the international competitiveness of the export sector and inflation rates were kept rather high (Pekkarinen and Vartiainen, 1993, p. 19; Huber and Stevens, 2001, pp. 134–40). Andersson, Kosonen and Vartiainen describe a typical Finnish business cycle in the following manner:

> During export-led booms, incomes have increased fast and the domestic cost level and wages level have risen, thereby undermining competitiveness. At this stage, public demand and private investment have also increased fast. When export growth falters, the economy moves into recession. The open sector's profitability worsens and the markka is devalued. Fiscal and monetary policy are rather tight during the recession. As export growth accelerates again, incomes policies are used with mixed success to contain wage inflation and investment increases heavily, boosted by the entrepreneurs' appreciation of improved profitability. (Andersson et al., 1993, p. 19)

This economic policy worked in the sense that it produced fairly rapid, although cyclical growth, and a rapid structural transformation. Compared to Sweden and Denmark, the variation of economic cycles was greater, particularly in the 1970s when growth fluctuated between 0 and almost 8 per cent of the GDP (Andersson et al., 1993, p. 24). Another feature of the Finnish economy was that real interest rates were rather low and sometimes even negative. Therefore, according to Andersson, it was necessary to generate forced saving via the public sector through tax exemptions as low interest rates would otherwise have made bank deposits unattractive (Andersson et al., 1993, p. 20).

The major difference between Finland and Sweden can perhaps be pinpointed by the fact that the labour movement only became part of the corporatist system of decision making in the 1960s, whereas it had been part of the system in Sweden since the 1930s. In both countries the development of prophylactic social policies in the spirit of social engineering also seems to accompany the moment when the labour movement is incorporated in decision making. In Sweden Gunnar Myrdal's influence on the prophylactic principles of social policy can be traced to the 1930s, whereas a similar kind of influence can be detected regarding Pekka Kuusi in Finland in the 1960s. Kuusi's programme was also based on ideas of rationalist planning as it contained detailed projections of estimated economic, population and employment growth as a basis of social reforms. The development of prophylactic social security programmes was then incorporated in the tripartite system of decision-making where taxation, labour supply, wages, working conditions and social security programmes were decided upon.

In Sweden the agreements of the 1930s marked the end of workers' radicalisation. Nor in Finland was there an immediate threat of further worker radicalisation despite a slightly ambivalent relationship with the neighbouring Soviet Union. In Denmark, however, the radicalisation of workers continued after World War II and the Communists gained some significant electoral support in the late 1940s (Kaspersen, 2005, p. 64). From the point of view of the US – the Super Power of the West – this represented a threat and made Denmark a target of the Marshall Plan, which established to counteract the rise of communism and a possible Soviet invasion of Western Europe.

The Danish welfare state may be viewed as a fusion of a defence project and a social project – given the high priority to establish social stability in order to contain the communist threat (Kaspersen, 2005, pp. 64–5). It can, however, be argued that social stability was a key goal of any welfare arrangement, but nonetheless, the co-operation with the West and the US in particular was an important aspect of Danish post-war politics. Denmark created a mirror image of Finland, so to speak, since both countries managed a complicated foreign policy relationship, whereas Sweden enjoyed relative stability. The reception of Marshall Aid and NATO and OEEC membership were important aspects of Danish politics, as was the Pact with the Soviet Union on Mutual Co-operation and Friendship for Finland.

The communist threat was contained during the post-war period in Denmark, and the country gradually began – boosted by capital injection from the Marshall

Plan – to develop an industrial sector that was eventually to outgrow the agricultural sector in terms of exports in the 1960s. Thus, the Danish economy had a stronger restart after World War II compared to Finland, who was obliged to pay heavy war compensations to the Soviet Union. The industrial sector that developed in Denmark was, however, not of the heavy kind relying on forest and steel as in Sweden and Finland, but of a significantly smaller scale (Huber and Stephens, 2001, p. 140). This was reflected in the management of the employment relations in at least two ways. Firstly, the wage setting system was slightly different compared to both Finland and Sweden where the strong unions of the heavy export-oriented industries of mining and forestry played a significant role in industrial relations. Benner and Vad describe the Danish wage setting system in the following manner:

> Wage determination proceeds through five stages. First, there are direct negotiations between individual unions and employers' associations. If they are unable to agree, the dispute goes to the central federations, the LO and DA. If no agreement can be reached at this level either, the dispute moves on to a state mediator. The mediator then has three weeks to reach a settlement between the parties before a strike or a lockout can begin. All settlements must be ratified by a vote of the members … The government may also intervene, however, if mediation proves unsuccessful. (Benner and Vad, 2000, p. 413)

Every round of bargaining in the post-war period ended in mediation, which indicates the somewhat dysfunctional character of Danish industrial relations (Benner and Vad, 2000, p. 413). The wage setting system was associated with major conflicts and the system was not very efficient in preventing wage drift either, as various sectors competed with each other for ever higher wage increases. Also characteristic of Danish industrial relations was the fact that collective agreements did not cover more than half of all employees as legislation did not automatically extend an agreement to an entire industry (Benner and Vad, 2000, p. 411). The Danish system did not, however, produce large income differences despite not being as harmonious as the Swedish system.

Secondly, what also distinguished to some extent the management of the Danish employment relationships from that in Sweden and Finland was the presence of comparatively liberal dismissal rules and the absence of Swedish-style ALMPs (Huber and Stephens, 2001, p. 143). In other words, it was fairly easy for the small Danish industries to adjust to economic fluctuations, which was something the people involved in managing these industries probably preferred. In alliance with the Social Liberalist Party (Radikale Venstre), the Social Democrats pursued, however, the establishment of institutionalised welfare arrangements and by the 1970s the Danish welfare state was about as generous as the Swedish one.

In principle, Nordic labour market policy, together with other social policies and the tax system sought to ensure that the societies remained inclusive in spite of sometimes quite rapid economic growth. In other words, to the extent that these policies were successful, the fruits of economic growth did not consolidate the position of a wealthy and powerful minority, but instead, benefitted societies on a larger scale. Nordic post-war policies have gained much international attention for successfully combining the aims of equity and efficiency, but as noted already, these policies can be said to have 'inherited' some of their features from earlier periods – not in the sense that they existed as such before, but in the sense of carrying on with emancipation that was previously associated with different aspects of societal development (e.g. modernisation of agriculture and redistribution of landownership). As a consequence, the income distribution in the Nordic countries remained comparatively narrow throughout the post-war period, and the majority of the population was allowed similar opportunities for economic and social participation.

Chapter 5
New Constraints and the Renegotiation of the Post-war Collectivist Order

At a time when Nordic welfare institutions had been developing in a fairly stable and continuous manner, Western societies again faced a breaking point in societal development. As with the two World Wars, many of the discontinuities associated with the 1970s are well known. Usually the two so-called 'oil crises' are both symbolically and concretely referred to as a break in stable economic growth and the progress of modern societies. But the challenges of the 1970s were more complex than suddenly rising oil prices. The simultaneous rise in unemployment and inflation, suggested that old ways of understanding the economic and social order were no longer valid. Again, as after the Wars, new economic and political ideas emerged internationally, and for a while there was uncertainty about the direction societal development would take.

Nordic post-war bureaucratic structures and institutions were designed in such a way that the positions of individuals and the motives of their actions were defined from above – i.e. from the characteristics, functions and purposes of the organisation in question. The polity became differentiated into various organisations and institutions – schools, hospitals, social insurance and social service institutions, local and central administration etc. – each with their own purposes and functions. According to conventional wisdom at the time, an organisation performed its function whenever its individual members performed their predefined roles. These roles were defined independently of the characteristics and skills of the particular individual that fulfilled the role. Hence, collectivism was a defining characteristic of this type of organisation.

Collectivism as it is employed here should not be attached to any ideological positions that take the term too far from its analytical meaning. It refers in no way to any modes of ownership, for instance. By the term collectivism is here understood only (and nothing else but) a social order or an organisation in which the motivations for individual action are defined by the functions. This collectivism has manifested itself in Nordic societies in various ways – for instance in law. The civil law tradition in the Nordic countries has maintained collectivism by detailed codification and regulation of practically all aspects of social life.

As opposed to the common law tradition where courts of law have a stronger role in setting legal standards, legislation in the civil law tradition starts from the systemic level of society and like an octopus stretches its tentacles into the various parts of social life (for a review of different legal traditions, see Glenn, 2007). The individual, when placed in this legal system, has on the one hand been included in a larger whole, but on the other hand remained rather subordinated; the individual is presented in legislation often through varying categories – as a 'child', 'student', 'employee', 'office holder', 'pensioner', 'parent' etc. By contrast, the common law tradition is typically concerned with formulating a set of rights for the individual citizen, and observing the fulfilment and maintenance of these rights, mainly through settling disputes, is the task of the courts of law.

Nordic collectivism has evolved. After the World Wars, collectivism contributed to a widened understanding of the position of the individual in society – a position where socio-economic background no longer played a decisive role. Thus, the collectivism inherent in the post-war organisation of Nordic societies was initially associated with emancipating societal development.

From the initial characteristic of collectivism (widening the conception of the individual) evolved another, perhaps even more crucial characteristic in the post-war years. The more individual creative potentials were liberated and enhanced compared to previous conditions, the more the collectivist characteristic itself turned into a limit to a further liberation and enhancement of creative potentials. This evolution of collectivism created a need to renegotiate previous principles of organisation, and the discontinuities associated with the 1970s (questioning of previous ideas, trying to solve new economic, social and environmental challenges) may be interpreted as perceptions of problems in the existing order, followed by efforts to find a new source for social order.

New Forms of Organising Work

Collectivist bureaucracy was not limited to the public sector alone but was an organisational feature of post-war private sector businesses as well. Therefore, the point made above may be exemplified by reviewing the case of reorganising private sector work since the 1970s. Boltanski and Chiapello (2005) have studied the management literature of both the 1960s and the 1990s, i.e. literature both before and after the renegotiation of the post-war collectivist order. Boltanski's and Chiapello's study concerns mainly France, but many of their observations are no doubt shared by all Western countries.

In the early 1990s, management literature was concerned with an intensified competitive atmosphere resulting from an increase in the number of actors in the increasingly open economy. In order to respond to new challenges and continue to make profits in the increasingly competitive market, it was perceived that managers must 'teach giants to dance' (Boltanski and Chiapello, 2005, p. 71). As a consequence, a completely new way of thinking about the organisation of work has emerged during the period in which the previous hierarchical and collectivist order was renegotiated.

The shift in principles from hierarchy to flexibility may initially sound as if the individual would be given more room to act on her/his own terms, but as Boltanski and Chiapello point out, this transformation has not been straightforward or without complications. Once the fundamentals of a previous social order are questioned, a need arises to find a new source for order if some kind of purpose in collective action is to be maintained. Thus, the re-emergence of the problem of social order is something which characterises the renegotiation process.

At the grassroots level, the significance of communication technologies and automatisation technologies can hardly be over-estimated when looking at further changes in the organisation of work since the 1970s, but on the other hand, they should by no means be regarded as the only changes. In any case, information has acquired a completely new relation to work, to the extent that a great deal of work since the influence of new technology occurs *within* the constant stream of information (Kallinikos, 2006). This is obviously a great contrast to older forms of work that were to a great extent manual and repetitive and concerned with concrete tasks in a particular environment. Whereas previously, work was associated with carrying out concrete tasks as specified by those above in the hierarchy, work during the so called 'information age' tends to be more about creating *innovative solutions* that might give the firm in question a competitive advantage in the market (for detailed analyses of changes in modes of economic production, for instance on the change from 'Fordist' to 'post-Fordist' production, see Jessop, 2002; Julkunen, 2008).

However, new dilemmas arise when work acquires new forms. The ideal worker in the new flexible work organisation is a dynamic team player that does not need orders from above. Instead, it is assumed that the worker constantly, and at her/his own initiative adapts to and acquires new systems of information, knowledge and meaning. In such a situation it is expected that these workers put their entire being including their fundamental values in life at the service of the employer. In such a situation motivating the worker and finding reasons for long-term commitment is a completely different matter compared to the old form of organising work when formal systems of incentives and rewards were easier to construct. Money tends to be perceived as a fundamental source of motivation for workers to the extent that it functions as a means to attaining goals outside the formal sphere of work. There is, however, a limit to the extent to which money can constitute a motivation for work. Therefore money alone (in the form of great income differences which provide 'incentives' and motivation) cannot provide the solution to the problem of order.

These dilemmas take a slightly different shape in the public and private sectors of the economy. In the private sector, another essential ingredient in the restructuring processes is a focus on so-called 'core competencies'. In order to further squeeze out profits, and in order to further increase flexibility, firms are increasingly focusing on the areas in which they have a competitive advantage, and tend to subcontract or outsource other activities. This has allowed firms to dispose of entire layers of the old hierarchical structures and create 'networks' instead (Boltanski and Chiapello, 2005, pp. 70–86; for a comprehensive study of networks, see also Castells, 2004). A network of contractors and subcontractors is able to function more flexibly than an old-fashioned hierarchical organisation due to its ability to better respond to fluctuations of demand. Being employed by a subcontractor may, however, be less secure than by a contractor as terms and conditions of subcontracts are frequently renegotiated.

Regarding the public sector, concerns about problems in hierarchy and subsequent demands for increased flexibility have often been translated into demands for more operating space for market principles. What is commonly termed *New Public Management* is concerned with imitating the logic of the private market in public sector organisations (Temmes, 1998; Green-Pedersen, 2002). However, public sector restructuring has been clearly less straightforward than a simple dismantling or removal of collectivist structures and an expansion of the operating space of markets. Although this certainly has been one aspect of the renegotiating process probably in all Western countries, undergoing a similar type of socio-economic change, creating markets and quasi-markets does not, however, automatically solve the problem of order. The problem of social order does not go away in spite of a requirement to renegotiate the collectivist order.

Theories and discussions around *New Public Management* tend to look at the problem of order at the collective level, but seen from the individual perspective matters look slightly different. The collectivist organisation may turn into a source of empty, meaningless routines that have lost their purposefulness. Giddens, for example, has shown how de-traditionalisation is associated with the emptying out of meaning from routines in modern institutions, and also how institutions are disembedded from their previous purposes and meanings (Giddens, 1991, 1994). Such a situation may come about when the individual sense of purposefulness is in a conflict with the rigid requirements of the collectivist organisation. In such cases, the individual in question is likely to maintain and participate in the empty routines out of a sense of duty. Changing the organisational environment is not an option if all organisations are in a similar phase of development. When such a situation becomes widespread, it appears as a logical and natural reaction to express concern about inefficiency and a distant bureaucracy in order to explicitly make the issue subject to reform.

Expressed from the point of view of the organisation as a whole, the collectivist organisation may find itself in a completely different environment compared to the one in which it was established, so that it simply cannot go on performing the same functions that it used to perform. From the point of view of the manager, such an organisation becomes unsteerable and inefficient – unable to perform the tasks that management would require. Such a situation may also arise as a consequence of endless specialisation and diversification.

Thus, concerns about inefficiency in the public sector may reflect the maturation of collectivist organisations. In such cases, there is a temptation to look for solutions in the private sectors of the economy, as these sectors have been slightly ahead with restructuring their bureaucracies. A simple option is to shift public sector duties over to the private sector. Once this is done, the implications for individual workers are significant. Terms and conditions of employment in the Nordic countries differ quite markedly in these two sectors, and they are even subject to different regulations. In line with the civil law tradition, the rights and duties of civil servants tend to be regulated directly by law, whereas the terms and conditions of other employees are typically regulated by collective agreements.

In addition to the new organisation of work, there are other, interlinked dimensions regarding the renegotiation of the post-war collectivist social order. As the transformation in question is of a rather fundamental nature, it is obvious that it also has a political dimension. Similarly to the perspective of the organisation of work, discontinuities in politics may also be interpreted from the point of view of perceptions of the problem of social order.

The International Competition State Paradigm

Internationally, it appears that the 1970s constituted a watershed regarding the maturation of the post-war collectivist order. A survey of international politics during this decade suggests that perceptions of problems in the post-war social order began to spread throughout the Western world. An array of phenomena may be interpreted in these terms – particularly those directly related to the economy. What is interesting in this respect is that these perceptions spread rapidly among the countries that were open to trade with each other. So, from the point of view of the Nordic countries it appeared that the post-war collectivist order began to mature earlier elsewhere in the Western world. The Nordic countries found it difficult to act completely independently vis-à-vis the international transformations. Closing their borders to Western influences (and trade) was never a realistic option for the Nordic countries.

A well-known phenomenon that triggered many problem perceptions was the oil crisis in the beginning of the 1970s. This event was associated with the demise of the Bretton Woods system of fixed but adjustable currency exchange rates – an essentially Keynesian construction that aimed to grant monetary policy autonomy for participating countries, including the Nordic ones (McNamara, 1998, pp. 93–7; Blyth, 2002, pp. 127–9). It is not possible here to provide a detailed survey of the events leading up to the oil crisis and the collapse of Bretton Woods. Instead, it must suffice to say that one of the main aspects associated with these events during the 1970s was a phenomenon previously unknown to economic policy makers – i.e. stagflation. This new phenomenon implied a simultaneous rise in inflation and unemployment – something which during the earlier post-war period was thought to be impossible, and something that contradicted the teachings associated with the Phillips curve. Governments around the Western world found through policy failure (McNamara, 1998, p. 171) and policy learning (Hall, 1993) that traditional Keynesian measures aiming to boost economic performance during an economic downturn only resulted in increasing inflation rates but not in lower unemployment rates. This represented the main anomaly to existing economic thinking, to use Kuhn's language describing scientific revolutions (Kuhn, 1966).

By the end of the 1960s, a new theory had been brought forward providing not only an explanation of the anomaly that economic policy makers world-wide fought with, but also a whole new paradigm in economic thinking, to continue to use Kuhn's concepts. In this respect, the work of Edmund Phelps (1967) and Milton Friedman (1968) proved to be particularly influential by suggesting that there was a 'natural rate of unemployment' below which inflation could not be kept under control with macroeconomic policy (McNamara, 1998, p. 146). This view was derived from monetarist theory according to which governments should only include the aims of price stability and a controlled increase of the money supply in their economic policy agenda. In other words, efforts to stimulate the economy by an increase in aggregate demand would only produce inflation – especially if the aim was to push unemployment below the 'natural rate'. According to proponents of the new theory, this explained the stagflation during the 1970s.

Monetarist theory went on to explain that workers and employers had learned, as rational actors, to anticipate future inflation rates and build them into their wage demands. This was a crucial assumption of the new economic paradigm. It was assumed that workers would not accept a job that paid less than the demanded wage – and this wage demand contained an anticipation of future inflation. Thus, if governments pursued policies that would be likely to increase inflation, the wage demands of workers increased accordingly, creating increasing unemployment as employers would not necessarily be able to meet the wage demands.

One thing seems particularly worth noting regarding the reasoning built into this new economic paradigm. The reasoning is individualistic at least in comparison with the reasoning of the previous Keynesian paradigm, which had dealt with economic equilibrium at the institutional and aggregate level. Thus, the Keynesian paradigm was essentially a paradigm of the collectivist era, whereas the new paradigm was individualistic focusing on the behaviour of individual rational actors (which it assumed to be utility maximising). The main consequence of this shift of focus from the collective level to the individual level was a reversal of many of the propositions developed within Keynesian thinking – particularly those that dealt with economic and social policy. The new paradigm postulated that the role of government economic policy should be quite different from what it had been during the Keynesian era – being only limited to maintaining price stability and a controlled increase in the money supply. Unemployment could, according to the new paradigm, only be targeted at the supply side of the labour market. This also put many post-war social policies under a completely new light.

Most importantly for the research interest here, the new way of economic thinking originating in the Chicago School in the late 1960s can be interpreted to represent a perception of problems in the post-war collectivist socio-economic order. Or to be more precise, the success of this way of thinking indicates more than anything else such perceptions. The new economic paradigm appealed to business interests, and in promoting it internationally, the role of organised business appears to have been quite crucial (Blyth, 2002, pp. 152–61, 209–16). It would, however, be wrong to assume that during the 1970s policy makers worldwide in a straightforward manner found a consensus in this new economic paradigm. Instead, during the 1970s the situation concerning the future socio-economic development of the Western world appears to have been rather contingent. One of the contestants in the revolution of previous thinking was the environmentalist movement, which sought to provide an alternative for industry-driven and growth oriented economic culture. A famous manifestation of this environmentalist movement was the *Club of Rome*, established in 1968, whose members published the book *Limits to Growth* (Meadows et al., 1972).

Environmentalist ideology did not, however, become the international blueprint of economic thinking after the contingent time of the 1970s. Instead, the kind of economic thinking associated with the Chicago School appears to have received international acclaim. The OECD began to endorse this way of thinking at the end of the 1970s (McNamara, 1998, p. 147) and European economic policy makers adopted most of the monetarist principles in establishing the European Monetary System (EMS) and the European Exchange Rate Mechanism (ERM) – agreements that later led to the European Monetary Union (EMU). Since these agreements, the concerns and aims of monetary policy in Europe have been price stability and a controlled increase in the money supply – at the cost of domestic economic policy autonomy (McNamara, 1998, p. 55). It should also be mentioned that the new monetary policy aims were made consistent with the remarkable increase in international capital flows that occurred after the 1960s. Economic policy makers contended that free capital flows were part of the new economic order, and thus national economies had to participate fully in international economic competition without the possibility of pursuing national policy goals by means of macroeconomic policy. This order was further consolidated in Europe by the Single European Act in 1986, which stated the so-called four freedoms: freedom of movement of goods, services, labour and capital (McNamara, 1998, p. 53; Wallace and Wallace, 2000, pp. 94–5).

What further indicated the international success of these new economic ideas was the electoral success of the Thatcher regime in the UK and the Reagan regime in the US, both coming into power during the early 1980s. This also signalled that the new economic ideas had not only remained elite thinking, but that they were formulated within a political ideology that owed much to traditional liberalism and laissez-faire ideas. Consequently, these two strong governments of Reagan and Thatcher were able to limit the authority of trade unions and reverse many of the policies pursued during the post-war era. Organised labour had been a strong party in formulating many of the policies consistent with Keynesian economic thinking aimed at promoting the well-being of the general population, but this party appeared unable to challenge the rising hegemony of organised business in providing ideas for the way forward after the 1970s. The new economic ideas about the relationship between states and markets were also expressed in the so-called 'Washington consensus', which became a cornerstone of the work of the World Bank and the International Monetary Fund (IMF) (Voipio, 2009, p. 346; Böckerman and Kiander, 2009, p. 105).

In the 1990s the new economic ideas that had challenged Keynesian economic policy were further consolidated into what can be labelled the *international competition state paradigm*. Academic economists and international organisations, such as the OECD and the EU began to express and promote this paradigm with increased intensity. One of the consequences of such ideological consolidation was that clear and concise policy suggestions were formulated – suggestions that were easily adaptable in principle throughout the world. In terms of economic and employment policy, the policy suggestions of the international competition state paradigm can be expressed in five main imperatives:

1. Passive unemployment insurance should be minimal;
2. The state should improve the availability of a labour supply for all sectors of the economy through bureaucratic means;
3. Tax rates should be as low as possible;
4. Wage negotiations should occur at the individual level instead of the collective level; and
5. Employment protection legislation should be as relaxed as possible (see for example Layard et al., 1991; Nickell, 2001).

These imperatives differ quite clearly from the logic built into Keynesian economic thinking on which many economic policies in the Nordic countries were based during the post-war period of 1950–1970. According to Keynesian thinking, redistribution of economic resources through progressive taxation and social security benefits was compatible with the aim of strong economic growth.

A key document in consolidating the international competition state paradigm was the OECD jobs study of 1994 (OECD, 1994ab, see also OECD, 2006), which was basically developed around the five imperatives referred to above. The EU Lisbon Strategy of 2000 contributed to the international consolidation of the competition state paradigm by aiming to make the EU the world's most 'competitive and dynamic knowledge based economy' (EU, 2000). In addition to the above-mentioned imperatives, the EU's Employment Strategy has contained emphases on education and training to improve human capital and 'flexi-curity' – a combination of flexibility and security.

There is, in fact, no consensus about the label of the new hegemonic way of economic thinking. One of the contestants is 'neoliberalism' – a term that is often used to denote the new rise of liberal ideas that were once put to one side by Keynesianism. Whilst this notion is not completely incorrect in the sense that both traditional liberalism and the new economic orthodoxy that spread after the 1970s both share a strong trust in the capacity of market forces to produce just and efficient outcomes, it appears, however, that the focus on the supply side of the labour market in the new paradigm may potentially contain elements that are not quite compatible with the classical liberalists' values of individual freedom and sovereignty. Theoretically, there seems to be no limits to what states can and ought to do to direct potential labour suppliers towards obeying the market forces.

Therefore, to call the new paradigm neo*liberal* may be somewhat misleading. These questions will receive further clarity when turning to the detailed analysis of how the problem perceptions of the post-war collectivist order have been encountered in the Nordic countries. This kind of analysis inevitably turns, at least partly, into an analysis of how this new economic paradigm has been received and applied and perhaps also challenged.

Drawing on a Polanyian framework of political economy, Blyth has termed the change in economic ideas as a shift from 'embedded liberalism' to 'disembedded liberalism', in which market forces are given a stronger role. The former term refers to a series of relations where the establishment of the (fictitious) commodity form of labour is balanced by a number of policies securing the well-being of workers. According to Blyth, who has analysed the historical transformations of economic policy in Sweden and the US, the Swedish Rehn–Meidner model is a prime example of a policy associated with 'embedded liberalism' (Blyth, 2002, pp. 119–23). Blyth also demonstrates clearly that the shift in economic ideas is an international phenomenon of great historical significance, and that individual countries must in one way or the other position themselves in relation to the grand international ideological currents.

Jessop has provided an interesting account about the changes in the role of the state and economic production, largely based on Marxist theory about the capital-labour relation. Adding to the terminological list of choices, he has analysed the changes in economic and public policy in terms of a shift from the Keynesian National Welfare Regime into a *Schumpeterian Workfare Postnational Regime* (Jessop 2002). Jessop's approach is fairly general and it manages to capture the complexity and thoroughness of the policies that have been associated with transformations of the Western economic production regime. In particular, the term 'Schumpeterian Workfare Postnational Regime' is worth attention. According to Jessop, the new economic order is 'Schumpeterian' because it is based on a new notion of competitiveness, that, with some links to the Austrian economist Joseph Schumpeter, postulates that 'competitiveness depends on developing the individual and collective capacities to engage in permanent innovation – whether in sourcing, technologies, products, organisation or marketing' (Jessop, 2002, p. 121). It is a 'workfare' regime because employment policy acquires a new function in managing the labour supply and ensuring that there are enough economic incentives for workers to join the labour force. 'Workfare' policies increase the conditionality of welfare benefits and establish links to programmes aiming to ensure the availability of a flexible work force (Jessop, 2002, pp. 152–62).

Kettunen has, in turn, studied the semantic and discursive shifts that have accompanied the socio-economic transformations since the 1970s – and particularly the shifts around the phenomenon called 'globalisation'. He points towards a number of intriguing tensions and even contradictions in trying to establish a competitive national 'us' in a global economic environment in which nation states as entities are supposed to be less relevant than before. Kettunen also sees a general demand for 'innovations' that can enhance economic competitiveness on the one hand, but a similarly general notion of economic decisions being determined, conditioned and constrained by external factors (Kettunen, 2008, p. 221). According to Kettunen, the shift from a 'welfare state' to a 'competition state' may, however, take place within remarkable institutional stability (Kettunen, 2008, p. 222).

Just as it is difficult to find a commonly accepted term for the new policy paradigm, so is it equally difficult to identify the emancipating and constraining elements of societal development since the 1970s. What seems clear, though, is that similar to earlier historical breaking points, new aspects become relevant and interesting from the point of view of societal development. Thus, it cannot automatically be assumed that welfare state institutions, for instance, carry on with their emancipatory functions after the 1970s. This is inherent in Kettunen's analysis, according to which old welfare state institutions are modified to serve the new purposes of the competition state (Kettunen, 2004, p. 133). Kettunen has, in fact, suggested that since the 1970s and 1980s one direction of social policy change in the Nordic countries has been back towards the pre-welfare state meanings of social policy, associated with keeping order and preventing idleness – in other words resembling times when major societal constraints were in place (Kettunen, 2004, p. 136). This is something Lødemel has also observed in his analyses of social policy reform in the 1990s (Lødemel, 2001, p. 298).

In principle, the shift of attention from the collective to the individual level could contain the possibility that old collectivist constraints are dismantled so that the liberation and enhancement of human creative potentials continues to be an aspect of societal development. Thus, regulations of individual behaviour would be loosened in such a manner that people would again, to an increasing extent, be able to direct their biographical time towards ends chosen by themselves. In theory, this dismantling of collectivist constraints could involve institutions and organisations where instead of fulfilling a role defined from above, the individual could to an increasing extent participate in defining her/his own role. In practice, however, the renegotiation of the post-war collectivist order appears to have been more complicated than this straightforward theoretical scenario. It is not at all clear that perceptions of problems of the social order since the 1970s have resulted in the dismantling of constraints associated with societal development.

In the following, reactions and solutions to the re-emerging problem of social order since the 1970s and 1980s will be analysed from the point of view of the Nordic countries at two levels. The first is the way 'workfare' reforms have been adopted as solutions to the re-emerging problem of social order. These reforms exemplify the shift of political attention from the collective to the individual level and from the demand side of the economy to the supply side. Although they may be regarded as one of the most important Nordic social policy reforms since the 1970s and 1980s, it is not at all clear that these 'workfare' reforms contribute to the emancipating aspects of societal development – in fact, the case might be the opposite. Workfare reforms appear to change the principles of Nordic welfare policy from universalism, inclusion and redistribution towards selectivism, targeting and work incentives (e.g. Kildal and Kuhnle, 2005). They also seem to be derived from the logic embedded in the international competition state paradigm, according to which public employment policy should focus on the supply rather than the demand side of the economy.

In addition to welfare state and social security reform, another dimension of the renegotiation of the post-war collectivist social order in the Nordic countries has been the ideological adaptation to the imperatives of the international competition state paradigm. In the following this adaptation process will be studied on the one hand by an analysis of domestic policy documents regarding the central ideas in public policy – ideas that may also shed light upon the rationales behind social security reform. On the other hand, the adaptation to the international competition state paradigm will be analysed by assessing the impact of OECD recommendations on the public and economic policy in Sweden, Denmark and Finland. In this respect the OECD will be regarded as a proponent of the international competition state paradigm. Whereas the ideas behind post-war Nordic welfare policies enjoyed widespread popular support, it is not clear that the new ideas which have dominated the new social order since the 1970s and the 1980s have emerged in accordance with public opinion. In the case of the Nordic countries, it appears that national policy elites have acquired the role of mediating between new ideas, past traditions and popular opinion. An analysis of policy documents will show the direction towards which this mediation has progressed.

Chapter 6
Establishing a New Social Order based on 'Workfare'

Sweden

*Beginning of the Renegotiation Process: Commercialisation and
Government Restructuring*

After the turmoil of the 1970s involving a loss of the 'spirit of Saltsjöbaden' through hostile industrial action and the economic worries associated with the oil crises, the re-elected Social Democrats attempted to find a new path for Swedish economic policy in the early 1980s. This new path was formulated as a *Third Road*, a compromise between Keynesian stimulus by deficit and Thatcherite monetarism, and it included a significant currency devaluation, attempts at wage restraint and control of public spending (Benner and Vad, 2000, p. 422). Although wage restraint turned out to be a more difficult goal than anticipated – centralised wage setting came to an end in 1983 – this economic policy strategy of the Social Democrats seemed successful at least in the early years of the 1980s.

Gradually, perceptions of problems in the post-war social order began to emerge in Sweden. Prime Minister Ingvar Carlsson has later expressed his feelings regarding the change of the ideological current:

> The ideas of community and solidarity associated with the People's Home were met by a slogan to "invest in yourself". The option of creating a better future through political decisions was rejected. Markets were to replace politics.
> The Timbro group constituted another bourgeois party to deal with, one more efficient and more difficult to reach than the parties in parliament. (Carlsson, 2003, p. 210)

As a think tank funded by organised business, Timbro was, together with SNS, rather active in changing the ideological current in Sweden by promoting ideas associated with the competition state paradigm (Blyth, 2002, pp. 215–16). The Swedish Conservative party was thus given an opportunity to benefit from ongoing ideological shifts. Their campaign preceding the 1985 elections may be interpreted as an attempt to take over the lead role in formulating a new social order for Sweden. The proposed privatisations and tax-reductions proved, however, to be too radical and the elections decided that it was not yet the Conservatives' turn to take the lead role in the renegotiation process. This did not, however, imply that renegotiation of the post-war collectivist order was postponed. Rather, the Social Democrats with their strong Finance Minister Kjell-Olof Feldt began to formulate some path-breaking policies including the deregulation of financial markets, and the commercialisation and privatisation of public enterprises. Government agencies were transformed into State-Owned Enterprises (SOEs) and Private Enterprises (PEs) – or into companies partly owned by the state. In addition the financial freedom of SOEs, such as the postal and telecommunications services, was increased so that they could to an increasing extent operate in the manner of private enterprises (Statskontoret, 2000, p. 181). Some of the areas dominated by state monopolies were also made subject to economic competition. These reforms paved the way for more thorough privatisations during the 1990s.

The early signs of the renegotiation of the Swedish post-war collectivist order were accompanied by some worrying economic trends. A wage-inflation spiral was one such trend, in addition to a decline in the household savings rate, increases in private consumption, and rapid increases in real estate building as credit became more easily available (Lindbeck et al., 1994, p. 3; Benner and Vad, 2000, p. 425). In Sweden tax reform also played a major part in these early stages of the renegotiation process. In 1989 a dual income tax system was introduced and capital income taxes, taxes on other incomes and corporate taxes were significantly reduced. At the same time the VAT base was broadened (Benner and Vad, 2000, pp. 426–7).

The experiences of the following few years were, however, to demonstrate that the timing of these tax reforms was quite unfortunate. The government was not quite able to interpret the economic signals of the time, and it went on to promise some further welfare benefits in 1988 (Huber and Stevens, 2001, p. 243), which for obvious reasons could never be delivered. The Finance Minister at the time, Kjell-Olof Feldt, reflected in his memoirs upon the failure to produce any stabilising measures in the late 1980s (Feldt, 1991, pp. 279–84, 288). Partly, the expansion of credit was interpreted not as a direct consequence of deregulation but as a consequence of the disappearance of a grey financial market. Partly, it appeared politically very difficult for a minority government to introduce measures that would curb private consumption.

In the early 1990s the over-heated economy began to collapse: the banking sector collapsed, house prices dropped, unemployment increased sharply and the krona became subject to speculation. The krona was allowed to float in 1992 but macroeconomic policy remained on the Swedish policy agenda as the country never joined the EMU.

A political regime change together with the economic crisis facilitated the continued renegotiation of the Swedish post-war collectivist order in the early 1990s. After persistent efforts, it was finally time for the Conservatives to take the lead role in formulating future directions for Swedish socio-economic development, and the new government appointed a commission to reconsider the role of welfare policies in the country. This commission, headed by Assar

Lindbeck, a renowned economist and a former Social Democrat, stated the need to renegotiate the post-war order in the following explicit manner:

> Old organizational models and conventional management methods have proved inefficient ... After an age of increased expectations, demands have grown for more freedom of choice and more personal integrity. Collective and uniform systems based on standardised solutions have great difficulties in satisfying increasingly differentiated demands. (Lindbeck et al., 1994, pp. 17–18)

In addition to strengthening perceptions about problems in the post-war order, the various processes initiated in the late 1980s also began to show effects. The consequences of the commercialisation and privatisation of public functions are demonstrated in Table 6.1

The table presents numbers regarding the reduction of employees in SOEs (State Owned Enterprises) during the crucial period of the 1990s. As state ownership in the enterprises concerned has varied, weighed figures are provided as well, in each case calculated according to the share of state ownership. All the different measures show a considerable decrease in the number of personnel in SOEs during the 1990s. Factors behind this decrease include privatisation, reductions in personnel in association with commercialisation and a focusing on core activities.

In addition to commercialisation and privatisation, the structure of government began to change as well. Decentralisation of government and increased municipal authority were included in this process. In Sweden decentralisation implied two things in particular. Firstly, the funding patterns of municipalities were reformed in 1992 (Bergmark, 2001, p. 63). Earmarked funding was transformed into block grants associated with caps on local government taxation (a system that

Table 6.1   Number of employees in Swedish State-Owned Enterprises 1990 and 1999 and relative change (%)

	Number of employees		
	1999	*1990*	*Change 1990–1999 (%)*
SOEs partly and completely under state ownership, unweighed	211,000	316,000	-33
SOEs partly and completely under state ownership, weighed	170,000	263,000	-35
SOEs with 50+ % state ownership, unweighed	156,000	258,000	-40
SOEs with 100 % state ownership	153,000	225,500	-32

Source: Statskontoret, 2000, p. 184.

redistributed state funding among municipalities) and with a way to assess the need for municipality funding (Hort, 2003, p. 255). This implied slightly greater autonomy for municipalities. After the reform, municipalities were no longer funded according to their past expenses, but according to estimations of future expenses. This increased the room for economic manoeuvre within municipalities, as they were able to choose their spending targets, as well as keep any possible surpluses for themselves.

The most important reform in the process of decentralisation was perhaps the so-called *ädelreformen* in the early 1990s, whereby the responsibility of elderly care and psychiatric care was shifted from the regions to the municipalities (Hort, 2003, p. 256). In addition to increased local government responsibility, the number of authorities in Swedish government was also reduced by merging authorities at the local level into greater entities – 'authority incorporations' (Statskontoret, 1999, p. 72). As a consequence, the number of government authorities was reduced during the 1990s by 774, partly due to the mergers, but partly also due to the privatisations mentioned above (Statskontoret, 1999, p. 74).

Moderate Reforms of Income Support and Unemployment Insurance

The renegotiation of the post-war collectivist social order also concerned the system of labour market policy. In the following, the legislative reforms in the areas of income support and unemployment insurance will be reviewed during the crucial period of the 1990s and 2000s. Particular attention will be paid to the question how the role of the traditional Swedish ALMP was changed as a consequence of the reforms, and how the individual benefit recipients are viewed in legislation. Will they be considered as a burden to society or as a potential resource for the economy? How will potential insider/outsider divisions in the labour market be managed? Of interest will also be how the insurance principle is maintained in Swedish unemployment insurance during the 1990s and what happens to the goals of redistribution in the social security system.

In the beginning of the renegotiation process the Swedish unemployment insurance system consisted of two tiers – a higher and a lower one. It was a voluntary system in the beginning of the 1990s in the sense that in order to qualify for earnings-related unemployment benefit, a person had to be a member of a trade union branch or an unemployment insurance fund (Edling, 2006, p. 99). Voluntary unemployment insurance administered by trade union-linked funds is usually known as the *Ghent system*. The name refers to the Belgian town of Ghent were this form of unemployment insurance administration first originated in 1901 (Clasen and Viebrock, 2008, pp. 433–4). This system was actually more widespread during the 1920s than after World War II, after which it remained a system unique to Denmark, Finland and Sweden.

In Sweden, in order to be eligible for unemployment insurance (higher tier) a person had to have a short work history. The lower tier of the Swedish unemployment insurance (the so-called *Kontant arbetslöshetsunderstöd,* from 1998 onwards *grundförsäkring* = basic insurance) was not tied to previous earnings, and was primarily intended for those who were not members of the voluntary earnings-related insurance scheme. Those who were unemployed, who did not qualify for either tier of the unemployment insurance system, were eligible for income support.

Rising unemployment rates and the economic crisis of the early 1990s created a pressure to reform the unemployment insurance system, but adjustments in Sweden were not of a large scale. Only (re)qualification criteria and replacement rates were adjusted in the unemployment insurance system during the 1990s (Regnér, 2000, p. 90). For instance, replacement rates were first decreased from 90 to 70 per cent in 1993 and then increased to 80 per cent. The re-qualification criteria of earnings-related unemployment benefit were kept more or less intact with the consequence that the insurance aspect of the unemployment insurance system actually strengthened. This was the case primarily as it remained possible to renew eligibility for earnings-related unemployment benefit through participation in Active Labour Market Policy measures.

What also indicates a strengthened insurance element in the unemployment insurance system in Sweden is that the share of unemployed receiving earnings-related unemployment benefit increased throughout the 1990s (Regnér, 2000, p. 92). In Sweden more than 70 per cent of the unemployed received earnings-related unemployment benefit in 1998 (Regnér, 2000, p. 92).

In addition to rising unemployment rates, the number of income support claimants and the costs of income support rose sharply after the beginning of the 1990s in Sweden. This created a need to adjust existing legislation in the field of income support as well. In 1998 two important modifications in existing legislation were made in Sweden regarding the conditions under which income support may be claimed. First, a nationwide norm was established concerning the level of income support, and second, the obligations of income support claimants were specified. Before the adjustments of 1998 the level of income support had remained unspecified in the Social Services Act (dating back to 1980) which regulated the scheme.

The second important revision in the Swedish Social Services Act made in 1998 concerned the obligations of the income support claimant. According to the previous law, income support could only be claimed in cases where the person in question was unable to support her/himself in any other way, and not eligible for any other existing benefits. In the paragraph defining the right to income support, the Swedish Social Services Act of 1980 stated the following:

> An individual has the right to support from the social services (*socialnämnden*) for her/his maintenance and general livelihood if her/his needs cannot be met in any other way.
>
> The individual shall through the income support be granted a decent standard of living. The support shall be designed in such a way that it enhances her/his

capacities to live an autonomous life. (Social Services Act 1980: 620 6 § as cited in Government, Sweden, 1996, p. 7)

A person claiming income support mainly due to the lack of work was, according to the Social Services Act, obliged to look actively for a job or, if a job could not be found, to participate in the Active Labour Market Policy (ALMP) measures offered by the employment services (Government, Sweden, 1996, p. 62). This was, at least, the interpretation of the government proposing the revisions to the existing law.

The government was, however, concerned with the fact that the previous act did not require (or indeed allow municipalities to require) individuals to take part in activities that were neither paid employment nor ALMP measures – in other words, activities specified by the municipalities themselves as conditions for claiming income support. There is a Supreme Administrative Court (*regeringsrätten*) ruling from 1995 (case nr. 6523/1994) enforcing this interpretation of the previous law. Yet, some municipalities had already in the late 1980s tested the limits of the law by introducing reciprocity in the area of income support (Milton, 1998).

The specifications made in the Social Services Act aimed at altering the existing practice of not requiring income support claimants to participate in activation measures other than those offered by the employment services. According to the revised law, the municipalities should be able to require individual income support claimants to participate in 'competence enhancing activities' should the employment services be unable to offer participation in ALMP measures *if*:

1. The claimant was below 25 years of age;
2. The claimant was aged 25 or above and for specific reasons was in need of 'competence enhancing' measures; or
3. Due to a break in studies the claimant was in need of income support (given that the studies granted eligibility to paid subsistence).

It was also specified that if without giving an acceptable reason an individual refused to participate in work practice or other 'competence enhancing' measures, the level of income support might be reduced or denied completely.

The following arguments were provided in the Government Bill for the revised act, giving reasons for the specifications listed above:

> The government's position is that, in principle, claiming income support for a longer period of time should always be combined with relevant requirements to support the individual to find a way to employment. It is another issue that in some cases it may be unrealistic to place requirements upon the individual to manage to support her/himself. In such cases the interventions made by the social services should be given another focus … It is also fair that an income support claimant in some cases should participate in other types of activities specified by the municipality, aiming at providing an enhanced competence for

a future position in working life ... These interventions may occur in the form
of "job seeker activities" aiming to improve the young person's knowledge of
society and working life, or in the form of writing applications or in other ways
contacting potential employers, etc. (Government, Sweden, 1996, p. 76)

Young people were the primary target group of the activation measures
specified in the revisions in the Social Services Act – although the revised act
maintained the possibility of extending these activation measures to other groups
as well. The revised law, despite specifying the conditions under which income
support may be claimed, still left many issues to the judgement of the social
services. It does not, for instance, specify which persons aged 25 or above should
have the obligation to participate in activation measures, nor for how long a person
should have received income support in order to be obliged to participate in such
measures. Neither does the revised act specify whether non-compliance should
be sanctioned by withdrawing the entire income support or reducing its level. In
other words, the revised act provides a framework under which social services
are expected to operate. The major difference compared to previous legislation
was, of course, that social assistance might be conditional upon the participation
in schemes designed by the social services. This was a major transformation in
Swedish social policy (Johansson, 2001; Hort, 2003, p. 249).

What the above quotation also shows is an interesting starting point in
targeting activation measures to income support claimants. In the first sentences
of the quotation a vague distinction is made between persons claiming social
assistance under 'normal circumstances' and persons on whom it would be
unrealistic to place expectations to support themselves at least in the shorter term.
In other words, a vague reference is made to people capable of working in the
ordinary labour market, and people in need of other kinds of assistance in order to
perhaps attain this capacity in the future. When interpreting the political reaction
to the process of renegotiating the post-war social order, it is crucial to see in
what ways these various groups of people are conceptualised, and what their
duties and rights are thought to be. Such conceptualisations within the political
sphere are of key importance when it comes to the moral order imposed by the
institutional framework.

The vague distinction between capable and less capable social assistance
claimants is maintained, specified and further developed in a few key government
documents that followed the above mentioned revisions of the Social Services
Act. Towards the end of the 1990s, the Swedish government became ever more
conscious of the rising numbers of social assistance claimants, and proposed a new
policy in 2000. During the process of preparing for this proposal, the following
aims for this new activation policy were expressed:

Studies made during the preparatory work as well as experience shows that each
month there is approximately 30,000 of those who are unemployed and support
themselves through social assistance but who do not have, or have only limited

other social problems in addition to unemployment, who through consistent programmes and strongly individualised measures should be given great opportunities to enter and establish a position in the labour market. I judge that through such measures – i.e. an Extended Development Guarantee – comprising wider age groups than young people a great proportion of this group would find employment, build an independent personal economy and escape dependency on social assistance. (Government, Sweden, 1999, p. 101)

The proposal of an Extended Development Guarantee was eventually developed into an Activity Guarantee (Government, Sweden, 1999). However, what is interesting here is that the preparatory committee was able to define a group of people – not insignificant in size – that did not claim social assistance due to social problems but due to unemployment. These people were, obviously, for various reasons not entitled to unemployment insurance – for instance because they may not have fulfilled the membership criteria or the work criteria associated with unemployment insurance eligibility. Thus, the earlier vague distinction between more capable and less capable social assistance claimants was developed into a distinction between people who claimed social assistance due to unemployment and people who claimed social assistance due to social problems. The distinction was developed to such an extent that the preparatory committee felt able to estimate the exact number of persons belonging to the former category, and to recommend new measures to deal with their situation.

When the proposal above was developed into an Activity Guarantee, no major alterations to existing legislation were made. In the Government Bill it was stated that unemployed social assistance claimants and those with other social problems should not receive a different kind of treatment from the employment services than those who are covered by unemployment insurance (Government, Sweden, 1999, p. 57). This aim may be interpreted as an explicit aim to counteract any possible insider/outsider divisions that may emerge due to the lack of coverage of unemployment insurance.

Other aims behind the government's proposal to establish an Activity Guarantee included the aim to counteract circulation between unemployment benefit and activation measures. The proposal acknowledged that according to the existing system it was possible to renew eligibility for unemployment benefit through participating in ALMP measures (Government, Sweden, 1999, p. 56) – although this possibility had been reduced in 1996 by preventing an initial qualification for unemployment insurance by entering the labour market straight into an ALMP programme (Government, Sweden, 1999, p. 21). The idea of the Activity Guarantee was that individuals should not go back into receiving passive unemployment benefit, but instead should enter the regular labour market – or, by their own choice, leave the labour market completely. As no major alterations in existing legislation were made when introducing this new policy, the previous sanctions for non-compliance remained in place. The Activity Guarantee was abolished in 2007 by the Conservative government and replaced by a Job and Development Guarantee (Government, Sweden, see also Sjöberg, 2011).

The number of legislative reforms in Sweden was not large during the 1990s. In the field of unemployment insurance not many significant changes were made. The possibility too of renewing eligibility through participation in ALMP measures was retained throughout the 1990s, and altered slightly only in the beginning of the 2000s. In the field of income support, only one major reform was carried out during the renegotiation of the post-war collectivist social order – that of 1998. This may indicate a resistance towards reform pressure, but on the other hand, by widening the obligations of income support recipients, the 1998 reform did represent a change at the level of principles. The reform represented a step away from universalism towards targeting. The scale of this transformation will become more evident when compared to corresponding reforms in Denmark and Finland, as the starting points of social policy reform were fairly similar in all three countries in the beginning of the 1990s.

Furthermore, it is worth noting that although the new obligations for income support recipients were enforced by sanctions, they were formulated in the legislation on a fairly general level. In other words, the legislation left room for a great deal of interpretation at the local level, where the law is implemented. The legislation also seems to have included aims to counteract any insider/outsider divisions that may emerge between uninsured and insured job seekers.

The Swedish government appears to have recognised a multiplicity of causes behind claiming income support: unemployment, substance abuse, social problems, psychiatric problems etc. (cf. Government, Sweden, 1996, p. 64). Thus, the impression that the legislation gives is that if a person is capable of working, the obligation to work or look for a job should be taken seriously and if necessary, be enforced by sanctions. However, if there are other causes behind claiming income support, there may be other channels in the social services that may be more appropriate for improving the situation of the claimant.

Ideological Shifts: Abandoning the Third Way

As legislative reforms in the area of labour market policy were rather moderate, this raises the question whether the international competition state paradigm has indeed had a strong role in the Swedish renegotiation of the post-war collectivist social order. This issue will receive further clarity by reviewing some of the ideological shifts during the 1990s and early 2000s.

The newly elected 1991 right wing government appointed a committee to formulate a point of view on some very fundamental questions about welfare provision, the scope of government and ways of financing the state (Hort, 2005, p. 151). As mentioned in the beginning of the chapter, this so-called Lindbeck Commission was fairly clear and conscious regarding the problem of social order. The Lindbeck Commission's awareness of the need to renegotiate previous collectivist institutions included the social insurance system as well (Lindbeck et al., 1994, pp. 103, 116). What further accelerated the renegotiation process and the establishment of a new order was, of course, the process leading to joining the EU in 1995 and adopting the rules of the Single European Market (freedom of movement for goods, labour, capital and services) and adjusting monetary policies more in line with European ones.

It would, however, be too simplistic to conclude that Sweden rushed head over heels to adopt the international competition state paradigm under conservative leadership in the early years of the 1990s. The ideas articulated by the Lindbeck Commission were probably slightly overenthusiastic about the national adoption and adaptation of the international competition state paradigm. The Swedish Lindbeck Commission did manage to capture the shared perception of a need to renegotiate the post-war collectivist order but most of its suggestions aimed at tailoring Swedish society in a fairly crude and simple way into a favourable environment for business. This part of the Commission's proposal apparently did not capture the views of the general population, and the situation backfired in the 1994 elections with the consequence that the Social Democrats returned to power and were largely given the responsibility to formulate the directions of the emerging social order for the next 12 years to come.

When the right-wing government had been elected in 1991, the top trade union LO did not remain passive, but mobilised on the grass roots level organising around 2,500 meetings and study groups throughout the country. In these meetings citizens were able to express their views on ongoing social changes (Hort, 2003, p. 156). According to Hort this endeavour contributed, in fact, to the return of the Social Democrats to power in 1994.

LO's endeavour in the early 1990s had sought to redefine the concept of national equality from the way it was understood during the post-war collectivist era (Lindberg, 1999; Hort, 2003, p. 157). In other words, similarly to the Lindbeck Commission, it represented a departure from the conceptions associated with the collectivist era. As it operated without the kind of government mandate that the Lindbeck Commission had been given, its results were largely formulated as a critique and alternative towards the existing policies that the right-wing government was pursuing. It should, however, be noted that new policies following from the renegotiation of the post-war order had emerged already before the election of 1991. One of the most important policy changes was the tax reform of the late 1980s whereby basic tax rates for most tax payers were reduced to 30 per cent (Benner and Vad, 2000, p. 426; Blyth, 2002, p. 225). Top marginal rates were reduced at the same time as well. In addition, the Social Democratic government had in 1990 announced that its number one economic policy priority was to fight inflation instead of pursuing full employment. Both of these policy reforms were consistent with the demands of the new international competition state paradigm, and they were significant as high taxes and full employment had been major cornerstones of the post-war collectivist order.

Thus, LO's Social Justice Committee was in a slightly ambivalent position. On the one hand it did not take much into account the emerging new policies and ideas that had begun to enter Swedish politics since the mid 1980s. This was possible as it operated 'outside' the formal government so to speak. On the other hand, with its close connection to the grass roots level of Swedish society, it managed more closely to reflect the views of the general population compared to the Lindbeck Commission. Thus, in a way, the differences between the Lindbeck Commission and the LO's Social Justice Committee may be interpreted as reflecting the ideological cleavage between the Swedish bureaucratic and political elite and the general population. But in any case, the latter had a channel through which it could influence political life at the very top. This was reflected in the outcome of the 1994 elections.

In addition to the two Committees mentioned above – the intra and the extra governmental ones – a third large-scale committee was also established in Sweden during the 1990s. This was the research project headed by Hans Zetterberg that included a variety of intellectuals and political activists (Hort, 2003, p. 154). This project, too, managed to provide an alternative vision of Swedish socio-economic development in the midst of the renegotiation process. Zetterberg's project departed from the conceptions of the collectivist era by discarding the concept of total equality and replacing it with a conception of 'human dignity' (Zetterberg and Ljungberg, 1997; Hort, 2003, p. 155). This conceptual turn led the project to deliberate about what would happen to the vulnerable in society after the concept of equality had been abandoned as the normative basis of socio-economic life. The answer was that social support could come from elsewhere than the state, for instance from the market or civil society (Hort, 2003, p. 155). Zetterberg's project was politically in a difficult position as it was neither supported by the government, as the Lindbeck Commission was, nor did it clearly aspire to appeal to the general public like the LO Commission. It was largely ignored by centre-left authorities, but its very existence shows that there was room for alternative visions about future socio-economic development in Sweden.

Despite the re-election of the Social Democrats in 1994, the Swedish renegotiation process progressed during the 1990s towards a national adaptation of the international competition state paradigm. One of the clearest ways to observe this is by looking at the changes of the so-called Rehn–Meidner model of balancing economic and employment policy during the post-war period. As noted in the previous chapters, the Rehn–Meidner model was developed in order to maintain both the goals of full employment and stable growth. The goal of full employment, in turn, became associated with the normative and ideological goals of securing a 'right to work' for everyone. As this full employment goal was associated with policies aiming at an equal distribution of income, the entire system of economic and social policy contributed to a general feeling of solidarity.

Part of the technical implementation of the Rehn–Meidner model had been that fiscal policy was geared towards redistribution of resources and restriction of consumption in order to prevent the economy from overheating. In practice, this occurred through the tax-benefit system. High taxes slowed down the economy and social security benefits redistributed income between various groups in society in accordance with the Social Democratic ideology of the time. Monetary policies were, in turn, geared towards growth in the sense of boosting the economy through low interest rates or low exchange rates whenever there seemed to be a need for investments or an increase in competitiveness in the export sector. This was possible due to controls on capital inflows and outflows and a political control of the central bank. Gradually, however, this relationship between fiscal and monetary policy began to turn around so that in the 1990s it was reversed: as a consequence of the renegotiation of the post-war collectivist order fiscal policy became geared towards growth and monetary policy towards price stability. This turn in economic policy making was associated with changed perceptions of the roles of both public and employment policy. Thus, in the process the roles of fiscal and monetary policy associated with the Rehn–Meidner model was reformulated as well.

The Swedish tax reforms of the early 1990s and the release of the central bank from political control are signs of the changed relationship between fiscal and monetary policy (it must, however, be noted that some taxes, most notably property and income taxes, were raised in 1994 in order to reduce the public budget deficit; Benner and Vad, 2000, p. 428). When this relationship is changed, it appears important to have as low as possible tax rates in order to stimulate the economy, as fiscal policy becomes geared towards growth. At the same time, a balanced public budget also becomes important, which in turn puts restrictions on public service expansion. From a social policy point of view, cash benefits start to appear to an increasing extent as disincentives for participation in the economic sphere. In the Swedish case this concern was expressed by the Lindbeck Commission, and indeed by the entire Swedosclerosis debate (Blyth, 2002, p. 245; for a summary of the debate, see Korpi, 1992) largely initiated by think tanks with close relations with organised business.

Furthermore, employment policies were also cast in a new light as the relationship between fiscal and monetary policy was reversed. During the era of the Rehn–Meidner model employment policies had been designed to compensate for the unemployment created by restrictive fiscal policies. In practice, this had occurred through the information provided by employment agencies, as well as ALMP measures providing re-training and subsidised work. Once economic policy started to change as well as the ideologies coupled with these policies, the old administrative apparatus including the cash-benefit system and employment administration received a new function that was in accordance with the new relationship between fiscal and monetary policy. As fiscal policies were now geared towards growth, so, it was thought, should social and employment policies be as well. During the course of the renegotiation of the collectivist post-war order, employment policies received the task of managing the labour supply, for instance through enhancing job-seeking activities among those at the margins of the labour market. This was a completely new function for the employment policy administration that only had to be modified in content, not in structure in order to meet the new demands. In any case, the new function of Swedish employment policy since the renegotiation of the post-war collectivist order differed significantly from that associated with the Rehn–Meidner model.

A document produced by the Swedish Central Bank confirms that the policy goal of price stability has persisted until the early 2000s:

> The goal of monetary policy is not and should not be a higher employment rate or faster growth. What monetary policy can achieve instead is an inflation rate that over a number of years is in line with the inflation target, in addition to contributing to alleviating fluctuations in the real economy. (Sveriges Riksbank, 2008, p. 7)

The goal of price stability was consolidated during the 1990s in Sweden when the central bank was released from political control and when the country began adjusting its policies in accordance with the requirements of the EU. Sweden's EU membership was confirmed in 1995 but the country never joined the EMU due to a negative referendum result. Nevertheless, the policy goals of the Swedish Central Bank resemble to a great extent those of the European Central Bank.

Although the tax-benefit system never underwent system-changing reforms, the following quotation from the Social Democratic government shows that at the end of the 1990s employment policy goals were still subordinate to the goal of price stability:

> How great the employment rate can be without endangering price stability depends on the efficiency of employment and commodity markets. An efficient labour market, increased competition in the product market and a stable wage setting are factors that allow a strong increase in employment with stable prices. In order to combine an increasing employment rate with low unemployment and low inflation a well functioning and flexible labour market is thus required. Such a labour market is created through strengthening individuals' positions in the labour market through training measures and work practice, in addition to enhanced professional and geographic mobility. (Government, Sweden, pp. 32–3)

As noted in the previous chapters, full employment together with price stability used to form the fundamentals of the post-war Rehn–Meidner model of employment policy. During the 1990s the goal of full employment became, however, subordinate to the goal of price stability along with the shift in the relationship between fiscal and monetary policy. Hort has offered an optimistic interpretation about the return of the goal of full employment, stating that despite certain streamlining with the European monetarist path, full employment has remained high on the Swedish policy agenda (Hort, 2003, p. 271). It is true that the Social Democratic government, after having in 1990 explicitly announced that price stability was the number one economic policy priority, reannounced in 1996 that its goal was to establish full employment in a situation where unemployment still remained persistently high. The documents quoted above show, however, that this goal of full employment remained subordinate to the goal of price stability throughout the 1990s and until the 2000s. Thus, the announcement of the Social Democratic government is perhaps best interpreted as a rhetorical appeal to those voters who approved of the old full employment policy goal of the post-war period. Indeed, this policy goal had been associated with normative values, such as equality and solidarity.

Increasing capital mobility was part of the more general process whereby post-war collectivist models of finance were questioned. This was to a great degree an international process, and only a decision to isolate oneself completely from the international economic order would have created complete autonomy regarding to the renegotiation process in any country. Ingvar Carlsson, Prime Minister at the time of the deregulation of the financial markets has later, however, regretted that the important decisions were never publicly discussed – and that no debate emerged regarding the causes of economic overheating in the late 1980s:

> The entire Swedish democracy had been hit by a fundamental structural problem.
> A "coalition" of politicians, civil servants, industry, economists and the media,
> who could not or would not meet reality face to face, created a silence instead of
> a debate regarding what was going on in the Swedish economy.
> How could things go so wrong? (Carlsson, 2003, p. 306)

Sweden decided to join the European Union and became a member in 1995, which to some extent attached the country to the Western socio-economic order. It would be wrong to suggest, however, that this decision would have determined the contents of the important transformations at hand. On the contrary, the renegotiation of the post-war collectivist order is better illustrated as a narrative about the national adaptation and adoption of the international competition state paradigm that began to dominate worldwide.

Expressed from another point of view, in the new Western economic order it was no longer possible to operate with a monetary policy that was entirely directed towards domestic policy concerns (McNamara, 1998, p. 44). In an environment of free capital mobility, states could only choose between a fixed exchange rate and domestic economic policy autonomy. But designing the new functions of fiscal policy together with employment policy and the cash-benefit system represents the national adaptation of the international competition state paradigm in Sweden's case. Managing the labour supply through activation measures the way it was expressed by the Social Democratic government in 1999 is perfectly in line with the imperatives developed by Layard, Nickell and Jackman, for instance (Layard et al., 1991; Nickell, 2001). Swedish policy makers also appear to have adopted notions about the relationship between inflation and unemployment that are in line with the competition state paradigm. As noted, the latter postulates that unemployment levels below a 'natural rate' will cause inflation.

The international dimension of the competition state paradigm becomes evident when, for instance, policy suggestions issued by the OECD are reviewed. In the 1970s the organisation began to endorse already market-centred ideas that significantly differed from post-war Keyenesianism (McNamara, 1998, p. 147). The 1994 White Paper on Growth, Competitiveness and Employment (OECD 1994b) has further strengthened this ideological commitment of the organisation. According to the OECD[1] itself:

> The OECD is a unique forum where the governments of 30 democracies work together to address the economic, social and environmental challenges of globalisation. The OECD is also at the forefront of efforts to understand and to help governments respond to new developments and concerns, such as corporate governance, the information economy and the challenges of an ageing population. (OECD, 2007a, p. ii)

The OECD's core activity consists of the publication of various publication series, such as the Economic Surveys, Reviews on Regulatory Reform, and Employment Outlooks.[2] These publication series compare the OECD member countries in various fields and provide detailed policy suggestions for each country. Although they cover a great variety of topics, including for instance economic competition, privatisation, public policy, social security, employment policy, housing, construction, administration and so on, the reports are constructed in a fairly mechanical way. Without much exaggeration it can be said that the various country reports are so constructed that the competition state paradigm is taken as a starting point, and then a selection of policy areas in a specific country is identified that do not conform completely to the imperatives and rationales of the paradigm. After that, policy suggestions are formulated so that they conform to the competition state paradigm, but also so that they are applicable in the country-specific context that has been dealt with in the particular report.

It must also be noted that policy suggestions even within a single OECD country report may vary and even contradict one another. This may be due to the fact that a single report is drafted by a number of different people – each with her or his own personal relationship with the competition state paradigm. Individual authors are, however, not identified in the country reports. As the legitimacy or

---

1 OECD member countries include Australia, Austria, Belgium, Canada, the Czech Republic, Denmark, Finland, France, Germany, Greece, Hungary, Iceland, Ireland, Italy, Japan, Korea, Luxembourg, Mexico, the Netherlands, New Zealand, Norway, Poland, Portugal, the Slovak Republic, Spain, Sweden, Switzerland, Turkey, the United Kingdom and the United States.

2 The OECD Employment Outlooks have been excluded from the analysis because they deal with the OECD countries in general and do not include any country-specific reports.

accuracy of policy suggestions of the reports is not the concern here, this particular issue does not constitute a problem.

What makes the OECD publications interesting for current purposes is that despite their mechanical approach towards cross-national comparisons, they do make an effort to take local cultural, political and economic arrangements into account when formulating their policy suggestions. In practice, the preparation of the publications occurs in association with national government officials, who have the opportunity to communicate with the relevant OECD officials about national policies and traditions. Therefore, although the competition state paradigm is the common denominator of each country report, the reports can be interpreted to reflect – if observed in the appropriate way – the national adaptation of the competition state paradigm. If national officials have endorsed the competition state paradigm very strongly, they are expected to find the same problem areas in their country as the OECD officials would have done from the perspective of their paradigm. In such cases, the policy suggestions could be expected to be fairly strongly articulated and oriented towards fundamental reforms without much consideration of national traditions or past policies. If national officials have remained critical towards the competition state paradigm, this would be expected to lead to stronger emphases on national traditions in the reports and milder policy suggestions, given the OECD's commitment to co-operate with national officials.

Two of the OECD's publication series will be reviewed here in the light of the Swedish case – the OECD Review of Regulatory Reform and the OECD Economic Surveys. The former series is based on a 2005 report on the *Guiding Principles for Regulatory Quality and Performance* and aims to 'assist governments to improve regulatory quality – that is, to reform regulations to foster competition, innovation, economic growth and important social objectives' (OECD, 2007a, p. 3). The OECD Economic Surveys 'identify the main economic challenges faced by the country and analyses policy options to meet them' (OECD, 2008abc). In other words, the Regulatory Reform series deals with state involvement in the economy and the Economic Survey with the economy itself. By conforming to the competition state paradigm, both of these publication series strongly favour the application of the laws of supply and demand, in addition to economic competition, wherever possible. In the case of labour markets the policy suggestions essentially include low taxation (in selected areas of the economy), relaxed employment protection, individual level wage setting and low levels of social security contributions and cash benefits.

The Swedish OECD Review of Regulatory Reform opens in the following way:

> Economic success, which has enabled Sweden to develop and maintain high levels of social welfare, remains an essential support for the achievement of social goals. These include economic security including full employment, and equality through the reduction of income differences and the mitigation of poverty, as well as homogeneity of living conditions throughout the country. Swedish ambitions for a high quality environment have also grown steadily.

Swedish governance has developed around a strong and pervasive role for the state as guardian of society, and a large tax-financed public sector, reflecting citizens' traditional willingness to pay for quality social services through taxation. The welfare system is extensive and generous. Public ownership and production are substantial. Sweden is also distinguished by a political and societal culture which is particularly strong on transparency and integrity, reflected in the fact that consensus building is the cornerstone of decision making.

...

Sweden's core challenge is to ensure that the current strong economic performance can be sustained so that its ambitious social goals and welfare system can be maintained, against a background of increasing demand for higher standards, especially in public services. (OECD, 2007a, p. 11)

The tone in which Swedish policy priorities are discussed remains largely the same throughout the entire report. Towards the end of the report it is stated that:

Although performance in the past has been impressive, the Swedish economy has not yet regained its pre-crisis per capita income ranking. It still lags a number of countries in this respect, including neighbouring Denmark. Thus, living standards could still be improved. Sweden's public policy goals are ambitious and demanding in terms of the economy's capacity to support them. They emphasise the importance of social cohesion through a reduction of income differences and equality of living conditions across the country, based on an unusually generous welfare system. (OECD, 2007a, p. 77)

The term 'pre-crisis' refers here to the period before the crisis of the early 1990s. The policy suggestions provided in the report on Regulatory Reform in Sweden are rather detailed (grouped under the headings of regulatory governance, competition policy, market openness, multi-level regulatory governance and environment) and never question the fundamental policy priorities identified in the beginning of the report. There is also a suggestion that entrepreneurial activity should be encouraged in Sweden (OECD, 2007a, p. 58). The tone in the other OECD report analysed here – the OECD Economic Survey (OECD 2007b) – is slightly less enthusiastic about Swedish welfare policy goals. However, the policy suggestions in this report also tend to be rather specific, containing, for instance, a suggestion to lower the level of unemployment benefits (OECD, 2007b, p. 75) – but only after an extensive discussion about the pros and cons of the Swedish in-work tax credit. Even demands for a more flexible labour market are quite specific, focusing only on the so-called first-in-last-out rule that is applied in the Swedish labour market (OECD, 2007b, p. 92; Kananen, 2012a, p. 461).

In the Economic Survey of 2011 the OECD continued to support traditional Swedish public policy commitments, but proposed nonetheless tighter sanctions in cases of non-compliance in unemployment insurance. Other proposals included further decentralisation of the wage setting system (OECD, 2011, pp. 88, 90; Kananen 2012a, pp. 461–2).

In Sweden the aim during the renegotiation process has been to participate in the economic development occurring in the rest of the Western world. This was indicated by EU membership in 1995 and subsequent reforms (privatisation and commercialisation) of the economy. Refusal to join the EMU indicates, however, taking a certain distance from the EU and the rest of the Western world, perhaps best interpreted as an effort to create a space within which international ideas and imperatives might be adapted to Swedish traditions and applied within the Swedish particular context. This is also what an analysis of OECD documents suggests. Regardless of whether the same course of action was taken in the domestic political arena, Swedish government officials appear to have been eager to defend national traditions in communications with OECD officials. An interesting contrast was revealed by reviewing both domestic policy documents and OECD recommendations. Although ideas associated with the new international competition state paradigm could be detected in domestic policy documents, OECD documents appeared to support the defence of traditional Swedish values and institutions.

Denmark

Beginning of the Renegotiation Process: European Impulses and Domestic Policy Challenges

The Danish economy was hit harder by the effects of the two oil crises in the 1970s than Sweden and Finland. In fact, the 1970s was a challenging decade in Denmark both from a political and an economic point of view. Taxes had been increased prior to Denmark joining the European Economic Community (EEC) in 1973, adding to public discomfort. This discomfort was probably also related to the fact that a great deal of Danish social expenditure was financed by various taxes instead of earmarked employer and employee contributions as in Sweden and Finland. It was also in 1973 that the first oil crisis shook the world economy, and at the same time a new tax-revolt party (*Fremskridtspartiet*) gained 16 per cent of the votes in the Danish parliamentary elections (Iversen and Andersen, 2008, p. 313), contributing to a fragmentation of the parliament. Coalitions, and effective consensus and consequently effective policy responses to the economic challenges thus became more difficult to achieve (Nannestad and Green-Pedersen, 2008, p. 44). During the 1970s the country moved from full employment to an unemployment rate of 10 per cent. Nannestad and Green-Pedersen have described the mounting economic pressures in the following way:

> By 1982, the economic situation looked even bleaker than ever. Unemployment and inflation each stood at the 10-pct. mark. Long-term nominal interest rates

were close to 20 pct. Private investments were at an all-time low. The balance of payment deficit was 4.5 pct. of GNP, and the foreign debt was exploding. So were interest payments on foreign credits as a proportion of the total government budget. The budget deficit had grown to about 10 pct. of GNP with no end to its continued growth in sight. There was a real anxiety that the imbalances in the Danish economy were getting out of control. As a former Social Democratic minister of finance remarked already in 1979, Denmark was standing on "the brink of the abyss". (Nannestad and Green-Pedersen, 2008, p. 44)

Such a description of standing 'on the brink of the abyss' could quite easily be associated with Sweden in the early 1990s. Denmark, however, faced its own abyss in the early 1980s rather than in the 1990s. The Social Democratic-led government resigned voluntarily in 1982 acknowledging a loss of political direction in the middle of the challenging economic situation. A Conservative-led government headed by Poul Schlüter took over and this government stayed in power until 1993.

The regime change of 1982 gave a clear voice to perceptions of problems in the post-war collectivist social order, and the political momentum of the Danish conservatives was enhanced by the simultaneous radical reform agendas of Margaret Thatcher in the UK and Ronald Reagan in the US. The Danish minority government was not, however, in the position to implement a fully-fledged privatisation agenda and the initial rhetoric of privatisation was turned into a more neutral rhetoric of 'modernisation' (Green-Pedersen, 2002, p. 282). The year 1982 indicated a gradual shift in political ideology accompanied by a number of reform programmes produced by the government (Ejersbo and Greve, 2008, p. 36). As in Sweden, public sector expenditure and the functioning of the public sector became key issues in efforts to formulate new directions in policy making. But despite this ideological change, practical reforms were few during the 1980s. This is indicated by the fact that when the Ministry of Finance – one of the key actors in public sector restructuring in Denmark – published an evaluation report in 1992 entitled *The Public Sector 1982–1992* descriptions of practical results of public sector restructuring remained on a theoretical level (Ejersbo and Greve, 2008, p. 43).

Among the most crucial concrete policy reforms relevant to the renegotiation of the post-war social order in Denmark during the 1980s was the introduction of framework steering in state budgeting (Ejersbo and Greve, 2008, pp. 84–9). This policy reform increased the influence of the Ministry of Finance in relation to other government departments as this Ministry began to coordinate the negotiation of budget frames. There was also another trend which in turn increased the influence of central government in relation to the political parties. This trend was an increase in the role of 'expert committees' preparing policy proposals brought to the parliament with the backing of the entire government coalition. In Denmark this policy style was first established in the field of education policy (Mathiesen, 2000, p. 12). What was similar in comparison with Sweden was that despite the increase in central government authority, the general public had the opportunity to follow closely the ideological underpinnings of the direction towards which the government wished to steer the country. This was ensured by the numerous publications and reports to the Parliament that the government produced during the 1980s (for a list of these publications, see Ejersbo and Greve, 2008, p. 36).

Thus, despite few concrete policy reforms, the beginning of the 1980s constituted the beginning of a gradual renegotiation of the post-war collectivist social order, which to an increasing extent began to be perceived as a cause of the economic and political problems that the country was facing. The Danish renegotiation process was more gradual compared to that in Sweden as the banking crisis that hit the Sweden in the early 1990s created a clearer transition period. A few years before the Swedish banking crisis, the Danish government had introduced a number of economic policy measures popularly termed the 'potato cure' (*kartoffelkuren*), which were intended to deal with the persistent problem of a deficit in the balance of payments. Capital markets had been liberalised in Denmark in a similar way to Sweden, but the 'potato cure' contributed to curbing private consumption in such a way that the increased availability of finances was not accompanied by the emergence of an economic bubble of the Swedish kind. Among the most significant economic policies in this respect was the tax reform of 1987, which significantly reduced the deductibility of home mortgage interest payments (Nannestad and Green-Pedersen, 2008, pp. 50–51). This reform decreased loan-financed consumption and contributed to cooling down the economy – a trend completely opposite to that in Sweden. The 'potato cure' also resulted in a decrease of real estate prices to the extent that many foreclosures occurred as the debts of home owners became unmanageable. But, in retrospect, from the point of view of avoiding a banking crisis the timing of measures restricting private consumption appears appropriate.

Having avoided the banking crisis did not, however, mean that the Danish economy was problem-free in the late 1980s. After a brief decline in the mid 1980s, the unemployment rate climbed back towards 10 per cent. Nonetheless, the current account deficit turned into a surplus before 1990 and the more active phase of renegotiating the post-war social order began without the kind of financial crises seen in Sweden. This phase occurred under new political leadership. Poul Schlüter's Conservative-led government had to resign in 1993 due to a political scandal and a new Social Democratic-led government with Poul Nyrup Rasmussen as Prime Minister began its period of office. This new government was also able to continue after the general elections in 1994.

In addition to the differences mentioned above, another major difference between Denmark and Sweden concerning the renegotiation of the post-war collectivist order was, of course, that Denmark had been a member of the EEC since 1973 and was subject to European impulses in a different manner from Sweden and Finland, which only joined the EU after the Maastricht Treaty of 1992. In 1986 the EEC drafted the Single European Act (SEA) granting the four freedoms of the movement of capital, goods, labour and services. The SEA constituted an impulse for the renegotiation of the post-war order in Denmark as it clearly contested the sheltering of the economy from competition in the manner public provision of various goods had done in the Nordic countries during the post-war period. In Denmark a referendum on the SEA was held and 56.2 per cent of the Danish population expressed their support for the Act. Six years later, however, the population rejected the Maastricht Treaty producing a number of Danish exceptions in the Treaty that established the European Union. This rejection of the Maastricht treaty can be interpreted as popular dissatisfaction with the direction the EU was pursuing in creating a new European social and economic order, but it also indicates the existence of a public debate about possible directions in the renegotiation of the Danish post-war collectivist order. In 1998 the European path towards a new social and economic order was once again rejected in Denmark when the Economic and Monetary Union (EMU) did not receive public support (Iversen and Andersen, 2008, p. 319). Denmark thus, like Sweden, stayed out of the EMU retaining both its own currency and the option to pursue domestic monetary policy.

Corporatisation, commercialisation and privatisation of public functions occurred in Denmark roughly during the same period of time as Sweden. As noted in the previous chapters, these processes were crucial for the renegotiation of the collectivist order as employment relationships changed from public 'offices' to private employment contracts. Between 1992–1997 public functions in the areas of energy production, telecommunications and postal services were corporatised and/or privatised (Christensen and Pallesen, 2001; Iversen and Andersen, 2008, p. 319). Local government restructuring – another area of crucial significance for the renegotiation process – showed slightly different patterns in Denmark and Sweden, despite many similarities between the local government structures in the two countries. Firstly, in Denmark the transition from earmarked funding to block grants was not associated with the post-expansive phase of service development as it was in Sweden. Block grant financing had been established in Denmark after a major municipal reform in the 1970s (Mouritzen, 2008). But when public expenditure became a major concern in Denmark during the 1980s, the number of these block grants was reduced. The reform was politically slightly sensitive but the central government managed to avoid blame for the cut back. This was because the targets of the cut backs had to be specified at the local level and in Denmark it was the health care sector that suffered in particular (Pallesen and Pedersen, 2008, p. 247). However, health care expenditure started to increase again in the 1990s (Pallesen and Pedersen, 2008, p. 245).

Innovative Reforms in Income Support and Unemployment Insurance

As in Sweden, labour market issues became part of the renegotiation of the post-war collectivist social order in Denmark in the 1990s. As mentioned already, unemployment had been a pressing issue in Denmark since the 1970s but co-incidentally labour market issues forcefully entered the political reform agenda at the same time as unemployment had become a pressing issue in Sweden.

This co-incidental simultaneous timing of new labour market policy agendas across Sweden and Denmark may be partly associated with the evolution of the international competition state paradigm. It was not until the 1990s that concrete policy suggestions in line with the international competition state paradigm were developed in relation to labour markets. When such concrete policy suggestions emerged, they could be adapted in Sweden and Denmark in various ways as parts of a process whereby the post-war collectivist social order was renegotiated.

The new Danish labour market policy agenda was, however, not solely introduced by the initiative of the new government that took over in 1993. A year before a working group commonly referred to as the 'Zeuthen Committee' had developed a comprehensive assessment of the 'structural problems of the labour market' (Ministry of Finance, 1992) and the Rasmussen government was able to develop its new labour market policy agenda based on the assessment of the working group. The reforms that were introduced after 1993 drew heavily on the foundations developed by the Zeuthen Committee (Jensen, 2008, p. 129). Danish labour market reforms after 1993 focused on two key aspects:

1. The role of Active Labour Market Policies; and
2. The balance of rights and obligations of benefit recipients.

Traditionally, Danish unemployment insurance had been, as in Sweden, in line with the Ghent system – i.e. insurance payments were voluntary and they were administered either by insurance funds or trade unions. The unemployment insurance system consisted of only one tier – the earnings-related benefit that was paid to unemployed persons who fulfilled the membership and employment criteria (one year of membership and 26 weeks of employment within the last three years). Unemployed persons who did not meet the eligibility criteria could apply for a variety of other social security benefits administered by the municipality (Jensen, 2008, pp. 119–20). Until the early 1990s the role of ALMP had primarily been that of a gateway to a renewed period of unemployment benefit. In principle, the maximum duration of earnings-related unemployment benefit was two years, but in practice, if the duration of unemployment approached 18 months, the person in question was offered a placement in an ALMP measure for 6 months and eligibility was renewed (Jensen, 2008, p. 122).

Danish labour market reforms proceeded in three waves after 1993 but in terms of a renewed role for ALMP and a new definition of the balance between rights and obligations the directions of future reforms was already set by the first wave in 1993–94 when a new Act on Active Labour Market Policy was established (Act on Active Labour Market Policy, 434/1993). This act explicitly stated both the rights and obligations of an unemployed benefit recipient and it was enforced in the beginning of 1994. After this reform an unemployment benefit recipient had the right to earnings-related benefit for a maximum period of seven years – given that the eligibility criteria were met. The seven-year period was further divided into two sub periods (4+3 years) and the rights and obligations were defined differently in each of these periods. During the first four years the benefit recipient had a right to participate in activation measures for 12 months in total. Concerning the second sub period (i.e. the last three years of the maximum period) the Act of 1994 stated that 'the aim was that benefit recipients would attend activation measures full time' (Act on Active Labour Market Policy, 434/1993, §33, Kananen 2012b, p. 563).

In addition to these rights, the new Act also defined the obligations of unemployed benefit recipients – or to be more specific how the obligation to participate in work activation measures would be enforced (for a critical view of these policies, see van Oorschot and Abrahamson, 2003). Paragraph §35 of the Act stated that if an unemployed person refused to co-operate with benefit administrators regarding individual action plans, the unemployment insurance fund would be informed about this refusal. Paragraph §36 stated the same rule concerning unemployed income support recipients (Act on Active Labour Market Policy, 434/1993, §35–26). In 1995 the formulations in the Act were changed so that the Act now defined a *right and obligation* to participation in activation measures during the last three years of the maximum seven-year period (Act on Revising the Act on Active Labour Market Policy, 1085/1994, §33). In practice this meant that refusing to participate in work activation measures during the second sub period implied exclusion from the benefit (Kvist, 2003, p. 235).

The labour market reform of 1994 created a path along which later legislative reforms proceeded. Between 1994–1998 the maximum duration of earnings-related unemployment benefit was gradually reduced from seven to four years (1+3). In 1996 the employment requirement was increased from 26 to 52 weeks of work within three years, and in 2003 the division between the two sub periods was abolished completely (Kvist, 2003, p. 235; Kvist and Pedersen, 2007, p. 103). Thus, the labour market reforms of the 1990s gradually introduced the obligation to participate in ALMP measures for all unemployed people.

Moreover, the Act on Active Labour Market Policy changed the purpose of ALMP measures from having been a gateway to renewed benefit eligibility to being part of a unique system that emerged as a result of creating the act. Two of the three essential parts of this novel system had existed prior to the reforms of the early 1990s – and they were largely preserved throughout the decade. Firstly, in international comparison, the level of compensation in earnings-related benefit was on a high level, and secondly, as mentioned in the previous chapter, Danish employment protection legislation had traditionally been relaxed at least in comparison with Finland and Sweden. Thus, in combination with the renewed purpose of ALMP a system based on three essential parts emerged. Such a combination of generous earnings-related unemployment benefit, relaxed employment protection legislation and ALMP in this form existed only in Denmark. Falling unemployment rates added to international interest in this system of employment policy, which has since become known as 'flexicurity' (a combination of flexibility and security) (Kvist and Pedersen, 2007, p. 99; Bredgaard et al., 2005, 2009).

Simultaneously with the Act on Active Labour Market Policy an Act on Municipal Activation was presented in Denmark (Act on Municipal Activation, 498/1993). This act was applicable to uninsured unemployed income support recipients who were entitled to support as specified in the Act on Social Assistance. It specified a right to offers of job training and education as outlined in the Act on Active Labour Market Policy. Paragraph §22 contained regulations for cases in which an income support recipient refused to participate in activation measures in a similar manner to paragraph §35 of the Act on Active Labour Market Policy.

Participating in ALMP measures counted towards renewed benefit eligibility criteria in Sweden, whereas this gateway function was abandoned in Denmark with the reforms that created a genuine maximum duration for earnings-related unemployment benefit. On these grounds, it also seems that the insurance principle was slightly weaker in Denmark compared to Sweden, it was actually strengthened during the 1990s – although the maximum duration of unemployment insurance remained, initially, at seven years in Denmark.

It is also worth paying attention to the connections between the level of unemployment and adjustments in the maximum duration of unemployment benefit. In Denmark the latter was reduced from seven to four years between 1994–98 and at the end of this period unemployment was at a level of 4.6 per cent (Eurostat, 2009). Thus, in Denmark the system changing reforms were carried out at a time when unemployment was already decreasing. Some might even credit the labour market reforms for falling unemployment rates, but often the causal mechanisms are more complex than this. In any case, it may be concluded that despite shortenings of the maximum duration of unemployment insurance, the insurance principle remained fairly strong throughout the 1990s in Denmark.

A new Act on Active Social Policy came into being in 1998. The preparation of this act was accompanied by some controversy and an initial proposal presented by the government was met with criticism that led to the formulation of a Law on Equal Rights and Administration (Torfing, 1999, p. 17). This law was referred to in paragraph §98 of the Act on Active Social Policy, which established a system of treating complaints on decisions made by the municipality in matters relevant to the Act.

After the new Act on Active Social Policy was passed, it stated its purpose in the following manner:

> The purpose of this Act is:
> 1. To secure that persons having or who will possibly have difficulties in remaining employed may receive support for their livelihood and
> 2. To establish an economic safety net for anyone who cannot in any other way attain the means to a sufficient livelihood for her/himself or her/his family.
> The purpose of providing support is to help the recipient to achieve a state where she/he may support her/himself. The recipient and her/his spouse should

therefore according to their capabilities utilise and develop their working capacity by accepting offers of work or activation.

The recipient should in accordance with her/his needs and capacities have the opportunity to influence and take responsibility for the administration of the support. (Act on Active Social Policy, 455/1997, §1)

Chapter 4 of the Act on Active Social Policy specified the connections between income support and activation. It contained a recognition of the various situations in which a person may be forced to claim social assistance:

The municipality provides support in the form of cash benefit and activation.
The conditions for providing support are:
1. That the recipient has been subject to changes in her/his living conditions, e.g. due to sickness, unemployment or separation
2. That the changes mean that the claimant does not have the possibility to provide for her/himself or her/his family, and
3. That the need cannot be met through other benefits.
...

Not having a realistic offer of employment is a condition for receiving support. Accepting a realistic offer of activation or other offers that may improve opportunities to gain employment (employment promoting measures) is a condition for receiving support. (Act on Active Social Policy, 455/1997, §11, 13)

Article 13 went on to describe situations in which it would not be reasonable to require recipients to accept employment offers. Such situations would be, for instance, a severe illness or pregnancy, or if the recipient was obliged to look after her/his children.

It was also stated in the Act that persons above 30 years of age should be offered participation in activation measures after having received income support continuously for a period of 12 months. For persons below 20 years of age the offer was to be made after 13 weeks of receiving income support.

As described in the previous chapter, the activation measures concerning uninsured job seekers was not regulated in Swedish legislation. Instead, the Activation Guarantee that was implemented in the early 2000s had more of an administrative character. In the Danish legislation income support and activation measures are more explicitly associated with each other with the phrases 'utilising and developing their working capacities' and 'achieving a state where she/he may support her/himself', as expressed in the first paragraph of the act. It may be interpreted that the entire act is about how to regulate and implement these aims.

It is interesting to compare the formulations concerning sanctions for non-compliance in the legislation in each country. The Swedish case stands out by only providing broad frameworks to be implemented in a more detailed manner at the front line of service delivery. In other words, in Sweden the legislation gives considerable room for manoeuvre for front-line service administrators also when it comes to sanctioning non-compliant behaviour.

By contrast, the Danish legislation specifies in detail the steps taken should an individual not participate in the ALMP measures:

> If a person fails without an acceptable reason to participate in the activities specified in an offer of activation or other employment promoting measures, the municipality may reduce the support specified in §25. The reduction should occur within 3 months after the event in question.
>
> The support specified in §25 is reduced in relation to the number of hours that the person in question has failed to attend. The reduction is calculated in relation to all offers of activation or other employment-promoting measures made within a month. The monthly support specified in §25 may be reduced by a maximum of 20 per cent.
>
> ...
>
> The support ends if the recipient or her/his spouse without an acceptable reason declines an offer of work, activation according to §16, section 2, no. 1–5 and 8, or other employment-promoting measures for a period corresponding to the period when the offer is available. (Act on Active Social Policy, 455/1997, §39, 41)

In other words, the legislation regulates two kinds of cases. Firstly, if an income support recipient fails to attend the activation measures designed for her/him, the sanction is a reduction of the benefit by up to 20 per cent. Secondly, if the income support recipient *rejects* an offer if activation measures altogether, the benefit is suspended for the corresponding period when the offer is available.

In Denmark paragraphs §39–41 of the Act on Active Social Policy were contested in the parliamentary procedures. The Parliamentary Committee on Social Affairs (*Folketingets Socialudvalg*) put forward a query whether the above artcles contravened article 75 of the Danish Constitution. This article states that one who cannot support her/himself is entitled to public support (Constitution of Denmark, §75). The article also states an obligation to obey the duties that this support is associated with.

The government Justice Department (*Justitieministeriet*) was assigned to reply to this query and it referred to the original government proposal which stated that demands should be stricter for persons with unemployment as their only problem (Folketinget, 1997).

Interestingly, the Justice Department also referred to historical interpretations of the Constitution, and particularly the last part of the paragraph stating the 'obligation to obey the duties that the law ascribes in such cases' (Folketinget, 1997, p. 2). Historically, receiving income support in Denmark was, as in Finland and Sweden, associated with a limitation of citizenship rights, such as the right to marry, the right to own property and the right to vote, and in its reply the Justice Department explained that the limitations of such rights were the 'obligations' that the Constitution referred to. Although not making this explicit, the impression made in the reply was that accepting activation offers could be assimilated with these 'obligations', which since 1965 were no longer applicable.

In addition, the Justice Department referred to an existing interpretation according to which municipalities could deny support from 'work shy' persons who were not available for the labour market (Folketinget, 1997, p. 2). The Justice Department concluded that the proposed Article 41 was not in contradiction with the Constitution. In its statement, it argued that it was not specified in the Constitution what form public support should take, given that the person in question is guaranteed a minimum level of existence. The Justice Department thus indicated that activation offers may also constitute the kind of public support mentioned in the Constitution (Folketinget, 1997, p. 3).

Although backing up a historical return to reciprocity in the criteria for claiming income support, the statement of the Danish Justice Department is defensive in many aspects. It states, for instance that 'the offer should not be made illusory' (referring to the activation offer), 'that demands should be stricter for those persons with unemployment as their only problem' and that 'the claim that the recipient should utilise her/his employment prospects should be adjusted individually with respect to the capacities of the person in question' (Folketinget, 1997, p. 3). In the Danish case articles 39–41 appear as logical consequences of the obligation to participate in ALMP measures. If this obligation is not fulfilled by the income support recipient, the consequence is suspension of the benefit.

There is yet another crucial aspect which makes Danish activation measures different in comparison to Swedish activation measures – at least in the beginning of the 1990s. This aspect is the significance of activation measures for local communities. Between 1989–1991 there was a development programme entitled *Det sociala udviklingsprogram* (SUM) (The Social Development Programme) which aimed to combine aspects of activation and rehabilitation. This programme had a strong bottom-up focus, which was later reflected in some of the administrative reforms that accompanied the policy reforms of the 1990s. There was a strong effort to involve voluntary organisations working in local communities and third-sector organisations in activation measures. New forms of organisation – such as self-help groups and organisations established by the unemployed themselves – were combined with traditional formal social work. Within the framework of the SUM projects, the unemployed were also granted the opportunity to participate in voluntary work so that the third sector was made into an arena of participation and empowerment (Salonen-Soulié, 2003, p. 79).

Once the Active Labour Market Policy had been established in legislation after 1994 a number of administrative reforms were carried out whereby the former National Employment Board (*Landsarbejdsnævn*) was replaced by a new National Employment Council (*Landsarbejdsråd*) and the 14 regional Labour Market Boards (*Arbejdsmarkedsnævn*) were replaced by Regional Labour Market Councils. These reforms temporarily increased the influence of the local level in administering the resources associated with ALMP and, in line with the earlier SUM projects, the idea was to combine the needs and interests of the local communities with the needs and interests of the individual job seeker (Jensen, 2008, p. 132). However, towards the end of the 1990s the administration was recentralised so that the influence of the local level decreased (Bredgaard et al., 2003, pp. 68–9).

In 2001 a new government coalition was formed headed by the Conservatives and Prime Minister Anders Fogh Rasmussen. Although unemployment levels had decreased significantly compared to the early 1990s, labour market policy reform retained high priority on the government's reform agenda. A labour market reform entitled *Flere i arbejde* (more people in work, Ministry of Employment, 2002) was initiated in 2002 and as a consequence of this reform the title of the Act on Active Labour Market Policy was changed to an *Act on Active Employment Policy.* This semantic change was perhaps above all a result of the new government's efforts to take a critical distance from the previous government's labour market policy. But the reform process implied some changes in the content of policy as well. For instance, the influence of the local level was further weakened by merging the 14 Regional Labour Market Boards into four Employment Councils (*beskaeftigelseråd*, BER).

The Conservative-led government made some changes in income support legislation as well. A number of revisions in the Act on Active Social Policy were made during the first period of office of Fogh Rasmussen's government so that in 2005 the Act on Active Social Policy already differed quite significantly from the original act of 1997. The revised act contained two kinds of general sanctions – one applicable to all income support recipients (article 39) – and one applicable to persons claiming income support only due to unemployment (article 38a). Article 41 stated that rejecting a work offer would lead to withdrawal of income support for the period when the offer was open, as in earlier versions of the act. In other words, benefit administrators had more ways than before to sanction non-compliant income support recipients as the obligations specified in the act were widened. In addition, the conditions for people with an immigrant background claiming income support were tightened (Revised Act on Active Social Policy, 1009/2005, §8).

In 2005 the Conservative-led government launched an initiative entitled *En ny chance til alle* (a new chance for everyone, Government, Denmark, 2005). The overall aim of this new initiative was to improve the opportunities of income support recipients to find regular employment and at the core of the initiative was a requirement that all those who had not received an offer of activation within the previous 12 months would have their situation reviewed by benefit administrators. Associated with the initiative was an acknowledgement that income support could be claimed for a multiplicity of reasons. As a result of the 2005 initiative sanctions remained unaltered in the Act on Active Social Policy.

In 2010 the maximum duration of earnings-related unemployment insurance was reduced from four to two years as part of an austerity package (Kvist and Greve, 2011, p. 152; Kananen, 2012b, p. 564). Seen together, the reforms in employment policy and income support under the Conservative-led government can be interpreted to have taken the legislation a few steps away from the preceding aims to combine local and individual needs and interests towards a broader range of obligations for income support recipients.

The amount of legislative activity in Danish labour market policy during the 1990s and 2000s was significantly larger than that in Sweden. What was similar to the Swedish case was, however, that behind the legislative reforms recognition of a multiplicity of causes behind claiming income support could be detected. In addition, the combination of different policies – generous unemployment insurance, low levels of job protection, extensive ALMP – distinguishes the Danish system from the Swedish system of labour market policy, as highlighted by the many studies of 'flexicurity'. Still, as regards the Swedish case, many aspects point towards efforts to counteract any potential insider/outsider divisions in the labour market.

Danish labour market policy reform has been an ongoing process since the 1990s and it appears that the goals of labour market policy in general and ALMP in particular have evolved throughout the reform process. At first, ALMP were recalibrated from being a gateway to renewed unemployment benefit eligibility towards decentralised policies aiming to combine local and individual needs and interests. Later ALMP evolved towards creating an increasing variety of obligations for unemployed benefit recipients. This evolving character of Danish labour market policy becomes more evident when the ideas and goals behind the various policies are looked at in more detail.

Ideological Shifts: A Danish Competition State Paradigm

When the *Socialkommissionen* (Social Commission) (1993) and the *Zeuthen Committee* (1992) were appointed, there seemed to be a fairly strong awareness of the prescriptions of the international competition state paradigm in Denmark. At first, the influence of the new paradigm remained modest, but it gained strength during the 1990s and 2000s.

What clearly indicates an awareness of the new paradigm in the early 1990s is that the problems in the Danish labour market were labelled 'structural problems' (Torfing, 1999, pp. 13–15; Larsen and Andersen, 2009, pp. 244–8). The term 'structural unemployment' (see e.g. Torfing, 1999, p. 10) is one of the key terms in the competition state paradigm, as it contains assumptions about the causes of unemployment and suggestions as to the best solutions. As noted earlier in the analysis, generous benefits, high taxes, centralised wage setting and detailed employment protection legislation are according to the competition state paradigm among the main factors causing 'structural unemployment'. The prescriptions of the competition state paradigm were not, however, applied without reservations in Denmark in the early 1990s. A White Paper on the Structural Problems in the Labour Market from 1989 shows an awareness of the competition state paradigm (Torfing, 1999, p. 14) but the Zeuthen Committee report included discussions about the validity of the remedies of this paradigm (Ministry of Finance, 1992, pp. 11–12). Thus, the early 1990s may be regarded as a period when the ideas of the competition state paradigm began to make their way into Danish politics, and when policy makers began to work towards a particular Danish way of adopting and adapting these ideas.

One aspect of the reforms in the 1990s that was clearly influenced by the prescriptions of the international competition state paradigm was the new role of ALMP. Previously, when ALMP was used as a gateway to renewed unemployment benefit eligibility, it represented almost the exact negation of the logic of the competition state paradigm, according to which unemployment benefits of long duration increased the level of unemployment and were thus undesirable. Thus, the reform whereby a genuine maximum duration was established for earnings-related unemployment benefit, and whereby the purpose of ALMP was changed, can be interpreted as a reform inspired by the international competition state paradigm.

As noted in the above analysis of employment policy reform, once the genuine maximum duration of unemployment benefit was established, the maximum period during which unemployment benefit could be received was split into two. The labels 'active period' and 'passive period' were directly derived from the competition state paradigm, according to which unconditional unemployment benefits have the tendency to render recipients 'passive'. In addition, the competition state paradigm suggests that 'passive' unemployment benefits cause 'structural unemployment'. The various reforms whereby the duration of earnings-related unemployment benefit was shortened – from seven to four years between 1994 and 1999 – may also be interpreted as following the logic of the international competition state paradigm.

In the previous chapter it was also noted that as a consequence of the policy reforms of the 1990s, the Danish employment policy system was quite unique compared to the Swedish and Finnish systems, and indeed internationally as well. The combination of relaxed employment protection, generous unemployment benefits, high taxes and extensive ALMP did not exist anywhere else – although parallels have sometimes been made to the Netherlands (on Dutch characteristics and employment policy reforms, see e.g. Cox, 2001, pp. 483–9; van Oorschot and Abrahamson, 2003, pp. 289–93, 295–8; van Gerven, 2008, pp. 123–74). It may be further interpreted that this uniqueness was a consequence of the negotiated adaptation of the international competition state paradigm that was achieved as a consequence of political efforts to adapt its imperatives to local Danish policies and traditions. There was, of course, one key element that was in place already before the renegotiation of the post-war collectivist social order, and this element was the employment protection legislation that left hiring and firing of employees fairly unregulated (Huber and Stephens, 2001, p. 143). This historical element was – one might almost say co-incidentally – in accordance with the international competition state paradigm.

The element that most strikingly indicates the negotiated adaptation of the international competition state paradigm in the Danish employment policy system is, of course, the level of compensation of the earnings-related unemployment benefit. The international competition state paradigm quite clearly asserts that generous unemployment benefits cause structural unemployment as they create disincentives to take up work on the open labour market. This is supposedly because employers cannot offer wages below the level of the unemployment benefit which prevents low productivity jobs from emerging in the labour market.

The level of compensation of Danish unemployment benefit was not subject to reform during any of the labour market reforms of the 1990s – indicating that this was the most persistent element that was maintained despite the suggestions of the logic of the international competition state paradigm. Another element that indicated not only adaptation but also policy innovation, was the effort to combine the needs and interests of local communities and the third sector with the needs and interests of the individual unemployed person in the early 1990s.

Thus, the institutional characteristics of the Danish employment policy in the 1990s already point towards a negotiated adaptation of the international competition state paradigm. This notion receives further support with a closer look at the rationales and discussions of the second of the two committee reports preceding the 1994 labour market reform – that of the *Socialkommissionen*, which published its suggestions in 1993 (see also Torfing, 1999, pp. 14–15; Cox, 2001).

In some respects, the work of the *Socialkommissionen* overlapped with the work of the Zeuthen Committee. Both had a strong focus on labour market issues and were preoccupied with the challenges associated with the high levels of unemployment. Therefore, it is interesting to consider the extent to which the high levels of unemployment were perceived by the Commission as a threat to social order.

One aspect is particularly striking when the propositions of the *Socialkommissionen* are considered. This is the attention that is paid to the ideal of a citizens' income as one of the possible outcomes in the process of the renegotiation of the post-war collectivist order (Socialkommissionen, 1993, pp. 33, 84). The Commission brought forward the argument that unless the employment policy system was reformed, it would develop towards an unconditional citizens' income. The requirements to be available for work in the open labour market were beginning to erode and in practice, the Commission argued, the system allowed people to lead their lives independently of economic demands. This was a worrying development according to the Commission, and as one of the reasons behind this development it pointed out the fact that ALMP measures had become an automatic gateway to renewed unemployment benefit eligibility (Socialkommissionen, 1993, p. 19).

The way the *Socialkommissionen* wanted to prevent the Danish employment policy system from evolving into an unconditional citizens' income was, of course, by increasing the conditionality of unemployment benefits. As noted already, this was also what happened after the 1994 reform when a clear maximum duration of earnings-related unemployment benefit was established, and when the purpose of ALMP was changed.

In the report containing the proposals put forward by the *Socialkommissionen*, there is a discussion whether 'unemployment should be made voluntary'. This discussion is carried out under the heading 'Why not learn to live with unemployment?' (Socialkommissionen, 1993, pp. 83–9). The arguments that the *Socialkommissionen* acknowledges (without, however, endorsing them) show the distance that it took from the rationale of the competition state paradigm. One of such arguments is that there is simply not enough employment for everyone in the open labour market and that it should be made acceptable that some people who cannot find work, should choose to be unemployed rather than compete for the few jobs that are open. The right to choose 'unemployment' – or more accurately, the right to choose not to be employed in the open labour market – would be guaranteed by an unconditional citizens' income. This idea is, however, not defended by the Commission, who maintains that the 'right and duty' to work as established by §75 of the Danish Constitution should be adhered to (Socialkommissionen, 1993, p. 82; Cox, 2001, p. 479).

However, although not fully supporting the idea of an unconditional citizens' income, the *Socialkommissionen* wished to maintain some elements of it in establishing a degree of conditionality in the employment policy system (Socialkommissionen, 1993, p. 84). This element of a citizens' income would, according to the Commission, be maintained if the choices of the individual unemployed were respected. As far as possible, participation in ALMP measures should be made voluntary, and the impression was given that no conflict of interest between the individual unemployed person and the political aims presented by the Commission existed.

Thus, the Commission proposed that for unemployed people that are not at risk of being excluded, participation in ALMP measures should be made voluntary. Similarly, the choices of those at risk of being excluded from society would be respected, but for these people the consequences of turning down an activation offer would be different from the consequences of those not at risk of exclusion:

> Those at risk of exclusion should not have the same right to refuse an activation
> offer ... If the individual in question refuses to participate in activities designed
> to improve her/his chances to be employed later on, there is according to the
> *Socialkommissionen* nothing dubious in this choice. But in such cases it would
> appear to be a completely natural consequence that the public support in question
> is withdrawn. (Socialkommissionen, 1993, pp. 86–7)

According to the *Socialkommissionen*'s proposal, unemployed people not at risk of being excluded should be able to decide for themselves whether or not to participate in an ALMP measure offered. The idea of the Commission was also to design a similar kind of autonomy for those it defined at risk of exclusion as well, only with the consequence that refusal to participate in an offered ALMP measure would lead to the withdrawal of the right to unemployment benefit.

It may also be interpreted that the actual employment policy system that emerged after 1994 in Denmark was actually in line with the rationale of the *Socialkommissionen* presented above. Participation in ALMP measures was voluntary for those unemployed people who had been out of work for less than four years. For those unemployed people out of work for longer than four years, refusing to participate in ALMP measures implied losing the right to earnings-related unemployment benefit. In other words, within the system, it was legitimate to decline an activation offer, but the consequence was that the right to unemployment benefit was lost.

The arguments and rationales presented by the 1993 *Socialkommissionen* further strengthen the image of a negotiated Danish adaptation of the international competition state paradigm. This negotiated adaptation proceeded during the 1990s in line with the legislative reforms described above, and the ideological foundations were discussed and reformulated in new committees. After the new Social Democratic-led government started in office, another commission dealing with the challenges of the welfare state was appointed, now under the name of the *Velfærdskommissionen* (Welfare Commission). This commission produced a number of reports the total length of which amounted to 2,585 pages. According to Jørn Henrik Petersen the basic perceptions of the challenges and solutions of the welfare state were in the *Velfærdskommissionen* similar to those of the Zeuthen Committee and the *Socialkommissionen* (Petersen, 1995, p. 295). The same questioning and reserved acceptance of the imperatives of the competition state paradigm can also be detected from a later document issued by the Ministry of Labour in 2000 about the effects of the labour market reforms in the 1990s (Ministry of Labour, 2000, p. 21).

As noted above, the composition of the government coalition changed in 2001 and a coalition headed by Conservative Prime Minister Anders Fogh Rasmussen entered office. This regime change appears to have been associated with a slight ideological shift as well – pushing Danish employment policy more towards the ideas of the international competition state paradigm. This shift can be observed in the *Velfærdskommissionen* report published in 2005. The tone of the report, when describing the aims and purposes of employment policy in general and ALMP in particular, is fundamentally different from that of the 1993 *Socialkommissionen*. In the 2005 report activation measures were associated with testing the willingness to work among the unemployed:

> Activation measures also have a significant perspective with regard to testing work availability, but activation in many cases takes place only after a certain period of time, and not as frequently as the face-to-face contact discussions ... Therefore, contact discussions can be regarded as complementing the activation measures by testing the genuine availability of labour among the unemployed. (Velfærdskommissionen, 2005, p. 475)

While the passage above is aimed at justifying regular face-to-face meetings between the unemployed and employment officials, it shows one of the main aims and purposes that the *Velfærdskommissionen* associates with ALMP measures: testing the willingness to work among the unemployed. The same aims and purposes can be detected in the recommendations made in the direction of tougher and more detailed sanctions for non-compliance with employment officials:

> In fact, sanctions should be stricter as a consequence of repeated non-compliance, and a kind of a ticket system could be applied, whereby a certain number of failures to show availability results in reductions in unemployment benefits. These principles are already part of the existing system, but they can be made stricter. (Velfærdskommissionen, 2005, p. 478)

An increased stress on sanctions indicates a stronger adherence to the ideas of the competition state paradigm, according to which 'passive' unemployment benefits create a disincentive to look for work in the open labour market. 'Activation' measures are therefore designed to counteract these disincentives through the testing, monitoring and controlling of the availability of the unemployed. In order for ALMP measures to function effectively in this way, they must be associated with sanctions that quite concretely remove the disincentives to look for work.

The *Velfærdskommissionen* of 2005 also proposed some reforms to the earnings-related unemployment benefit, and these proposals aimed to push Danish employment policy further towards the ideas associated with the international competition state paradigm (Velfærdskommissionen, 2005, p. 490).

According to the *Velfærdskommissionen*, the maximum duration of earnings-related unemployment benefit should be reduced from four to two and a half years. After the shorter maximum period, a new basic compensation would be available for the unemployed (see also Velfærdskommissionen, 2005, p. 511). The basic compensation proposed by the *Velfærdskommissionen* would not depend on the income of other family members, but it would still in practice imply a reduction in the level of unemployment benefit. This proposal was quite clearly in line with the competition state paradigm, as it was thought that by reducing the amount of unemployment benefit incentives to look for work become stronger.

In 2006 a *Welfare Agreement* was established by the government and this agreement was, to some extent, influenced by the proposals of the *Velfærdskommissionen*. For instance, a more intensive period of activation was introduced after two and a half years of unemployment (Kvist and Pedersen, 2007, p. 103). As noted above, the duration of earnings-related unemployment benefit was eventually reduced to two years in 2010, indicating drift towards a more orthodox adaptation of the ideas of the international competition state paradigm.

It is also interesting to look at an article by Hans E. Zeuthen (Zeuthen, 2005) who, as noted already, chaired the committee set to deal with Danish employment policy in the early 1990s. The article, written 13 years after the work of the committee, appeared in a book entitled *13 Reforms of the Danish Welfare State*

(Petersen and Petersen, 2005) and can be described as a pragmatic reflection on the past of, and possible future directions for, Danish employment policy. The article is interesting because in terms of its positioning against the international competition state paradigm it contains the same elements that could be detected more generally in Danish employment policy: acknowledgement of some ideas of the competition state paradigm, doubts about some other ideas, and extension and further development of key ideas associated with the paradigm. Thus, the article manages to summarise much of the Danish political relationship with the international competition state paradigm.

In the article the author connects wage setting, productivity, income differences and 'structural unemployment' largely in accordance with the logic of the international competition state paradigm:

> It is difficult to deny that the level of structural unemployment would most likely be lower if wages to a larger extent, both in the shorter and the longer term, reflected the differences between employees' qualifications and productivity. (Zeuthen, 2005, p. 209)

Likewise, the connection between 'passive' unemployment benefits and 'structural unemployment' is made in line with the international competition state paradigm:

> There is little doubt that lengthy passive maintenance, i.e. payment of daily allowances or cash benefits for a longer period of time, in many cases will increase structural unemployment. (Zeuthen, 2005, p. 206)

However, concerning to the level of unemployment benefit, the article reflects the negotiated adaptation of the competition state paradigm that the Danish employment policy itself represents. Arguments for and against the negative consequences of high replacement rates are acknowledged, but it is not concluded that high replacement rates would without doubt increase 'structural unemployment' (Zeuthen, 2005, pp. 207–8).

The author also extends and develops the ideas associated with the international competition state paradigm in a rather interesting way:

> There is little doubt that there are quite a few employees that, although they would receive initial help, would find it difficult to remain in employment on normal terms and conditions. Demands for efficiency are great and with liberalist eyes one should say that the wages that are paid in the Danish labour market are significantly higher than what these people are worth as workers to the employees. It would be specious to consider more permanent subsidies for these people, but it should not be kept a secret that such arrangements would, from a humane and from other perspectives too, not be without problems.

If those concerned would be old fashioned war invalids with visible impairments, such as missing legs and so on, it would not be difficult to distinguish between those entitled to the subsidy and those not. It is much more difficult to recognise those people who due to more invisible reasons are not fully worth their wage ...

To grant subsidies to people because they are less productive, less, reliable, slower or less intelligent than the "average employee" would without doubt in many cases also imply that these recipients of subsidies would be despised by their colleagues at the workplace. And this would most likely be the case even if the employment policy diagnosis were formulated in the most politically correct language. (Zeuthen, 2005, p. 210)

The underlying assumption behind the reasoning in this excerpt is that a number of people in the labour market are not 'worth what they are paid' in the sense that their productivity is lower in monetary terms than what the employer pays them in wages. This assumption is more or less directly derived from the competition state paradigm, which contains the idea that 'structural features' such as high income taxes, centralised wage negotiations and high 'passive' benefits keep the reservation wage at a high level and prevent employers from paying employees in accordance with their 'productivity'.

Subsidised work is one of the central ALMP measures and this measure is based on the idea that the state subsidises an unemployed person's salary so that the costs of employing the person are reduced. ALMP measures are usually, however, only of a limited duration and the speculation in the article referred to here refers to the possibility of 'adjusting' the labour market permanently in such a way that costs for employers would correspond to the gain they receive from the employees. The labour supply is viewed in a rather instrumental fashion as a group to be shaped and managed in order to meet the needs and demands of the employers and the labour market.

What is also indicative of the relation between the leading political ideas in Danish policy making and the ideas associated with the international competition state paradigm is the way recommendations made by the OECD are formulated in reports dealing specifically with Denmark. As noted in the previous chapters, OECD recommendations operate in the interesting realm of on the one hand trying to promote the ideas associated with the international competition state paradigm, and on the other hand trying to take into account national and local traditions and characteristics – a process in which national officials are often consulted and given the opportunity to discuss ideas promoted by the OECD.

As in the case of Sweden, useful observations can be made based on the OECD Economic Surveys of Denmark (OECD, 2008b; OECD, 2009b) and the OECD Review of Regulatory Reform in Denmark (OECD, 2000). In terms of its general approach to the Danish political system, the OECD expresses its understanding in the following way:

OECD indicators consistently show that Denmark is more comparable to the English-speaking countries than to continental European countries with respect to trade- and competition-friendly regulation in markets for goods and services ... Moreover, market efficiency is supported by a high degree of transparency in business dealings and government affairs ... and, unlike other Nordic countries, Denmark never had large-scale public ownership in the business sector ... Combined with a well-trained labour force, and institutions focused at actively moving benefit recipients into work, Denmark has the right policy settings to allow all parts of society to gain from globalisation ... Thus, the analysis and policy recommendations given in this *Survey* are not about radical changes to deal with deep flaws in the Danish economy, but about building on its existing strengths. With high social ambitions and strong public demands for expansion of publicly funded services, there is little room for complacency. (OECD, 2008b, p. 29)

The OECD also seems to approve, in principle, of the Danish employment policy system – especially an account of the good results that have been seen in the past decades (OECD, 2008b, p. 79). The general approving approach concerning the fundamental aspects of Danish public policy does not imply that the OECD would not be aware of the aspects of Danish policy that are not in accordance with the international competition state paradigm. The organisation has a clear view on the positive aspects of Danish labour market policy:

When the pure flexicurity model with limited employment protection legislation and generous long-lasting unemployment benefits existed in the 1980s, it led to rising unemployment; when the duration and generosity of unemployment benefits was reduced and tougher job-search and activation requirements were introduced in the 1990s, it led to falling unemployment ... (OECD, 2008b, p. 36)

In other words, in accordance with the logic of the competition state paradigm, the OECD associates generous benefits with high unemployment and tough conditionality about benefits with falling unemployment. As noted earlier, Danish unemployment benefits have remained rather generous throughout the process of renegotiating the post-war collectivist social order, and the OECD expressed its concerns about (OECD, 2008b, p. 37).

By steering the discussion into details concerning part-time unemployment, the OECD finds a way to recommend, in accordance with the competition state paradigm, a shorter maximum duration of earnings-related unemployment benefit in Denmark (OECD, 2008b, p. 92). In addition to being mildly critical about the generosity of Danish unemployment benefits, the OECD promotes, in accordance with the logic of the competition state paradigm, a lower tax rate for Denmark (OECD 2008b, p. 38; cf. Kananen, 2012a).

The Danish reports show a similar kind of recognition of local traditions, aims and policies as the OECD reports dealing with Sweden. The main difference is that recommendations in the Danish case are more far-reaching and thoroughgoing than in the Swedish case. Recommendations for Sweden tended to be rather specific and of a nature that was not in stark contradiction with existing Swedish public policy. Recommendations for Denmark appeared more radical although the strengths of existing policies were acknowledged. The OECD approved of policies that pushed the country towards more competition and away from traditional practices involving co-operation and informal correspondence in government.

To the extent that OECD documents can be seen as a proxy for national policy officials' relationship with the international competition state paradigm, the Danish policy recommendations may be interpreted in the following way. Acknowledging Danish local traditions and policies implies that Danish officials have succeeded in communicating these traditions and policies in a convincing nature to OECD officials. At the same time, Danish officials have to some extent acknowledged the goals of the international competition state paradigm, and expressed a degree of approval, which in turn has encouraged the OECD officials to include rather strong policy recommendations in the reports. This interpretation is also in line with the interpretation that Danish policy reforms represent a negotiated adaptation of the international competition state paradigm. Indeed, the communication between local Danish officials and OECD officials can be regarded as part of this negotiation process. In the following chapter we shall see how OECD recommendations for Finland can be compared with the recommendations for the two other countries dealt with so far.

In Sweden there was, as in Denmark, in addition to the perception of a need to renegotiate the post-war collectivist order, a rather strong awareness of the recommendations associated with the competition state paradigm in the early years of the 1990s. Initially, this awareness had in Sweden been strengthened by think tanks affiliated with organised business during the 1980s (Blyth, 2002, pp. 216–19). In the following decade the right-wing government led by Carl Bildt had made an effort to translate this awareness into policy.

What may have been a decisive difference between Denmark and Sweden in the 1990s was that the Swedish right-wing government tried to push its reform agenda closer to the competition state paradigm than the general population was willing to accept. In Denmark the Social Democratic-led government was both able to find a more negotiated adaptation of the paradigm and to maintain continuous electoral support throughout the decade. In Sweden the right-wing government's efforts backfired and power was handed over to the Social Democrats, who pursued a more 'conservative' reform agenda. The competition state paradigm was applied to a lesser extent than what the Conservatives would have most likely done, had they remained in power.

Despite the Danish Social Democratic-led government's ability in the 1990s to find a negotiated adaptation of the competition state paradigm and to maintain electoral support and to communicate its perceptions about the problem of social order, a certain gap between the general population and the political and bureaucratic elite appeared in Denmark, just as it had emerged in Sweden as well.

In 1996 and two years later in 1998 the Danish Social Democratic leaders tried to find support for an agenda of further privatisations of public functions at the party General Assembly. In this the leaders did not, however, succeed. That the party leaders responsible for the government of the nation declared themselves thereafter no longer in need of support from the General Assembly, and pursuing their own reform agenda without support from their own party members (Mathiesen, 2000, p. 7), indicates an ideological gap between the party leaders and their constituency. Another indication of the same phenomenon is the increased role of expert committees, rather than wider consensus-seeking in Danish policy making (Mathiesen, 2000, p. 12).

In Sweden, adapting to the ideas of the competition state paradigm implied abandoning for good the economic policies associated with the classic Rehn–Meidner model, but legislative reform in the area of employment policy was more limited than in Denmark. In Denmark the negotiated adaptation of the ideas of the competition state paradigm led to an original model of employment policy in the 1990s, but in the 2000s the country has drifted towards a stronger adherence of the paradigm.

Finland

Beginning of the Renegotiation Process: The Need for Strong Political Leadership?

In retrospect, it seems quite remarkable how dense the various post-war socio-economic transformation processes have been in Finland – particularly those occurring between the 1960s and 1980s. Creative potentials were liberated fully from the provision of basic needs only in the 1960s and many rapid transformation processes, such as urbanisation, followed from this. The institutions of social policy were still being developed and shaped during the 1980s when a new order began to make its way into Finnish society. The following analysis of the renegotiation of the Finnish collectivist social order will show that behind these rapid socio-economic developments have been both perceptions of problems in the domestic social order and an aspiration towards Western political ideas.

Signs of the beginning of a Finnish renegotiation process regarding the post-war collectivist order can be detected from the 1980s onwards. The transformation process did not originate at the grass roots level of society. On the contrary, most of the aspects of the Finnish renegotiation process followed a top-down logic. The policy elite played a significant role in initiating reform fairly independent from the general public and from any public debate. Restructuring of the public sector[3] and the transformations in the Finnish financial system during the 1980s

---

3   The series of reforms dealing with public sector restructuring were thorough and lengthy and continued throughout the renegotiation process. Here they will be reviewed only

and 1990s – the key elements in the Finnish renegotiation process – followed this logic.

As in Sweden and Denmark, the early stages of the renegotiation process involved public sector restructuring – in the Finnish case particularly decentralisation and commercialisation. In the mid 1980s the government appointed two significant committees – a Committee on Government Decentralisation and another on State Enterprises (Committee on Government Decentralisation, 1986; Committee Report on State Enterprises, 1985). The *State Enterprise Act* was among the first pieces of legislation in the new wave of reform that followed the work of these committees (State Enterprise Act, 627/1987). This act defined the structures of state enterprises, and it represented the first step in the commercialisation of government services. According to the act, state enterprises should have a distinct budget, partial self-funding and they should operate in a competitive market. In the process that followed the act, the fields of transport and telecommunications were commercialised amongst others. In many cases government agencies were first transformed into state enterprises, and later into state-owned companies and finally into privately owned companies. This kind of commercialisation occurred mainly between 1991–1998 (Julkunen, 2001, p. 108).

Decentralisation of government was, in addition to commercialisation another key process in the renegotiation of the collectivist order within the public sector. However, the term decentralisation is slightly misleading in this respect. The reform process, that was initiated by the above-mentioned committee report and government bill, in fact implied a transfer of authority from intermediate levels of government not only to the local but also to the central level as well. The first act in this process came in 1987 (Act on the Government Development Centre, 110/1987) affecting a small part of government. More thorough reforms across all government sectors were carried out in the 1990s, and former central government agencies were transformed into development centres (*kehittämiskeskus*) and their former authority was divided between local municipalities and central government. In the previous system, a great deal of bureaucratic exchange was required between the municipalities and the central government agencies, which in turn were accountable to the ministries. This exchange was perceived as cumbersome and unnecessary and the need for reform is clearly reflected in the committee report of 1986. A practical consequence of this restructuring was that the size of government shrank (Alasuutari, 2004, p. 14).

Finnish public sector reforms, and in particular the commercialisation of public services, were in many cases consistent with the international ideas of liberalisation and market orientation, but virtually no political discussion was carried out at the national level about how these international ideas should be applied in the Finnish context (Alasuutari, 2004, pp. 11–14).

---

to the extent which is necessary in order to establish when and under what circumstances the Finnish renegotiation was initiated.

Decentralisation (and restructuring) of government increased, mainly in the early years of the 1990s, the room for manoeuvre in municipal administration. In 1993 the funding patterns of municipalities were reformed and Sweden followed suit two years later (Kröger, 1997, pp. 144–67; Helin and Oulasvirta, 2000, pp. 108–26; Julkunen, 2001, pp. 115–23). Earmarked funding was transformed into block grants, which increased the managerial and financial responsibilities at the local level.

However, after the reform of the municipal funding structure, the central government dramatically reduced the share of its financial aid to municipalities and the increased room for manoeuvre was practically translated into a freedom to choose what services to cut. Between the years 1994–1998 the share of state funding of the total expenses in municipalities dropped from 40 to 25 per cent (Julkunen, 2001, p. 119). Although a direct comparison cannot be made, it is useful to note that in Denmark health care expenditure rose in the beginning of the 1990s (Pallesen and Pedersen, 2008, p. 245). As distinct from Denmark, Finland in the early 1990s was hit by an economic depression possibly of an even larger scale than in Sweden. In addition to being a time of serious economic downturn, the early 1990s also represents, firstly, a shift to a post-expansionary phase of welfare state development (Kröger, 1997, pp. 144–59; Helin and Oulasvirta, 2000, pp. 108–21), and secondly, an important time period in the renegotiating of the post-war collectivist order.

The transition to the post-expansionary phase of welfare state development occurred within the context of strong popular support for the maintenance of public welfare services (Blomberg and Kroll, 1999ab; Ervasti, 2001, p. 18; Kantola, 2002, p. 314). Cuts in the financing of welfare services were usually legitimised with arguments regarding the state of the public budget. Yet, these fundamental political manoeuvres were never quite subject to ideological or moral consideration.

As in Denmark, reforms of Finnish local government in the early 1990s were also associated with an increase in the relative influence of the Ministry of Finance in central government. It was mainly the Ministry of Finance that took the responsibility for tough financial decisions whereby the share of public spending was cut. This suited the political parties as they could avoid any blame that tough decisions might incur (Kantola and Kananen, 2013). Through reform of local government, the tough political decisions about cutting services had to be made at the local level, which also made it easier for the Ministry of Finance to cut the state funding of municipalities (Lehto, 2006, p. 20). At the same time, reforms in state budgetary policies were carried out as well. With the introduction of the new framework budget mechanism, a major proportion of government spending was decided at the beginning of the four-year tenure of each government. These budgetary frames were determined by the Ministry of Finance, who had to approve the total four-year expenses of each government department at the beginning of the election period. As a result of the introduction of this steering mechanism, expansionary reforms were thus unlikely to succeed unless specified in the framework budget (Harrinvirta and Puoskari, 2001).

In addition to reforms in public administration, the beginnings of the renegotiation of the collectivist order may also be recognised when looking at developments in the financial markets in Finland. Collectivist models of banking and financing had been an integral feature of the Finnish economy during the post-war period. Interest rates and terms and conditions of financing were subject to central government planning and the market mechanism played only a marginal role in the economy (Kantola, 2002, p. 103; Alasuutari, 2004, p. 5). During the 1980s the economy began to change. Much of the evidence available points towards the conclusion that Finnish economic policy makers were aspiring towards the West (Kantola, 2002, pp. 110; 116, 138), where the new economic order of free capital mobility combined with supply-side economic policies had already developed for some time. The question how this new economic order should be applied in Finland, or in what ways Finland should participate in the emerging new international economic order, received little attention. Instead, during the 1980s credit market regulations were simply gradually abolished as a technical procedure without the majority of the general public being aware of what was going on (Kantola, 2002, p. 93).

The liberalisation of credit markets began by allowing first a limited group of lenders to take loans tied to foreign currencies. Once the gates were opened, there was little policy makers could do to prevent the inflow of capital. Thus, the amount of money in the economy began to increase. At this stage, due to the lack of a systematic plan, policy makers did nothing to counterbalance the inflow of capital. Private consumption increased rapidly and savings rates decreased. Banks began to compete for customers by increasing risk taking to unrealistic levels with the consequence that the economy began to overheat (Honkapohja and Koskela, 1999, p. 407; see also Honkapohja et al., 2009).

From the early 1990s onwards, Finland experienced a severe economic depression. The collapse of the Soviet Union coincided with the burst of the economic bubble and trade with the east significantly slowed down. At the time of the crisis, economic policy makers were faced with only bad options. The government first tried to maintain a stable exchange rate but was forced to devalue the currency in 1991 by 12 per cent, and in 1992 the currency was floated. This was obviously disastrous for those with loans tied to foreign currencies and the situation resulted in numerous personal bankruptcies. As Honkapohja and Koskela note, the international economic upswing during the 1980s had further contributed to the economic boom caused by increased credit availability. Very few, if any, counterbalancing policy measures were carried out during economic boom, and it appears that policy makers did not at the time perceive the development as unhealthy in any way.

Perceptions only began to change once the bubble had burst, unemployment rates skyrocketed, the banking sector collapsed and when the public and private financing catastrophe was evident. The Finnish economy shrank in size during the few years of depression and the government had to introduce a series of austerity measures to maintain the stability of the national economy. When the crisis was most severe, the country was close to applying for a loan from the International Monetary Fund. Most importantly, however, policy makers began to rethink the social and economic order – remarkably only *after* individualistic modes of financing had been introduced as a technical measure during the 1980s (Kantola, 2002, p. 139).

Faced with the realities of the new international economic order, policy makers were forced to adjust their beliefs after the economic crisis of the early 1990s. As the renegotiation of the post-war collectivist order had proceeded further in the rest of the Western world following the lines of the new competition state paradigm, Finnish policy makers became increasingly sensitive to new perceptions regarding the relationship between the state and markets (Kantola, 2002, pp. 111–13; 138). In 1995 Finland was accepted as a member of the European Union, and old economic policies were abandoned for good after 1996 when Finland joined the European Exchange Rate Mechanism (ERM).

The renegotiation of the post-war collectivist order began roughly during the same period of time in Denmark, Sweden and Finland. In all three countries concerns about public sector efficiency emerged in the 1980s – in Denmark after an experience of being 'on the brink of the abyss' and in Sweden and Finland just before a similar experience. Judging from the contextual elements reviewed above, the politicisation of the renegotiation process was similar in Sweden and Denmark in the sense that government coalitions openly discussed the ideological aims of their policies. The Danish Conservative government actively pushed for a 'modernisation' of the public sector in a manner that met forceful resistance, but eventually opened up opportunities for the Social Democratic government to utilise in the 1990s. In Sweden the 1980s was characterised by efforts to find a 'Third Road' between Keynesianism and Thatcherism, but there was also simultaneous increase in the influence of competition state ideas promoted by business think tanks.

In Finland the key processes of corporatisation, commercialisation, privatisation, local government restructuring and EU/EMU membership were largely dealt with without public discussion. An understanding of a new social order emerged only at the top level of political decision making. Neither were the changes in policy makers' perceptions about the relationship between state and market accompanied by a political regime change. Throughout the crucial years of the 1980s and 1990s the coalition government included two of the three major political parties – the Centre Party (former Agrarian Union), the Social Democratic Party, and the conservative National Coalition Party – but the changes in the compositions of government were not associated with changes in the main political ideas. Perhaps the most crucial political reforms regarding the renegotiation of the post-war collectivist order were carried out under the rule of the so-called 'rainbow government' between 1995–2003, headed by a Social Democratic Prime Minister (Paavo Lipponen) and including parties representing the entire political spectrum (for a summary of the aims of social policy during this period, see Saari, 2006).

Thorough Income Support and Unemployment Insurance Reforms

During the post-war period, the prevailing idea had been that means-tested income support would only play a minimal role in the inclusive and collectivist system of Nordic social insurance. Although a latecomer in political and legislative reforms, Finland shared this aspiration with the other Nordic countries. The numerous social security benefits were thought to prevent anyone from having to rely on means-tested income support, which was supposed to be the last resort benefit preventing people from falling into absolute poverty. In the Social Services Act of 1984 (1982) the right to income support was established in the following manner:

> A person has the right to receive *income support*, if she/he is in need of support and cannot get this support by means of employment or entrepreneurship, or from other income or means, or from a person who is responsible for her/his maintenance, or in any other way. (Social Services Act, 710/1982, 30§)
>
> When deciding upon granting social assistance, the Social Services Board (*sosiaalilautakunta*) may at the same time order that the income support, or part of it, shall be claimed back:
> ...
> 2) from the income support recipient, if she/he has on purpose disregarded her/his duty to support her/himself. (Social Services Act, 710/1982, 34§)

Establishing the right to income support in this manner left room for some interpretation – for instance concerning when exactly a person cannot gain their necessary maintenance from employment – or in what cases a person has disregarded her/his duty to support her/himself. In other words, the legislation only provided the broad principles under which income support was to be implemented. The act did not, for instance, specify explicitly whether denying a work offer made by the employment services was compatible with the right to claim income support. These aspects are important to note from the point of view of the changes that were to be carried out during the latter part of the 1990s.

Along with the economic recession a new political situation emerged in Finland in the 1990s. Previously, long-term reliance on income support had been rare (cf. Kananen, 1985). In the early years of the 1990s this began to change, and in 1995, according to figures reported by the government, 12 per cent of all households received income support (Government, Finland, 1997, p. 9). In absolute figures this is in excess of 300,000 households. What made the situation specifically intriguing was that, after the depression had ended and the economy started to grow again, unemployment remained stubbornly high at levels well above 10 per cent of the labour force. The government was in a situation where high unemployment rates could not be sustained, either from an economic or a social point of view. Prolonged unemployment was often associated with personal tragedies, and from a financial point of view the unemployed also represented a double cost in the form of benefit expenditure and lost tax revenue. In 1996 54 per cent of households receiving income support also received unemployment benefit. In 1990, the corresponding figure had been 17. Thus, during the 1990s, income support became a benefit that also concerned those who in principle were available for the labour market (Julkunen, 2001, p. 185).

This was the context when the Finnish Social Democratic-led 'rainbow government' began to reform the income support and unemployment insurance systems in 1995 when it entered office. For the first time since the beginning of the renegotiation of the Finnish collectivist order, the connection between income support and the take up of work was reinforced through a negative incentive (a sanction) in 1995, when it was stated in the law that if an income support recipient refuses a job offer or refuses to participate in active labour market policies, the level of income support may be decreased by up to 20 per cent. In the legal paragraph in question, the phrase 'unless the reduction can be considered unfair' was added after stating the possibility of sanctioning the income support recipient (Government Decree, 1995).

What is important is that in the decree issued in 1995 the relationship between the rights and the obligations, as stated in the 1982 Act, was not altered or revised in any way. Instead, the 1995 decree stated the following when regulating the *amount* of income support:

> If a person's need for income support arises from her/his refusal without a valid reason to accept an individually made job offer or an offer to participate in ALMP measures, the basic part of income support may be reduced in her/his case by up to 20 per cent, if the reduction cannot be considered unfair. (Government Decree, 1676/1995, 3§)

It is not possible in a straightforward manner to assess whether the sanction quoted above should primarily be understood as an *obligation* to participate in ALMP measures. In principle, when it comes to social legislation, an obligation should be accompanied by a corresponding right; in the case of income support it would be expected that the obligation to participate in activation measures would be balanced by the right to receive income support and vice versa. When income support legislation was reformed in Sweden and Denmark, the reforms affected in particular the realm of rights and obligations. In the Finnish case, sanctions do not appear to be formulated in order to enforce an obligation. In 1995 when the above decree came into force, existing legislation had already specified the rights and obligations of income support recipients. Each person had an obligation (and indeed a right, as specified in the constitution, Kettunen, 2008, p. 156) to support her/himself through work, and if this was not possible, and if there were no other sources of income available, a person was entitled to income support. Therefore, in order to understand the underlying motivations, the reforms following this decree must be analysed.

In 1997 a new Income Support Act was drafted by the government. In this new act the right to income support remained unaltered compared to the 1982 Act, but the opening paragraph of the new act was, nonetheless, quite revealing regarding the direction towards which the income support system was intended to develop. The previous opening paragraph was transformed into the second paragraph. The new opening paragraph was formulated in the following way:

> Income support is, being part of social services, the economic benefit of last
> resort intended to secure the income of the person or the family in question, and
> to promote their independent survival. Through income support the necessary
> economic support is provided for a person or a family in order to lead a dignified
> human life ... (Income Support Act, 1412/1997, 1§)

The key words to understand the legislative reform that was enforced in March 1998 are the words '*and promote their independent survival*' in the first sentence. It seems clear that the way in which the Act is intended to promote individual survival is through the sanctions that are established in later sections of the Act.

In the decree of 1995 the unwanted behaviour it intended to sanction through a reduction in the level of income support still remained fairly unspecified – and neither did the decree give any clues as to why this kind of behaviour would be unwanted. Both of these aspects were elaborated in the 1997 Act, which stated the following:

> If a person's need of income support arises from her/his refusal without a valid
> reason to accept an individually made job offer or an offer to participate in ALMP
> measures that for a reasonable period of time would secure her/his income, or
> if she/he through neglect has caused a situation where work or participation in
> ALMP measures cannot be offered, the basic part of income support may be
> reduced by up to 20 per cent.
> In connection with reducing the basic part, a plan for action promoting the
> independent functioning of the client must always, if possible, be produced in
> association with the income support claimant and if necessary in cooperation
> with employment services or other officials.
> If a person has repeatedly refused without a valid reason to accept a job offer
> as specified in the 1st paragraph, or through continuous neglect has caused
> a situation where such a job cannot be offered, the basic component of this
> person's income support may be reduced by a greater amount than stated in
> the 1st paragraph, and in total by up to 40 per cent. A similar reduction may
> be carried out if a person has been subject to the reductions specified by the
> 1st paragraph but has repeatedly refused without a valid reason to participate
> in an offered ALMP measure, or if she/he has through her/his actions caused a

situation in which such an offer cannot be made, and if she/he in addition refuses without a valid reason to participate in actions promoting her/his functioning capacity in the manner specified in the 2nd paragraph.

The reductions specified in paragraphs 1 and 3 may only be carried out if the reductions do not endanger the income that is needed for the security that a dignified human life presupposes, and if the reductions may not in any other way be considered unfair. The reductions may last for up to two months from the time of the refusal or neglect. (Income Support Act, 1412/1997, 10§)

As in Denmark, the reform of income support legislation resulted in parliamentary debates regarding the compatibility of the reform proposal with the Constitution. The Constitutional Committee of the Finnish Parliament gave a statement about the compatibility of the new Income Support Act in comparison with the Constitution, in which the right to income support was also specified in cases where a person was unable to support her/himself. While stating that the new act was not in contradiction with the Constitution, the Committee also gave an interpretation indicating that the obligation to participate in ALMP measures had, in fact, been part of the legislation before the new act. The Committee stated that 'if a person has been offered a possibility to attain her/his livelihood through work or through participating in ALMP measures, it can be said that she/he would have been able to attain the livelihood referred to in the Constitution' (PeVL, 1997, p. 4). In other words, the Constitutional Committee seems to interpret that an offer of work or participation in ALMP measures implies the *possibility* of supporting oneself, and if this possibility exists, the person is not necessarily entitled to income support. What the new legislation then creates is a new sanctioning mechanism for non-compliance if a person refuses to participate in an offered ALMP measure.

The 10th paragraph of the Finnish 1997 Income Support Act almost depicts a heated battle between the income support claimant and social services. First, the Act enables social services to sanction an income support claimant by reducing the amount of income support by up to 20 per cent if the claimant has refused a job offer or an offer to participate in ALMP measures. Then, when such a sanctioning has been carried out, the Act requires that the sanctioned individual together with social services produces a plan that is supposed to promote the income support claimant's functioning capacity.[4] The act then goes on to elaborate what further action must be carried out if the sanctioned person continues to act in a way that shows non-compliance towards social services. It states that if the sanctioned person still continues to refuse job offers or offers to participate in ALMP measures, or indeed if the person refuses to cooperate when producing

---

4   The term 'functioning capacity' has here been translated from the Finnish terms *toimintakyky* and *itsenäinen suoriutuminen*. The latter term, which is used in the 2nd paragraph of the 10 § of the *Income Support Act* also contains the meanings of (individual/ independent) survival and performance. The opening paragraph of the Act uses the term *selviytyminen*, which also contains the meanings of both survival and performance.

the individual survival plan, the amount of income support may be reduced by up to 40 per cent. Thus, what the act vividly pictures is an income support recipient who behaves in a way that does not comply with the procedures designated to the social services. This kind of behaviour is specified as strongly unwanted in the Act, and a range of measures is constructed by which such behaviour should be combated.

Whereas the Swedish and the Danish reforms of income support legislation in the 1990s clearly contained a definition of the rights and obligations of income support recipients, it is unclear whether the new sanctions for non-compliance in the Finnish legislation are meant to enforce an obligation. If this were the case, it remains extremely unclear in the legislation what this obligation could be, and indeed how it differs from obligations in the previous legislation.

Although this difference may seem merely technical (after all, one might claim that the end result is the same in all cases – active job seeking on the part of income support claimants is desired), when followed up it reveals a fundamental difference in the perception of the causes of claiming income support, leading to fundamentally different attitudes towards income support recipients. The attitude embedded in the Swedish legislation contains aspects of compassion and understanding towards the situation of income support recipients, whereas the Finnish legislation primarily views benefit recipients as potential abusers of the system.

When preparing the new *Income Support Act*, the government expressed a concern that if income support is continuously claimed despite refusal of work offers and reductions in the level of benefit, the purpose of income support as a last resort only is dimmed (Government, Finland, 1997, p. 21).

In the Government Bill, where detailed arguments for the proposed Income Support Act are provided, it seems as if there is an awareness of cases where benefit recipients have continued to receive income support in spite of having been subject to the sanctions made possible in the previous reform in 1995. As noted, these sanctions included the reduction of income support by up to 20 per cent if the recipient does not accept a work offer or if they do not cooperate with administrators. As a solution to such cases, where it is likely that the benefit recipient experiences serious hardship, the government proposed that the level of income support could be further reduced by up to 40 per cent. The aim was thus to further strengthen the negative incentives to take up work and to prevent reliance on income support.

In the same section the relationship between the individual claiming income support and society are further specified. The first part of the quotation below refers to a case where the benefit claimant has refused to cooperate with administrators and has been subject to the sanctions specified earlier:

> When a person behaves in the way described in the paragraph, it may generally
> be assumed that she/he earns her/his immediate support in other ways. In such

cases it cannot be sustained that society provides an income in several different ways. (Government, Finland, 1997)

In the Government Bill it is interpreted that claiming income support and meeting the eligibility criteria is not always evidence of the actual need for the benefit. It suggests that in spite of the formally specified criteria and the income test that is involved there, the benefit administrator should have the opportunity to subjectively assess whether the benefit claimant actually needs the benefit. Clearly, avoiding long-term dependence on income support is the formal aim here, but the only reason that is recognised for prolonged benefit dependency in the case of the document here seems to be the failure of the claimant to support her/himself. In such a case, the proposed solution is to reduce the level of income support by up to 40 per cent on the grounds that prolonged benefit dependency distorts the status of the benefit as a last resort. Thus, instead of a serious concern for the economy and employment, the quotation reveals a rather cynical attitude towards income support claimants.

The paragraph of the Income Support Act stating these sanctions concludes with the following remark, which is similar to what was added in the 1995 law:

> The reductions stated in the first and third sectors of this paragraph may only be carried out if they do not jeopardise the immediate support required for leading a dignified human life, and if they cannot be considered unfair in any other way. The reduction of the level of benefit may last for up to two months from the of the refusal. (Income Support Act, 1412/1997, 10§)

Still, in practice, it is entirely up to the social worker in question to decide what may be considered fair or dignified. The reduction in the level of support that is considered to provide the absolute minimum standard of living morally acceptable in a welfare state is never in the immediate interest of the income support claimant but can only be regarded as a sanction, the aim of which is to impose a certain kind of behaviour on the claimant. Thus, whereas the Swedish and Danish reforms could be seen as widening the realm of obligations associated with claiming income support, the Finnish reforms can, as a contrast, be seen as aiming to control a certain kind of unwanted behaviour – that is in the legislation defined as, for example, non-compliance with requirements placed by the benefit administrators.

In 1994 the Finnish unemployment benefit system was reformed so that the new system was based on three tiers (Julkunen, 2001, pp. 174–84; Timonen, 2003, p. 92). The first tier consisted of an earnings-related unemployment benefit, which was payable for a maximum of 500 days to unemployed job seekers with a work history of 6 months or more who were members of an unemployment insurance fund. The second tier ('basic unemployment compensation', *peruspäiväraha*) was for unemployed persons who did not qualify for earnings-related compensation, for instance persons who wished to enter the labour market but had no work history. In the 1994 reform the eligibility criteria of basic unemployment compensation were tightened, so that a work history of 6 months was required in order to qualify for the benefit, and its maximum duration was limited to 500 days. In addition, a third tier was created – 'labour market support' – which was intended for those who did not qualify for either one of the two other tiers. The level of this benefit was similar to that of basic unemployment compensation, but it was made a means-tested benefit.

In 1997 the eligibility criteria of the first two tiers were further tightened. Previously, participating in active labour market policy measures that typically lasted for 6 months could renew eligibility. After the 1997 reform eligibility criteria were tightened so that a work history of 10 months was required in order to renew eligibility (Virjo et al., 2006, p. 25). This reform contributed to the weakening of the insurance principle of Finnish unemployment insurance as it enforced the two-year maximum duration of earnings-related unemployment benefit. As a consequence, an increasing number of unemployed people became dependent on means-tested benefits. At the turn of the millennium the share of the unemployed receiving earnings-related benefit in Finland was well below 50 per cent and this remained more or less stable during the first decade of the new millennium (TEM, 2008, p. 187).

Thus, simultaneously with weakening unemployment insurance, the Finnish government toughened income support legislation. This strategy was quite different compared to the strategies of the Danish and Swedish governments during the 1990s, as reviewed in the previous chapters. In Sweden, due to system maintenance, the insurance principle of unemployment insurance actually strengthened during the 1990s. As it was possible to renew eligibility for earnings-related unemployment insurance by participating in ALMP measures, the share of unemployed people receiving the earnings-related benefit actually increased in Sweden during the 1990s. In Denmark, the maximum duration of earnings-related unemployment benefit was kept comparatively long during times of high unemployment, and was reduced close to the maximum duration in Finland only when unemployment was on the decrease. Considering the aims of Danish and Swedish policy during the 1990s (as described in the previous chapters), the actions of the governments in these countries appears to have counteracted the emergence of insider/outsider divisions in the labour market. As an increasing share of people became dependent on means-tested benefits in Finland, the actions of the Finnish government appear, by contrast, to have contributed to strengthening these insider/outsider divisions.

It has sometimes been suggested that during the 1990s the Finnish unemployment insurance system retained a wider coverage compared to the Swedish system (Kautto, 2000, p. 101). The rationale behind this reasoning is that all unemployed people in Finland remained protected by at least some kind of unemployment benefit system, no matter whether they were eligible for the first tier or not, whereas in Sweden around a fifth of all unemployed remained uninsured. It is indeed the case that the third tier of the Finnish unemployment benefit system shortly after its establishment became the main pillar of the

Finnish unemployment insurance system, and soon afterwards it covered in fact more unemployed people than any other of the pillars of the system. But from a comparative point of view, the Finnish labour market support is primarily comparable with the Swedish (and Finnish) income support with its corresponding means tests and levels of compensation. Thus, the more correct interpretation of a comparison between the two unemployment insurance systems is that in Finland a great deal of the insurance principle was abandoned as a consequence of the 1994 and 1997 reforms, whereas in Sweden, the insurance element was maintained in spite of high unemployment and slow economic recovery during the mid 1990s.

According to the governments' own figures in Finland 290,000 households received income support during 1999 and about a third of them were long-term recipients (Government, Finland, 184/2000, p. 13). In the following year, the government responded to this situation by proposing a new law on rehabilitative work (Government, Finland, 2000). The aim of the new legislation on rehabilitative work was, among other things, to unify the activation measures for both labour market support recipients and income support recipients. According to the new law, all income support claimants would be required to register at an employment office. As a consequence, they would also be subject to the job seekers' activation measures. The same sanctions for non-compliance would remain. If an income support claimant refused to register at an employment office, their income support could be reduced by up to 40 per cent.

In addition, a new type of activation measure was introduced in the law on rehabilitative work. If a person claiming income support or labour market support for a considerable period of time failed to find employment, they would be subject to rehabilitative work organised by the municipality for participants under the age of 25 (Act on Rehabilitative Work, 189/2001). Non-compliance could result in up to a 40 per cent reduction in the level of income support.[5]

The aim to improve a person's 'functioning capacity', which is part of the legislation (Act on Revising the Act on Income Support, 191/2001, 10§) seems to imply subtle control. The usage of the term reveals that people are not quite treated as individual persons but as objects whose 'functioning capacity' should be improved. Increasing the influence of the social worker over the income support recipient might not be problematic regarding the individual sovereignty of the benefit seeker if an empathetic relationship between the two is encouraged. In such case, the social worker would sincerely assess what is in the best interests of the support seeker and recommend action accordingly. An empathetic approach is not, however, apparent in an interpretative reading of income support legislation in the reforms under review here. Instead, benefit claimants are regarded as potential fraudsters and exploiters of public resources, and one of the prevailing attitudes in

---

5   In October 2009 the Finnish government proposed, presumably as a reaction to the global financial crisis, to widen the sanctions to concern also potential participants above the age of 25 (Government, Finland, 2009). In 2011 the sanctions in the *Income Support Act* were widened to cover those under the age of 25 (Palola et al., 2012).

legislative reforms seems to have been a cynical attitude towards those who do not appear to conform to the mainstream of society.

The analysis above raises the question whether the reforms in income support and unemployment insurance could not be interpreted in a more positive way – for instance as reactions to the serious unemployment situation and efforts to increase the employment rate. It could also be interpreted that providing a range of activities for job seekers and income support recipients actually increases the rights of these groups, assuming that these activities are meaningful and that they actually improve the situations of those concerned.

It must be emphasised that the above analysis has only dealt with the level of intentions and ideas that have motivated legislators to carry out the reforms in question. It would be a matter of further empirical research to establish the effects that the legislation dealt with above has on the 'ground level'. Keskitalo (2008) has carried out such research on the Act on Rehabilitative Work Action by analysing interviews with staff and clients of the social services. She found that the legislative reform had a strong impact on the way staff dealt with their clients, and on the basis of the interviews analysed in her study it appeared that the social services staff followed the directions specified in the legislation (Keskitalo, 2008, p. 134). Keskitalo also found that participants in measures of rehabilitative work action appeared rather obedient and fairly uncritical towards the requirements placed upon them. As the researcher acknowledges herself, this result may have been a consequence of a bias in the selection of interviews, as social workers may have had an interest in selecting only 'successful' cases for interviews. It is, however, also possible to interpret these results as reflecting obedience rather than satisfaction, as the interviewees may be in a position in which it is extremely difficult and even hazardous to express a critical position towards the regulations they are subject to. Thus, silent obedience may be a survival strategy rather than an indication of satisfaction with regard to the legislative framework.

The reforms carried out between 1995–2001 were primarily not about increasing the employment level. Firstly, what was common to all of these reforms was that they sought to specify, elaborate and deal with a particular kind of unwanted behaviour – not wanting to work in cases where this would have been possible. Ultimately the aim of the measures was, perhaps, to increase employment rates but the methods whereby this was to be reached consisted of imposing ever more rigorous control mechanisms on job seekers and making benefit schemes so unattractive that the threshold of seeking whatever job in the open labour market became ever lower.

Thus, the Finnish reforms of 1995–2001 are best interpreted as being the political and bureaucratic elite's solution to a perceived problem of order that was thought to emerge along with mass unemployment. The source of the new order was to be a strong central administration that was modified in order to create and maintain an insider/outsider division within the labour market. Insiders consisted of those with a secure position in the labour market – including entitlement to earnings-related unemployment benefit. Outsiders, on the other hand, consisted of those at the margins of the labour market having to rely on insecure employment contracts and means-tested benefits in the case of unemployment (Timonen, 2003, p. 106). The rigorous control mechanisms were established so that neither group would have any exit options through the social security system. In such a way it was thought that the labour market insiders contributed to economic growth while the establishment of a group of outsiders supported the institution of wage work. At the same time, the threat of becoming an outsider has allowed the introduction of further control mechanisms for labour market insiders working either in the public or the private sector.[6]

When comparing Finland (and Denmark) with Sweden, Hvinden and Johansson (2007) have found that the right to 'activation' is more strongly articulated in Finland than in Sweden, where activation remains a measure to be carried out at the front line service's discretion. Expressing the difference between Finland and Sweden in this way suggests that it is perceived that the realm of rights is wider in Finland than in Sweden. It has also been suggested that the articulated right to activation is associated with autonomy (Keskitalo, 2007). This exemplifies the challenges associated with interpreting the legislation in the three countries. If the logic embedded in government rhetoric is followed, the legislative reforms appear to enhance incentives and opportunities to develop individual capacities. However, as indicated above, an interpretative reading of the legislation and associated government proposals shows that the main concern behind the Finnish legislative reforms has not been to alter the balance between rights and obligations in the field of income support. Instead, the main concern has been to sanction unwanted behaviour among income support claimants, specified in the legislation as non-compliance with requirements placed by benefit administrators.

Several observations of differences between Finnish, Swedish and Danish legislative reforms support this interpretation. Firstly, the Finnish reforms between 1995–2001 have one by one added to the range of detailed specifications regarding the relationship between income support recipients and benefit administrators. As Danish and Swedish legislation only provided a framework for this relationship, it seems likely that in the Finnish case legislators did not wish to leave the outcome open for different interpretations at the local level. Thus, sanctions play a much greater role in Finland than in Sweden or in Denmark. Secondly, as a result of the reforms, the Danish and the Swedish legislation still recognised a number of different causes behind claiming income support – causes other than unemployment (for instance, physical or mental illness, substance abuse, etc.). The Finnish reforms of income support legislation seemed, according to the review of government proposals, to be concerned merely with benefit abuse. Thus, the Finnish legislation as a consequence of the reforms became associated

---

6   Timonen (2003) has offered an explanation of the emergence of a new tier in the unemployment benefit system and the subsequent insider/outsider distinctions. She argues that the trade unions played a key role in defending what they perceived were their core constituencies (see also Rueda, 2007).

with a more cynical view of the individual income support recipient. Thirdly, the Finnish revised legal paragraphs talk about action that is intended to maintain the 'functioning capacity' of the individual income support claimant, and again, participating in this kind of action is encouraged by sanctioning non-compliance in the form of reduced income support. As a contrast, the Swedish paragraphs talk about 'competence enhancing' activities and aim to offer similar services to both insured and uninsured unemployed persons.

The Finnish legislation is not so much concerned with rights and obligations – after all, this relationship has remained unchanged since the 1980s in Finland. In comparison with Denmark and Sweden, however, the Finnish legislation appears to impose stricter control mechanisms in order to prevent unwanted behaviour among marginalised citizens.

Ideological Shifts: Towards a Finnish Low-Paid Service Sector?

Reforms in the eligibility criteria of unemployment compensation did provoke many discontented voices. And yet in the mid 1990s it was not entirely clear whether this creation of insiders and outsiders within the labour market was to become the final solution to the perceived threat of the problem of order. During the presidency of Martti Ahtisaari (Finnish Social Democratic Party), a fairly lively debate on the possible role of the 'third sector' emerged (Haatanen, 2000; Rahkonen, 2000). Although the precise meaning of the concept of the third sector was never systematically articulated – for instance in the form of a programme how it should be applied in the Finnish context – there seemed to have been a vague ideological feeling that the third sector might provide an alternative path for future socio-economic development. This sensation was probably based on a notion that the outsiders of the labour market and others outside the labour market could perhaps be able to find meaningful prospects within local civil society, outside the formal economy, if enough ideological and public support were created around the emerging idea. It appears that for a few years there was an ideological momentum to create alternative solutions to the perceived problem of order other than the emerging solution to create insider and outsider groups within the labour market. But no concrete plans were made how to deliver the promises of the 'third sector' and soon the ideological momentum faded away.

In Sweden Zetterberg's *Human Dignity* project and LO's *Social Justice* committee represented alternatives to the international competition state paradigm. In Denmark, there appeared to be more efforts to find local adaptations to the imperatives of the international competition state paradigm. In Finland, the brief momentum associated with the debate on the 'Third Sector' could have produced an alternative to the dominant paradigm. However, instead of developing discussions around the idea of the third sector, the competition state paradigm gained a dominant position in Finland during the early years of the twenty-first century. This paradigm, strongly favoured by organised business further contributed to consolidating the political strategy to impose control on vulnerable job seekers. But the paradigm of competitiveness was not only confined to the realm of organised business. Soon the rationale behind the ideology was spread within the government as well (Kantola and Kananen, 2013). It was perceived that as economic globalisation and post-industrialisation posed great challenges to society and the economy, an increase in national competitiveness by all possible means, and greater productivity of work and capital both in the private and public sectors were the best remedies against falling behind in international economic competition. As it was formulated in a prominent policy document produced by the government in 2004:

> In a global economy the most important, and the ultimate decisive factor from the point of view of competitiveness and standard of living – is productivity. It decides what kind of standard of living a country can achieve and what kind of welfare system it can maintain ... The key issue is to what extent underutilised labour resources can be made productive also within the labour-intensive fields with low productivity, while simultaneously maintaining the competitiveness of high skills and high productivity. (VNK, 2004, pp. 83–4)

The quoted passage is originally from a document produced by a government working group on 'globalisation', whose task was to recognise the key challenges to the Finnish economy and society, as well as to formulate general directions about how to tackle these challenges at the political level. What is important in this respect is the connection made between competitiveness, productivity, welfare and standard of living. It is thought that competitiveness and productivity determine welfare and standards of living, and that they should therefore receive a dominant position as policy goals. A similar kind of connection between competitiveness, productivity and welfare has also been made in documents and reports commissioned by the Ministry of Finance and the Ministry of Social Affairs and Health (Kuusela, 2007; Pohjola, 2007). The logic is also similar to that found in the article by Hans E. Zeuthen in Denmark stating that not all people are 'worth what they are paid' (Zeuthen, 2005).

In the competition state paradigm, it is also assumed that the evolution of the private service sector is of key importance when further economic and employment growth is concerned. This assumption is based on a notion that in a post-industrial economic order heavy industries do not provide a reliable source of further economic growth, and therefore attention has to be focused on the private service sector instead – and particularly to the end of the service sector where productivity is low. A style of reasoning of this kind encounters, however, the structures of the Finnish labour market that developed during the post-war period. Compared to many Anglo-Saxon countries, the Nordic labour markets did not, during this period, contain a low wage private service sector. This was due to solidaristic wage policies, systems of collective bargaining and wage setting, and high wage thresholds maintained by the tax-benefit system. It was possible to maintain and finance relatively generous social security benefits because the lowest wages were higher than the highest benefits – and the highest benefits still allowed for a decent standard of living in comparative terms. From the point of view of the competition state paradigm, a solidaristic wage policy and the entire structure of the post-war system are seen as a problem for employment growth. This is clearly expressed in an influential policy document produced by the Prime Minister's Office in 2005:

> Looking at the special characteristics of the service sector, and on the other hand looking at the structures typical of the Finnish labour market, attention is focused on a few potential problem areas. Firstly, the income distribution in Finland is in European terms narrow both with regard to gross and net wages ... Low productivity work tends to become too expensive in this situation with respect to productivity and the price that is paid on the market for these services. The problem is primarily that the lowest wages are too high in relation to average wages. (Sinko and Vihriälä, 2005, p. 16)

As discussed previously, the Finnish post-war system was based on many redistributory mechanisms that required progressive taxation and a certain kind of social security system that was at the same time collectivist and inclusive. This ensured that nearly all citizens faced more or less similar economic and social opportunities. One of the pillars of this system was the solidaristic wage policy that ensured comparatively high minimum wages across sectors. This is the system that is primarily attacked in the above quotation representing the Finnish adaptation of the competition state paradigm – particularly regarding the development of the service sector. Concrete proposals on how to reform wage setting follow from adapting the competition state paradigm:

> Wage flexibility so that worker specific wages reflect performance creates incentives for best possible performance and thus support productivity. Various incentives and performance-based systems are one way of trying to achieve this. Wage differentials associated in other ways with productivity may also create incentives for individual efficiency. (Sinko and Vihriälä, 2005, p. 32)

The competition state paradigm has gained a solid foothold in Finnish politics (Kananen, 2008). One ideological aspiration contained in this paradigm appears to be to create a low wage private service sector in the Finnish economy as a solution to increased global competition. This would inevitably increase income inequality but also strengthen and consolidate the earlier political strategy adopted partially as a solution to the perceived problem of order in the labour market during the 1990s – namely the creation of an insider/outsider division within the labour market, adjustments of the social security system and new mechanisms of control. Thus, it would establish a completely new order in society. The supply of workers to the low wage economy would consist of the outsiders of the present labour market – i.e. workers who are subject to various control mechanisms and uncertainties. The Globalisation Report quoted above argues, along with criticising existing structures, that 'work based' immigration is also a crucial condition for future economic success as all areas of the economy are not supplied with enough workers (VNK, 2004, pp. 70–71). This suggests, implicitly, that immigrants – together with local labour market outsiders are seen as a potential supply for the future low wage economy.

The Finnish competition state paradigm can be interpreted as an adaptation of the international competition state paradigm referred to in Chapter 5. Its imperatives are almost completely opposite those of the solidaristic and inclusive labour market policies of the post-war collectivist order in Finland. Taxation used to be strict and social security benefits generous, and wage setting was centralised and employment protection legislation fairly strict as well. Thus, the Finnish adaptation towards the competition state paradigm has by necessity been only gradual, but it is possible to see that each stage of adaptation, starting from the system-changing reforms in 1994, has indeed been consistent – despite the fact that the process represents a complete turn away from, or indeed reversal of, post-war policies and ideas. Weakening the insurance element of unemployment benefits between 1994–1997 in Finland was completely consistent with the demand to restrict the availability of social security benefits in order to increase the supply of workers. Introducing control measures between 1998–2001 was consistent with the demands to manage the supply side of the labour market and create administrative measures to ensure a sufficient labour supply. Aims to create a low wage service economy are consistent with the demands of the competition state paradigm according to which wages should be adjusted to be low enough to ensure the supply of labour also in areas where productivity is low. Due to the post-war structures of the Finnish labour market wages have not adjusted downwards precisely due to taxation, social security benefits and centralised wage negotiations.

It must be noted that the new competition state paradigm, of which the Finnish paradigm is an adaptation, does not trust in the sole capacity of the markets to generate wealth, prosperity and justice. It stresses that the market mechanism is the best way to achieve such goals, but without effective management by the state this market mechanism would not work perfectly. Thus, a number of administrative measures (often labelled 'activation' measures in political and administrative rhetoric) are needed to ensure the supply of labour in order to allow the markets to act as the main mechanism of distributing resources. To the extent that these administrative measures may be regarded as coercive and controlling – as in the Finnish case – this paradigm cannot be regarded as representing a version of liberalism, as it would be in contradiction with principles of individual autonomy and freedom. This point makes the new competition state paradigm somewhat controversial and delusive. As Kantola has pointed out (Kantola, 2002, p. 150), ideas about the market easily turn into ideas about freedom, but at the same time the market may be a source of discipline and may control the rules which the much heralded individual should obey even at the cost of their personal autonomy and integrity.

As noted in the previous chapters, in addition to documents produced by national governments, the search for a national adaptation of the international competition state paradigm could be analysed with the help of OECD recommendations. Some interesting observations can be made concerning the differences between OECD recommendations for Sweden, Denmark and Finland. The OECD Review of Regulatory Reform in Finland summarises the general characteristics of the Finnish political system in the following manner:

> The Nordic governance model remains a key feature of the Finnish political economy. In particular, the state remains a key player in the economy, through the provision of public services and the substantial ownership of economic assets. An enduring political consensus promotes the development and maintenance of high standards for the protection of Finnish citizens, including an extensive system of social services, many of which are delivered at the municipal level, and high standards of social, environmental and consumer protection. These policies are also aimed at ensuring the continued settlement of the northern region (including for security reasons). The core public services of social, health and education services remain tax-funded. That said, evolution toward a more market-oriented approach, a distancing of the state from commercial activities, and reforms of parts of the public sector have taken place since the 1980s. (OECD, 2003, p. 20)

The passage quoted above is the only time traditional Finnish policy commitments – other than those directly derived from the international competition state paradigm – are mentioned in the report. Shortly afterwards, the report goes on to question the entire foundation of Finnish socio-political arrangements:

> Unemployment has halved since 1994. But structural unemployment is a major issue, with unemployment highest (relative to other EU countries) at both ends of the age spectrum ... The job market is characterised by a low share of part-time employment, and a high share of temporary employment, together with an increasing polarisation between those with a low and a high chance of finding work. Long-term unemployment is a major issue.
> The structural problems can be linked to the Finnish governance model and value system, which promote equity and solidarity, with decisions based on consensus between the social partners. But the social cost of a high rate of unemployment contrasts with the aspiration to an equitable society.
> The regulatory regime for the labour market includes a number of features that militate against getting people back to work. These include a long maximum duration for unemployment benefits, high levels of support for long-term recipients of benefit, and a short waiting period before benefits can be claimed.
> Though the current wage system has often delivered aggregate outcomes, which have kept inflationary pressure under control, this feature could be preserved in

a reform. Changes are urgently needed, including more flexibility in the central wage bargaining system. (OECD, 2003, p. 20)

The same, rather critical tone persists throughout the rest of the report. Several times the entire Finnish public sector is deemed inefficient (e.g. OECD, 2003, p. 39), and the urgency to introduce new management techniques is stressed (OECD, 2003, p. 40). The OECD Economic Survey of Finland is less dramatic in tone, but identifies nonetheless wage setting, labour mobility (OECD, 2008c, p. 18) and high labour taxes (2008c, p. 62) as some of the main problem areas in the Finnish economy. In 2010 the organization proposed opening up municipal services for private providers, in addition to identifying a 'fiscal sustainability gap' and demanding cuts in public spending (OECD, 2010c, pp. 44–8; Kananen, 2012a, p. 460). Both of these themes were high on the Finnish government's reform agenda after the 2011 general elections.

The criticism presented in the OECD documents quoted above may be partly interpreted as the OECD's promotion of the international competition state paradigm, but partly also as local Finnish officials' consent to what kinds of reforms the OECD wishes to promote in the Finnish case. The subtle difference between these two aspects – OECD recommendations and local officials' positions towards local affairs – becomes more evident when comparing the recommendations for Finland with recommendations for Sweden and Denmark.

A comparison of the quoted OECD documents in the cases of Finland and Sweden reveals an interesting contradiction: in the Swedish case commitments to solidarity and equity are regarded as legitimate, although ambitious, policy goals, whereas in the case of Finland the same policy goals are turned into causes of serious structural problems in the labour market. Part of this contradiction may be explained by the different timing of the reports in question. The Finnish report was published in 2003 when the international economy was experiencing hard times following the burst of the IT bubble. The Swedish report, by contrast, was published in 2007 when there was not yet a strong awareness that the international finance bubble was about to burst. Therefore, the reports may have been more even and more compatible had they been published during similar economic conditions. In addition, it must be remembered that the reports have been drafted by different people.

Differences in the economic cycle do not, however, account for all of the differences in the Swedish and Finnish country reports. Above all, they do not explain the contradiction regarding the value systems and principal policy goals that the reports discuss – i.e. mainly the principles of equity and solidarity. The same policy goals are referred to in entirely different ways in the two reports. Therefore, what is the most likely explanation of this contradiction is that national policy officials have discussed national traditions and policy goals from quite different perspectives. In the Swedish case, it appears likely that the national officials have strongly defended the traditional policy goals of equity and solidarity, and spent a great deal of time explaining the benefits of their model of governance and social policy. In the Finnish case, it appears more likely that the national officials have firstly anticipated the strong favouring of the international competition state paradigm that can be associated with the OECD, and have attuned themselves to the paradigm when discussing specific features of Finnish politics and society. Thus, OECD officials have perceived a strong will among Finnish policy makers to reform the economy and society in accordance with the international competition state paradigm, and identified problem areas accordingly. In the Swedish case OECD officials have been convinced about the strong priority of traditional values and policy goals, which is reflected in the reports as great respect towards these values and only moderate policy suggestions derived from the competition state paradigm.

In light of OECD documents, the Danish case seems to be somewhere in the middle of Sweden and Finland judged from the point of view of adopting and adapting to the competition state paradigm. In the Finnish case, OECD recommendations were fundamental in nature without acknowledging the strengths of existing policies. Instead, the OECD saw in the Finnish case many existing policies as fundamental weaknesses despite the fact that these policies were rather similar to those in Sweden and Denmark (i.e. strong state involvement, regulation of markets, ambitious welfare goals). As noted in the previous chapter, Danish policy recommendations contained both of the elements that were absent in Finland and Sweden – i.e. recognition of local traditions and aims, and fundamental and far-reaching policy recommendations.

The ideological shift in Finland has primarily been possible due to a strong maintenance of a political rhetoric about preserving old welfare state ideals. These ideals are still present in all election manifestos (Nygård, 2006) and they are designed to appeal to public opinion. They have been obscured by a perceived necessity to redesign the post-war collectivist order – something that the general public may only vaguely relate to because these issues have never been formulated into understandable concepts and brought under the light of public debate. And indeed, the general public has continuously expressed support for the values behind post-war welfare policies (Blomberg and Kroll, 1999ab; Muuri and Mandelbacka, 2010), something that the political parties have willingly taken advantage of. Thus, the democratic legitimacy of the competition state paradigm that dominates elite thinking remains extremely questionable in Finland.

The result of the renegotiation of the Finnish post-war collectivist social order appears to be that certain cleavages started to appear in Finnish society. First, a cleavage appeared between the political elite and the general public, indicated by the fact that efforts to create a new order never quite reflected election outcomes. Secondly, part of the solution to the perceived problem of order implied creating a cleavage within the labour market so that the institution of waged work could be supported in a dialectic fashion by two distinct groups – those with an established position in the labour market and those in danger of marginalization. The marginalized group was targeted by policies aiming to control unwanted behaviour that allowed, to some extent, even a restriction of individual autonomy.

The Finnish solution to the problem of social order signals lack of trust between policy makers and citizens (Björklund, 2008).

All three countries included in the present analysis have undergone an ideological shift that has included a positioning against the imperatives of the international competition state paradigm. This positioning and adaptation has occurred in various ways in our three chosen countries. In Sweden, adapting to the ideas of the competition state paradigm implied abandoning for good the economic policies associated with the classic Rehn–Meidner model, but legislative reform in the area of employment policy has been more limited than in Denmark and Finland. In Denmark the negotiated adaptation of the ideas of the competition state paradigm led to an original model of employment policy in the 1990s, but in the 2000s the country has drifted towards a stronger adherence to the paradigm. In Finland, where the perception of the problem of social order was strongest in connection with the renegotiation of the post-war collectivist social order, the application of the ideas associated with the competition state paradigm has been most far reaching and orthodox, both with regard to ideology and with institutions of employment policy.

Chapter 7
The Reversal of Societal Development

Along with the shift from pre-modern to modern societies a 'modern process of liberating and enhancing human creative potentials' was actualised (Chapter 2). The less work was tied to the production of necessities (food and shelter), the more people were able to redirect their creative abilities and potentials towards self-chosen ends. At the same time, however, important constraints remained. Modern societal impulses, such as ideas of the modern polity and universal education had to 'penetrate through' pre-modern societal constraints that divided citizens into different classes of people.

The post-war Nordic model of welfare policy was associated with increasing equality of opportunity and, as demonstrated in chapters 2 and 3, with emancipatory societal development. Each new generation was, to an increasing extent, able to determine more individually the goals of their biographical life projects and the ways in which they wished to contribute to societal development. The Nordic model of welfare has usually been praised for its successful combination of economic growth and social equality. In the previous chapters another, often overlooked feature of Nordic welfare policies has been scrutinised – namely the particular way in which Nordic policies and institutions structured the relationship between individual and society.

Evolving collectivism became a feature of Nordic post-war societies. Modern political and administrative institutions defined the roles of people from above, through pre-defined characteristics derived from collective functions of institutions. People were expected to behave in different situations as 'parents', 'unemployed', 'sick', 'elderly', 'disabled' and so on. Initially, a collectivist social order contributed to increasing equality of opportunity. Whereas previously, opportunities had strongly been associated with socio-economic background, the link between fortune and birth status began to weaken in post-war Nordic countries – in a manner that afterwards received considerable international attention.

Around the 1970s and 1980s, collectivism began, however, to turn into a constraint. In retrospect this seems a somewhat unavoidable development: the more people were able to define their own goals in life, the less they seemed to conform to collective norms of behaviour. This led to a re-appearance of the problem of social order. Experiences of mass unemployment strengthened perceptions of problems in the post-war social order, and affected the attempted solutions in various ways.

The 1970s and 1980s therefore constitute an important turning point in societal development. Nordic societies were facing a situation in which new ideas were needed for the continuation of emancipatory development. Policy makers and leaders of the time were presented with a situation in which a dismantling of collectivist constraints might have led to continued emancipation of human creative potentials. Such a development would have, gradually, shifted the responsibility of solving the problem of social order from the collective level to the individual level. In a society with few collective constraints, it would be increasingly an individual choice in what ways to contribute to collective goals and shared purposes.

The post-1990 Nordic countries have witnessed a reversal of most of their post-war welfare policies through the adoption and adaptation of what was in Chapter 5 termed 'the international competition state paradigm'. This paradigm places economic goals, such as international competitiveness before social rights and places public economic and social policies in the service of business interests.

The competition state paradigm has evolved simultaneously on many levels. One level has been that of economic theory and model building, which has been dominated by new classical axioms and assumptions. New classical economics has gradually become the mainstream paradigm in the academic world, and changing its hegemony would be a slow process.

Another level is that of generating policy imperatives based on the models and results of economic analysis. At this level business lobbies and think tanks have been remarkably active (Blyth, 2002) and they have contributed to promoting the imperatives in public. Similarly, supranational bodies, such as the OECD, EU and IMF have played a crucial role in promoting the imperatives of the competition state paradigm. These bodies issue regular policy analyses and recommendations for national governments based on a rather unified understanding of how the economy works and how governments should or should not intervene.

The third level is that where governments adopt the policy imperatives promoted by business lobbies and supranational bodies. What is significant here is that governments do not necessarily announce this adoption publicly. Governments usually do their best in creating a positive spin on public policies to maximise their appeal among voters. Or alternatively, they create a sense of crisis and urgency, which serves as an excuse to policy reform. Governments do not necessarily benefit from opening up all premises of public policy for critical debate. Thus, without closer scrutiny, the underlying rationale of government policies may remain unnoticed.

What has here been termed the international competition state paradigm is not, therefore, a coherent political ideology formulated with the idealistic purpose of changing the world into a better place. It is rather a fragmented and multi-layered view of the world which has, in the Nordic countries, become an administrative rationale and source of policy reform. With a specific view on labour markets and the economy, the main imperatives of the paradigm may be described as follows:

1. Passive unemployment insurance should be minimal;
2. The state should increase the size of the labour supply by administrative means;
3. Income tax rates should be as low as possible;

4. Wage negotiations should occur at the individual level;
5. Employment protection legislation should be as relaxed as possible.

In addition to these items another one has been added more recently: i.e. that the state should maintain either a balanced or a surplus budget. This imperative is consistent with a general aim of reducing the size of the public sector and creating more operating space for markets and private actors. Privatising state-run activities is a way of reducing the level of public spending.

Although being reconstructed from public policy, the imperatives of the competition state paradigm listed above have an intellectual heritage in new classical and monetarist economic analysis (for discussions on neo-Schumpeterian influences on public policy, see e.g. Jessop, 2002; Kantola and Kananen, 2013). The imperatives may be reconstructed rather easily from the OECD's country specific economic policy recommendations and an analysis of Nordic social policy reforms since the 1990s shows that the governments in these countries have progressed along the path pointed at by these imperatives (see Chapter 6). Of course, one could think of counter examples where policy reform has not proceeded along the lines of the six imperatives listed above. But the important point is that the imperatives of the competition state paradigm capture the general direction of policy reform towards which the Nordic countries have progressed, notwithstanding the variations in pace and degree discussed in the previous chapter.

It was noted in Chapter 5 that the six imperatives of the international competition state paradigm constitute a reversal of Keynesian thinking that was the rationale for a great deal of policy reform during the post-war years in the Nordic countries. By international standards, the levels of social insurance benefits used to be quite high and coverage wide. To some extent, this was true even after two decades of reform towards the reversed direction, i.e. towards lower levels and smaller coverage of benefits. At the same time, the redistributive effects of social insurance have become weaker.

Similarly, the levels of income taxes used to be comparatively high in the Nordic countries, but since the 1990s reforms have progressed towards lower levels. The redistributive effect of progressive taxation has become weaker, the more these reforms have progressed. The consequences of increasing the labour supply through administrative means were reviewed in Chapter 6 in connection with the so-called 'workfare' reforms. Nordic governments have sought to strengthen conditionality of both social assistance and unemployment insurance benefits as part of an effort to change the behaviour of workers and job seekers. At the most extreme, particularly in Finland, measures have included tough sanctions for unwanted behaviour among benefit recipients in a vulnerable and precarious situation.

What tends to blur the consequences of 'workfare' in the Nordic countries is an administrative language of 'activation' that accompanies it. Nordic governments themselves do not use the term 'workfare', which is of American origin. Instead, by using the term 'activation' the governments imply that there is a continuity between the measures instituted since the 1990s and those in use in association with the Active Labour Market Policies of the post-war years. Assuming a continuity of this kind is, however, a grave mistake. Post-war activation policies were part of a very different package of labour market measures. In the post-war Rehn–Meidner model of employment policy, Active Labour Market Policy was used to combat the local unemployment arising from needs to rationalize production (Sihto, 1994; Blyth, 2002). This need was, in turn created by solidaristic wage policy, which implied equal pay for equal work across the country.

'Workfare' policies since the 1990s have been part of efforts to increase the size of the labour supply since Nordic governments have been reluctant to increase aggregate demand by economic policy. Workers are assumed to become dependent on unconditional benefits, and 'workfare' reforms are thought to improve the incentives to find work on the open labour market.

Furthermore, the moves toward more individualised wage negotiations and looser employment protection legislation constitute reversals of post-war Nordic welfare policy. Collective and universally binding agreements on wages and terms and conditions of work between the labour market parties were pivotal of Nordic welfare policies during the post-war period. Often, these negotiations were coupled with reforms in taxation and social insurance, so that employers gained a strike-free period in return for concessions in the form of benefits to wage workers. Collective wage setting also contributed to a comparatively narrow income distribution as minimum wages and the rates for wage increase were set for entire industries.

According to the dominant economic theories that have informed policy debates, collective level wage setting increases the level of 'structural unemployment', since inflation expectations are a part of wage demands at the collective level. According to these theories, wages should be set according to productivity, which is best determined at the industry, firm or even individual level. Performance-based salaries are a consequence of these new ideas of wage setting that reverse past ideas of Nordic public policy.

Finally, employment protection legislation used to be comparatively tight in the Nordic countries during the post-war years – although perhaps not as tight as in Western Europe. Especially in the public sector terms and conditions of officers were rather rigid and the scope for lay-offs small. As a contrast, the trend of reforms in the terms and conditions of work has been towards more temporary contracts and more precarious employment relations both in the public and the private sectors as part of demands for more flexibility among workers.

It is possible to conclude, that the adoption and adaptation of the international competition state paradigm in the Nordic context has not only been a technical reversal of post-war policies, but a reversal of emancipatory societal development as well (cf. Ben-Aharon, 2011). Collectivism was an important feature of post-war Nordic societies – a feature that in itself evolved from emancipation to constraint (Chapter 5). Collective constraints have been dismantled in the Nordic countries by an adoption of the international competition state paradigm. Previous collective constraints have, however, been replaced by new individual constraints and disciplinary mechanisms that are designed to affect the behaviour of individuals and increase their conformity towards existing power relations. The failure to find another source for social order than individualised control has reversed the general direction of Nordic societal development from emancipation to discipline. This development creates new hierarchies in the Nordic countries, with the lowest hierarchy being those subject to 'workfare' policies and tough sanctions in the case of non-compliance with benefit administrators. Immigrant workers have been often forced into positions low down in the labour market hierarchy (Jønsson et al., 2013), whereas a small fortunate elite at the other end of the hierarchy has been able to benefit from this new development.

The reversal towards increased constraints has, however, been somewhat non-linear. For instance in Sweden and Denmark, as demonstrated in Chapter 6, policies have, especially during the 1990s contained efforts to counteract insider-outsider divisions in the labour market. Such efforts amount to a counter example of a general trend towards increased constraints – a trend that was strengthened in the 2000s in all three countries analysed in this study.

'Workfare' measures are the most extreme and most visible manifestation of reversed societal development. Individual action is constrained whenever externally motivated behaviour is imposed upon without an opportunity to participate in the definition of the motives. 'Workfare' policies do contain efforts to involve clients in designing what they should do (van Aerschot, 2008), but such elements are in the Nordic countries eroded by the compulsion that is also built into these policies. Individuals are made to comply with external requirements by a threat of absolute hardship and even starvation. Thus, the implementation of compulsive 'workfare' possibly compromises some human rights – particularly the right to choose one's place of work (Dean, 2007).

It could be argued, that 'workfare' policies affect a rather small minority of Nordic citizens, and that these policies would therefore not signal a reversal of emancipatory societal development. It is true that societal emancipation has not disappeared overnight in the Nordic countries since the establishment of a social order based on 'workfare'. What is primarily argued here is, however, that the general direction of societal development has changed so that the longer Nordic societies continue along the same path, the more constraining elements dominate over emancipatory elements. This argument is based upon two observations: firstly, all of the imperatives of the competition state paradigm listed above work in the direction of gradually imposing new hierarchies and new individualised constraints in Nordic societies. For instance, a loosening of employment protection legislation reduces the scope for future action for individual workers in precarious employment relations. This is a constraint on action since a reasonably stable future outlook is a requirement for making individual choices and for developing individual initiatives. Similarly, individual level wage setting tends to render workers more compliant with given hierarchies at the work place – since their performance and salaries are determined by such compliance.

By contrast, previous Nordic collective constraints on action operated in a slightly different manner. By ascribing collective roles for individuals, they directed individuals towards fulfilling the norms associated with each role. Such collective norms were quite clear and they could even be justified with a collective sense of nation building. More recent individualised control mechanisms are more subtle and they are in a more abstract fashion grounded on existing power relations.

The second observation suggesting a more general significance of 'workfare' reforms in the Nordic countries is that the extreme compulsion built into these policies affects not only those directly concerned, but other layers of the labour market as well. Externally motivated action and control in the labour market and at workplaces is enhanced by the fact that there is a lower hierarchy – i.e. the subjects of 'workfare' – and their very existence serves as a threat to workers in the hierarchies above. People higher up the hierarchy will be more likely to comply with externally motivated action and existing power relations from a fear of being moved down (cf. discussion in Chapter 2 on Foucault and discipline). Therefore, hierarchies and control mechanisms presuppose each other. In practice, this means that people in the labour market are forced to accept worse pay and worse terms and conditions than they would otherwise have accepted – had the hierarchies and control mechanisms not been in place.

In addition, the most recent societal development tends to work in favour of those at the absolute top of the hierarchy. A small fortunate minority is able to benefit from a development towards new hierarchies, as wealth and power tend to concentrate at the top of the new hierarchical order – rather reminiscently to pre-modern societies.

We are now in a position to present the general direction of societal development during the three eras of the Nordic welfare state (Figure 7.1).

During the first period of modernisation constraining elements originating from medieval times were still quite visible in Nordic societies. As discussed in Chapter 3, these constraining elements gradually gave way to the modern impulses of modernisation of agriculture, establishment of universal education and a modern polity with modern political rights. The timing of these three impulses was special in the Nordic countries in the sense that they occurred rather simultaneously. This was, in turn, associated with an enhanced emancipation of creative potentials, as they could be redirected from the provision of basic needs under conditions of educational and political rights. Each individual was, to an increasing extent, given the ability to reflect upon their own abilities, to perfect them, and to put them in use. In contrast, in countries such as the UK, where the three modern impulses occurred with a clear interval, a quite distinct working class subject to various constraints emerged.

During the second era, emancipation was stronger than constraint in Nordic societies. As noted above, a collectivist order increased meritocracy and equality of opportunity. Welfare state institutions like social security and public services ensured an increasingly equal distribution of well-being including material and non-material resources. In the 1970s and 1980s emancipatory societal development

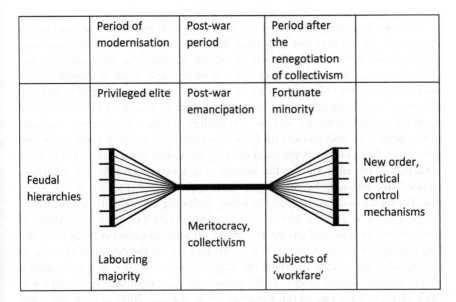

	Period of modernisation	Post-war period	Period after the renegotiation of collectivism	
Feudal hierarchies	Privileged elite ... Labouring majority	Post-war emancipation ... Meritocracy, collectivism	Fortunate minority ... Subjects of 'workfare'	New order, vertical control mechanisms

Figure 7.1   Emancipating and constraining aspects of societal development

was, however, reversed, so that constraining elements began to dominate again. This reversal was actualised through the adoption of the international competition state paradigm as the main rationale for policy reform. As noted above, the result has been the imposition of ever more individualised control mechanisms and new hierarchies in the labour markets.

The main question that inevitably arises from the discussion above is how or whether societal development could be re-reversed so that the constraining development of the third era of Nordic welfare states could be (re)turned into renewed emancipation. This is a question that points towards the future and as a conclusion to the study at hand, it is possible to outline a few ideas that might possibly work as alternatives to the dominant ideas associated with hierarchy and discipline.

As pointed out in Chapter 2, societies can be structured so that individual creative potentials are liberated from previous bonds. Later, it was argued that the Nordic welfare state institutions carried forward the emancipatory impulses manifested earlier in the form of modernised agriculture, universal education and modern political rights. A re-reversal of constraining societal development since the 1990s would not, however, imply a simple re-institution of previous welfare state institutions in the form they were in during the post-war period. Ever since the renegotiation of the post-war collectivist social order, there has been a need to re-invent societal emancipation in the Nordic countries. Admittedly, efforts during the first two decades after this renegotiation have not been successful, but in principle, the course of societal development could be turned.

A modest beginning in the direction of a re-reversal might be thought of at two levels: first, concerning those in a vulnerable life situation, and second, concerning organisational principles in the private sector. Contrary to the penalising and disciplinary policies and practices that are increasingly used in Nordic labour markets, those in a vulnerable position could be met with an empathic attitude. Policies could be designed according to the idea that each individual has the potential to contribute to society – regardless of past performance or past experiences. Care and services for those in a vulnerable position could, along the same lines, focus on developing and utilising individual capacities and individual initiatives – for example for the benefit of a local community (in a fashion outlined, for instance, by the 'capabilities' approach, Chapter 2). At the same time, the right to a decent standard of living, including a reasonably reliable future prospect could be granted, instead of maintaining a threat of absolute hardship. A sense of being useful and an opportunity for meaningful action is likely to be the best remedy for many obstacles individuals face during the course of their lives. A re-reversal of societal development might therefore amount to a re-invention of the 'Nordic welfare model' as the opportunity for continuing in the post-war spirit seems to have passed (cf. Kosonen, 1998; Kuhnle, 2000, p.54; Kuhnle and Alestalo, 2000, p.15; Rothstein, 2000; Hvinden et al., 2001; Kautto et al., 2001; Andersen et al., 2007).

The complex Nordic systems of social security were developed during a time when societies were quite different from what they are presently. Therefore, from the perspective of emancipatory societal development (see Chapter 2) a dismantling of past collectivist structures seems something of a need of contemporary times. People no longer behave according to the norms built into collectivist categories. However, instead of re-instituting control at the individual level, benefits could be developed with less conditionality in mind. This would probably take the benefit system even more towards an unconditional citizens' income (van Parijs, 1995; Offe et al., 1996). Nordic universalism is in principle an idea which is quite compatible with granting every citizen a decent standard of living (Julkunen, 2009).

A less penalising approach at the life situations of those in vulnerable situations would signal that temporary obstacles in life are common and tolerated. This would, in turn, be likely to contribute to emancipation as individual creativity requires a reasonably secure future outlook which allows for some risk taking in present ventures. Most importantly, dismantling individual constraints would reduce the pressure to conform to externally imposed behaviour and existing power relations and would thus contribute towards a dismantling of societal hierarchies.

Concerning organisational principles, both the collectivist state bureaucracies and competitive for-profit enterprises appear problematic from the perspective of emancipatory societal development. As noted, collectivism leaves little room for individual initiatives and agency. Collectivist action is oriented towards complying with norms derived from the functions that the norms are thought to serve (e.g. the role of a teacher in an educational system). On the other hand, competition and profit seeking is likely to encourage adversarial and abusive behaviour in organisations. Organisational principles could, therefore be developed more towards co-operation and away from hierarchy and competition. The Nordic countries have, in principle, a strong tradition of co-operative organisation to draw upon, and there are certainly lessons to be learned from the past in this respect. Co-operative organisations could be given a higher priority in regulations and in the allocation of resources. This would imply a dismantling of past employer–employee divisions, and a conception according to which each worker is seen as a potential entrepreneur.

Resilient Competition State Ideas

There are at least two main obstacles to a re-reversal of societal development back towards emancipation in the Nordic countries. The first one is the resilience of competition state ideas, which originally produced the reversal in the 1990s. The second one is associated with problems in democratic policy making. These two obstacles are somewhat interrelated and aspects of them will be discussed in the remaining parts of this concluding chapter.

The issue of resilient competition state ideas is complex. One might have expected a re-evaluation of past economic policies in 2008 when the international financial markets were on the brink of collapse, and afterwards, when the financial crises spread into the real economies of many countries. Competition state ideas, as discussed above, do not directly concern finance. Still, their international dominance after the 1980s and 1990s was associated with a 'financialisation' of the global economy (Calhoun and Derluguian, 2011).

Looked at from the perspective of finance and monetary policy, many of the imperatives of the competition state paradigm seem to be geared towards keeping price inflation at bay. Inflation targeting was also the main goal of monetary policy in many countries before the financial crises. According to the logic built into competition state imperatives, lower income taxes and lower social security benefits increase the supply of labour without creating the inflationary pressure that wage increases, for instance, would do. Similarly, according to dominant economic theory, individual level wage setting is a source of lower inflation than co-ordinated wage setting.

Indeed, inflation rates have been rather low before the global financial crisis in the Nordic countries and internationally, which signals an effective utilisation of competition state ideas in public and labour market policy. Consequently, central banks have been able to keep interest rates low resulting in cheap borrowing costs for private actors and unattractive prospects for saving. At the same time, the levels of real wages have grown rather slowly.

This development has, in turn, been associated with an increased tendency in financial markets to seek profits – not from returns in the real economy, or from the channelling of capital – but from fluctuations in asset prices. The developments described above have allowed such speculative activity to occur on an unprecedented scale with enormous profits being made by traders. In this sense, banks have gone beyond their traditional role of providing capital for the smallest possible transaction costs (Stiglitz, 2010). They have, instead, redirected their activities towards making gains from fluctuating asset prices. Indeed, if public bail out money is considered, banks have gravely failed this traditional task of providing capital for the smallest possible transaction costs. Banks have been protected by public deposit insurance schemes. They have also been rescued by governments in cases where risks have been realised – something which has not, however, reduced the tendency to speculate with asset prices.

In Europe banks have also benefitted from expanding sovereign bond markets. The European Central Bank has provided cheap loans to banks that have in turn bought government bonds in the euro area. The European Financial Stability Mechanism has secured at least part of these debts (with public finances), and the ECB has also purchased bonds from secondary markets so that banks' losses have not been great – in spite of the absence of a lender of last resort and some debt restructuring in the euro area.

At the same time competition state ideas have continued to play a key role in governments' public policy responses. Europe has been divided into those governments that choose to hold on to these ideas, and those that are forced to do so. A dividing line has emerged that goes across Central Europe so that Northern countries impose strict rules of austerity and 'structural reforms' on Southern countries that are struggling with debt, unemployment and recession.

A minority of professional economists has continuously been critical towards the foundations of the competition state paradigm. Since the financial crises after 2008 such criticism has become more widespread and subject to renewed attention. A growing body of evidence seems to support ideas and theories put forward by John Maynard Keynes and Hyman P. Minsky, and increasing efforts have been made to apply the ideas of these late economists to events after 2008.

Advocates of the Keynesian/Minskyan approach have put forward the argument that a lack of aggregate demand is a major problem in post-2008 economies worldwide (Davidson, 2009; Stiglitz, 2010; Galbraith, 2011; Wray, 2012; Krugman, 2013). As firms and households have reduced spending capacity, the solution to this problem would be to stimulate the economy by running a government budget deficit. By contrast, policy makers in charge of economic policies after 2008 in most European countries would say that problems are associated with the lack of competitiveness of private business. The solution to this problem is quite the opposite compared to the Keynesian approach: budgetary austerity combined with 'structural reform' in the direction of the imperatives of the competition state paradigm.

Post-Keynesians have also advocated a legal separation of investment and retail banking, something that would prevent the development of banks that are 'too big to fail'. They have argued that without such a separation banks will not have to face the consequences of reckless risk taking. Regarding international trade, post-Keynesians have argued for a reform of the international payments system so that countries running a permanent trade surplus would have to take a greater responsibility for increasing global demand (Davidson, 2009). This argument contains an underlying critique of German policies since the beginning of the 2000s.

It may seem slightly paradoxical to cling to competition state ideas after the financial crises since 2008. Yet this is more or less what policy makers of the world's leading economies did after 2008. Critics have been able to challenge the rationale behind the competition state paradigm,[1] but a political process whereby this rationale would have been replaced by another one has not occurred.

In the debate about policy response towards economic challenges since 2008 and about the foundations of the competition state paradigm, the policy makers and public intellectuals in the Nordic countries have been passive observers. Alternative policies or rationales have not been developed in the Nordic countries – a situation that differs from that after World War II when the unique Nordic welfare policies were instituted.

Nordic Corporatism under Pressure

As long as competition state ideas continue to dominate Nordic policy-making, a re-reversal of societal development will be unlikely. As challenging competition state ideas would be a political event, it is also an interesting question to what extent Nordic political institutions allow for a contestation of dominant ideas.

The Nordic (neo)corporatist model of policy-making is often thought of as democratic and efficient in international comparisons (cf. Lijphart, 1999). Corruption is usually not found and administration is thought to be open and transparent (for a discussion, see Götz and Marklund, forthcoming). At the same time, practical Nordic policy-making appears quite distinct from classical democratic ideals, such as the Montesquieuian ideal of the separation of judicial, administrative and legislative powers. This is the case because the labour market parties share many aspects of these three powers. This distinctive feature may underlie some of the challenges that the Nordic political systems have been facing since the adoption of the international competition state paradigm as a source of policy reform.

As noted in Chapter 4, Nordic trade unions and employers' organisations were highly involved in designing social and economic policy during the post-war years. In addition, these organisations gained a significant role in administering the policies they had been designing. Labour market policy (including the matching of employers and job seekers, unemployment benefits and pensions) was organised and implemented under the formal rule of the labour market parties.

---

1 A very illustrating and informative debate occurred between the European Commissioner of Economic and Monetary Affairs and the Euro Olli Rehn and Professor Paul Krugman in 2013.

Later on, when Nordic governments wished to change labour market policy, the labour market parties who administered these policies were consulted. Not only did corporatism extend to legislation and administration, but special labour market courts – with corporatist administration – were set up for settling disputes between employers and employees on collective agreements (Rothstein, 1992; Knudsen and Rothstein, 1994). Thus, the separation of powers in the Nordic countries remains subject to debate. On the one hand there are separate formal institutions for each form of power: parliaments, governments and courts. At the same time, important aspects of judicial, administrative and legislative powers have been rather concentrated with the labour market parties.

The efficient and legitimate aspects of the Nordic system of policy-making did, however, dominate until around the 1990s. Serious and disruptive conflicts were rare, and standards of living were rising among citizens – although critical contestation of those in power was also quite rare. The high density of trade union membership and the strong support of Social Democratic parties in parliamentary elections indicate trust and legitimacy among citizens with regard to the policies the various Nordic governments were pursuing.

As the international competition state paradigm became the leading rationale of Nordic policy making since the 1990s, the legitimacy of political decisions has been cast under new light. The new paradigm is clearly influenced by business interests, but it remains rather unclear through which channels this interest has been influencing political decisions. Competition state ideas have been promoted publicly by think-tanks funded by organised business (Blyth, 2002), but most crucially, the link between election outcomes and competition state policies remains unclear. Political parties have remained faithful in election campaigns to traditional Nordic welfare state ideals (Nygård, 2006), but once in government, they have pursued contradictory competition state policies.

Although unarticulated, the situation has become frustrating for the electorate. Despite variations in election results and changes in government coalitions, the direction of policy-making has not changed: election results have influenced at the best only the pace by which competition state reforms have been adopted. At the same time, a significant challenge towards Nordic political systems has emerged in the form of increasing support for what has been termed 'populist' parties. As traditional Nordic political parties from left to right have become increasingly similar in the public rhetoric, the more recent populist parties have appeared as critical voices contesting the idea that governments have acted in favour of the country and its citizens. The populist parties that have since the 2000s gained an increasing number of seats in Nordic parliaments have also channelled a significant amount of criticism towards EU policies.

Although Nordic populist parties also channel racist prejudice, their strong emergence can also be seen as a self-correcting mechanism of Nordic political systems that keep aspiring towards democratic ideals. Governments are forced to consider dissenting views that have the backing of citizens criticising elite policy making. The dividing line in politics is perhaps rather between bureaucratic and business influenced managerialism and frustrated citizens than between a tolerant majority and a prejudiced and nationalist minority. Many events suggest that the same problematique is a European-wide phenomenon. The fact that the protest against elite policy making takes the form of ethno-nationalist ideas may be explained by a lack of constructive alternative reform agendas or even analyses of dominant competition state orthodoxies. After all, prejudices are nothing new in the Nordic countries.

Thus, the Nordic corporatist model of policy-making is struggling to maintain legitimacy. In order to strengthen this legitimacy, the system could be made more open and transparent so that citizens could become more involved in political debates and the decision making process. For instance, the links between political parties in parliament and the corporatist labour market parties could be acknowledged openly. Traditionally, trade unions have been funding left-wing parties in the Nordic countries, whereas employers' organisations have been funding parties on the right. It remains, however, unclear to what extent the parties in parliament and the labour market parties that exercise the three powers of legislation, administration and jurisdiction share the same political agenda – or even what this agenda is in precise terms. To achieve greater openness, the amalgams of political parties and interest organisations – and indeed actors in the civil service – could be first thought of as unified 'advocacy coalitions' (Sabatier, 1998), sharing the same normative commitments in a given policy domain. The agendas and normative commitments of such advocacy coalitions could then be made public and open to contestation and debate.

The influence of business interests on political decisions should also be made subject to more open scrutiny. Defending and promoting particular interests is an important part of democratic policy making, but the general public should be aware of how and through what channels this influence occurs. For instance, large international corporations have a business interest in the privatisation of Nordic health care services, and accordingly, they have an interest in changing laws and regulations. If such reform agendas in health care or in any other domain exist, they should be announced publicly and political parties subject to electoral scrutiny should position themselves in relation to these agendas.

The establishment of independent constitutional courts might also strengthen the legitimacy of the Nordic corporatist system of policy making. So far, the absence of such a court has left the interpretation of the constitution to the parties who are proposing policy reform. It is difficult to think of these parties as totally neutral as regards to the reforms that they are proposing, and hence the interpretation of the constitution in question may be biased. Examples of problems of this nature were touched upon in Chapter 6 when the parliamentary contestation of Nordic 'workfare' reforms was discussed. A useful constitutional court in the Nordic countries would consist of officials recruited on the basis of legal expertise only. New legislation could be contested in the constitutional court before enforcement.

The Nordic countries have a unique political heritage that they may draw upon when making future political choices. Nordic societies continue to have an opportunity to develop towards modern ideals of freedom, equality and co-operation, but the obstacles to such a development should be recognised and collective efforts to overcome these obstacles should be made.

References

Aerschot, P. van, 2008. On the Right to Participation in Activation Processes in Three Nordic Countries. *Journal of Social Security Law*, 15(3), pp. 99–112.

Ahonen, S., 2003. *Yhteinen koulu. Tasa-arvoa vai tasapäisyyttä?* [A Common School – Equality or Equal Opportunities?]. Tampere: Vastapaino.

Alapuro, R., 1988. *State and Revolution in Finland*. Berkeley: University of California Press.

Alapuro, R., 2004. What is Western and what is Eastern in Finland? *Thesis, 11* 77(2), pp. 85–101.

Alasuutari, P., 1996. *Toinen tasavalta. Suomi 1949–1994* [The Second Republic. Finland between 1949–1994]. Tampere: Vastapaino.

Alasuutari, P., 2004. Suunnittelutaloudesta kilpailutalouteen. Miten muutos oli ideologisesti mahdollinen? [From a Planned Economy to a Competition Economy. How was the Transformation Ideologically Possible?]. *Yhteiskuntapolitiikka*, 69(1), pp. 3–16.

Alestalo, M. and Kuhnle, S., 1984. *The Scandinavian Route. Economic, Social and Political Developments in Denmark, Finland, Norway and Sweden* (Research Group for Comparative Sociology, No. 31). Helsinki: University of Helsinki.

Allardt, E., 1996. Hyvinvointitutkimus ja elämänpolitiikka [Welfare studies and life politics]. *Janus*, 4(3), pp. 224–41.

Åmark, K., 2006. Women's Labour Force Participation in the Nordic Countries during the Twentieth Century, in *The Nordic Model of Welfare. A Historical Reappraisal*, edited by N.F. Christiansen, K. Petersen, N. Edling and P. Haave. Copenhagen: Museum of Tusculanum Press, pp. 299–334.

Andersen, T.M., Holmström, B., Honkapohja, S., et al., 2007. *The Nordic Model. Embracing Globalisation and Sharing Risks*. Helsinki: The Research Institute of the Finnish Economy (ETLA).

Andersson, J.O., Kosonen, P. and Vartiainen, J., 1993. *The Finnish Model of Economic and Social Policy. From Emulation to Crash* (Nationalekonomiska institutionen ser. A:401). Åbo: Åbo Akademi.

Arendt, H., 1958. *The Human Condition*. Chicago: University of Chicago Press.

Baldwin, P., 1990. *The Politics of Social Solidarity. Class Bases of the European Welfare State 1875–1975*. Cambridge: Cambridge University Press.

Beck, U., 1992. *Risk Society. Towards a New Modernity*. London: Sage Publication.

Beck, U., 2000. The Cosmopolitan Perspective. Sociology of the Second Age of Modernity. *British Journal of Sociology*, 51(1), pp. 79–105.

Beck, U. and Beck-Gernsheim, E., 2002. *Individualization. Institutionalized Individualism and its Social and Political Consequences*. London: Sage.

Beck, U., Giddens, A. and Lash, S., 1994. *Reflexive Modernisation. Politics, Tradition and Aesthetics in the Modern Social Order*. Cambridge: Polity Press.

Beckett, J.V., 1986. *The Aristocracy in England 1660–1914*. Oxford: Basil Blackwell.

Ben-Aharon, Y., 2011. *The Event in Science, History, Philosophy & Art*. College Station: Virtualbookworm.

Benhabib, S., 1986. The Generalised and the Concrete Other. The Kohlberg-Gilligan Controversy and Feminist Theory. *Praxix International*, 5(4), pp. 402–24.

Benhabib, S., 1992. *Autonomi och gemenskap. Kommunikativ etik, feminism och postmodernism* [Situating the Self. Gender, Community and Postmodernism in Contemporary Ethics]. Gothenburg: Daidalos.

Benner, M. and Vad, T.B., 2000. Sweden and Denmark. Defending the Welfare State, in *Welfare and Work in the Open Economy*, edited by F.W. Scharpf and V.A. Schmidt. Vol. II. Oxford: Oxford University Press, pp. 399–466.

Berg, M., 1994. *The Age of Manufactures 1700–1820. Industry, Innovation and Work in Britain*. London and New York: Routledge.

Bergmark, Å., 2001. Den lokala välfärdsstaten? Decentraliseringstrender under 1990-talet [The Local Welfare State? Trends of Decentralisation during the 1990s], in Government, Sweden. *Välfärdstjänster i omvandling* [Social Services in Transition] (SOU 2001:52) Stockholm: Regeringskansliet.

Björklund, L., 2008. Kannustaminen ja moraali. Kannustamisen idea suomalaisessa yhteiskuntapolitiikassa 1990-luvulta lähtien [Incentivisation and Morality. The idea of Incentivisation in Finnish Activation Policies since the 1990s]. PhD Thesis. University of Helsinki.

Bjørn, C., 1988. 1810–1860, in *Det danske landbrugs historie III*, edited by C. Bjørn, T. Dahlerup, S.P. Jensen, and E.H. Pedersen. *1810–1914* [The History of Danish Agriculture. 1810–1914]. Odense: Landbohistorisk Selskab, 7–192.

Blomberg, H. and Kroll, C., 1999a. Do Structural Contexts Matter? Macro-Sociological Factors and Popular Attitudes towards Welfare Services. *Acta sociologica*, 42(4), pp. 319–35.

Blomberg, H. and Kroll, C., 1999b. Who Wants to Preserve the 'Scandinavian service state'? Attitudes to Welfare Services among Citizens and Local Government Elites in Finland, 1992–1996, in *The End of the Welfare State? Responses to State Retrenchment*, edited by S. Svallfors and P. Taylor-Gooby. London: Routledge, pp. 52–86.

Blomberg, H., Kallio, J., Kangas, O., et al., 2012. Attitudes Among High-Risk Groups, in *Contested Welfare States. Welfare Attitudes in Europe and Beyond*, edited by S. Svallfors. Stanford: Stanford University Press, pp. 58–80.

Blyth, M., 2002. *Great Transformations. Economic Ideas and Institutional Change in the Twentieth Century*. New York: Cambridge University Press.

Böckerman, P. and Kiander, J., 2009. Luova tuho. Miten suuren laman aiheuttama murros muutettiin käsitykseksi luovasta tuhosta? [Creative Destruction. How Was the Great Transformation Caused by the Depression Changed into a

Notion of Creative Destruction?], in *Ajatuksen voima. Ideat hyvinvointivaltion uudistamisessa* [The Power of Thought. Ideas and Welfare State Reform], edited by J. Kananen and J. Saari. Helsinki: Minerva/SoPhi, pp. 99–118.

Böckerman, P. and Kiander, J., 2006. Talouspolitiikka [Economic Policy], in *Suomen malli. Murroksesta menestykseen?* [The Finnish Model. From Transition to Success?], edited by J. Saari. Helsinki: Helsinki University Press, pp. 135–72.

Boltanski, L. and Chiapello, E., 2005. *The New Spirit of Capitalism*. London/New York: Verso.

Bredgaard, T., Jørgensen, H. and Larsen, F., 2003. Tanskan työmarkkinapolitiikka: Peruspiirteet ja ajankohtaista kehittämistä [Danish Employment Policy: Basic Characteristics and Current Shaping], in *Kannustavan sosiaaliturvan haaste* [The Challenge of Incentivising Social Security], edited by P. Kananen and U. Salonen-Soulié. Reports of the Ministry of Social Affairs and Health, 2003: 5. Helsinki: Ministry of Social Affairs and Health, pp. 55–74.

Bredgaard, T., Larsen, F. and Madsen, P.K., 2005. *The Flexible Danish Labour Market. A Review* (CARMA Research Paper 2005:1). Alborg: University of Alborg.

Bredgaard, T., Larsen, F. and Madsen, P.K., 2009. Flexicurity. In Pursuit of a Moving Target. *European Journal of Social Security*, 40(4), pp. 305–25.

Broman-Kananen, U.B., 2005. *På klassrummets tröskel. Om att vara lärare i musikläroinrättningarnas brytningstid* [On the Threshold of the Classroom. On Being a Teacher during the Transition Period of Music Schools]. Helsinki: Sibelius Academy.

Buchardt, M., Markkola, P. and Valtonen, H. eds, 2013. *Education State and Citizenship*. Nordic Centre of Excellence NordWel Studies in Historical Welfare State Research 4. Helinki: NordWel.

Burleigh, M., 2000. *The Third Reich. A New History*. New York: Hill & Wang.

Calhoun, C. and Derluguian, G. eds, 2011. *Business as Usual. The Roots of the Global Financial Meltdown*. New York: New York University Press.

Carlsson, I., 2003. *Så tänkte jag. Politik & dramatik* [How I Thought. The Drama of Politics]. Stockholm: Hjalmarson & Högberg.

Castells, M. ed., 2004. *The Network Society. A Cross-Cultural Perspective*. Cheltenham: Edward Elgar.

Castles, F., 2004. *The Future of the Welfare State. Crisis Myths and Crisis Realities*. Oxford: Oxford University Press.

Chernilo, D., 2006. Social Theory's Methodological Nationalism. Myth and reality. *European Journal of Social Theory*, 9(5), pp. 5–22.

Christensen, J., 1983. *Rural Denmark. 1750–1980*. Odense: The Central Co-operative Committee of Denmark.

Christensen, J.G. and Pallesen, T., 2001. The Political Benefits of Corporatization and Privatization. *Journal of Public Policy*, 21(3), pp. 283–309.

Clasen, J. and Viebrock, E., 2008. Voluntary Unemployment Insurance and Trade Union Membership: Investigating the Connections in Denmark and Sweden. *Journal of Social Policy*, 37(3), pp. 433–51.

Cox, R.H., 2001. The Social Construction of an Imperative. Why Welfare Reform Happened in Denmark and the Netherlands but not in Germany. *World Politics*, 53(2), pp. 463–98.

Daly, M., 2010. Families versus State and Market, in *The Oxford Handbook of the Welfare State*, edited by F.G. Castles, S. Leibfried, J. Lewis, et al. Oxford: Oxford University Press, pp. 139–51.

Davidson, P., 2009. *The Keynes Solution. The Path to Global Economic Prosperity.* London: Palgrave Macmillan.

Dean, H., 2007. The Ethics of Welfare to Work. *Policy and Politics*, 35(4), pp. 573–89.

Dean, H., 2010. *Understanding Human Need. Social issues, Policy and Practice.* Bristol: Policy Press.

Dombernowsky, L., 1988. 1720–1810, in *Det danske landbrugs historie II*. 1536–1810 [Danish Agricultural History II. 1536–1810], edited by C. Bjørn, T. Dahlerup, S.P. Jensen and E.H. Pedersen. Odense: Landbohistorisk Selskab, pp. 211–394.

Dwyer, P., 2010. *Understanding Social Citizenship. Themes and Perspectives for Policy and Practice.* Bristol: Policy Press.

Dybdahl, V., 1982. *Det nye samfund på vej 1871–1913* [The New Society on its Way 1871–1913]. Copenhagen: Gyldendal.

Edling, N., 2006. Limited Universalism. Unemployment Insurance in Northern Europe 1900–2000, in *The Nordic Model of Welfare. A Historical Reappraisal*, edited by N.F. Christiansen, K. Petersen, N. Edling and P. Haave. Copenhagen: Museum of Tusculanum Press, pp. 99–144.

Egidius, H., 2001. *Skola och utbildning. I historiskt och internationells perspektiv* [School and Education. In Historical and International Perspective]. Stockholm: Natur och kultur.

Ejersbo, N. and Greve, C., 2008. *Moderniseringen af den offentlige sector* [Modernisation of the Public Sector]. Copenhagen: Børsens Forlag.

Eräsaari, R. and Rahkonen, K., 2001. *Työväenkysymyksestä sosiaalipolitiikkaan. Yrjö-Koskisesta Heikki Warikseen* [From the Workers' Question to Social Policy. From Yrjö-Koskinen to Heikki Waris]. Helsinki: Gaudeamus.

Ervasti, H., 2001. Class, Individualism and the Finnish Welfare State. *Journal of European Social Policy*, 11(9), pp. 9–23.

Esping-Andersen, G., 1990. *The Three Worlds of Welfare Capitalism*. Cambridge: Polity Press.

Esping-Andersen, G., 1999. *Social Foundations of Post-Industrial Economies*. Oxford: Oxford University Press.

Feldt, K.O., 1991. *Alla dessa dagar ... I regeringen 1982–1990* [All These Days ... In Government 1982–1990]. Stockholm: Nordtedts.

Flora, P. ed., 1986. *Growth to Limits. The Western European Welfare States since World War II*. Berlin: Walter de Gruyter.

Flora, P., Alber, J., Eichenberg, R., et al., 1983. *State, Economy, and Society in Western Europe 1815–1975 vol.1. The Growth of Mass Democracies and Welfare States*. Frankfurt: Campus Verlag.

Foucault, M., 1977. *Discipline and Punish*. London: Penguin Books.

Freire, P., 1974. *Education for Critical Consciousness*. London: Continuum.

Friedman, M., 1968. The Role of Monetary Policy. *The American Economic Review*, 58(1), pp. 1–17.

Friisberg, C., 1998. *Den danske vej fra enevaelde til demokrati. Borger og bonde i overgangsårene 1830 til 1848* [The Danish Path from Authoritarianism to Democracy. Burgher and Peasant in the Transition Period of 1830–1848]. Varde: Vestjysk Kulturforlag.

Galbraith, J.K., 2011. The Great Crisis and the Finacial Sector. What We Might Have Learned, in *Aftermath. A New Global Economic Order?*, edited by C. Calhoun and G. Derluguian. New York: New York University Press.

Gerven, M. van, 2008. *The Broad Tracks of Path Dependent Benefit Reforms. A Longitudinal Study of Social Benefit Reforms in Three European Countries, 1980–2006*. KELA Research Department, Studies in Social Security and Health 100. Helsinki: KELA.

Giddens, A., 1984. *Constitution of Society. An Outline of the Theory of Structuration*. Cambridge: Polity Press.

Giddens, A., 1991. *Modernity and Self-identity. Self and Society in the Late Modern Age*. Stanford: Stanford University Press.

Gilbert, N., 1992. From Entitlements to Incentives. The Changing Philosophy of Social Protection. *International Social Security Review*, 45(3), pp. 5–18.

Glenn, P., 2007. *Legal Traditions of the World*. Oxford: Oxford University Press.

Götz, N. and Marklund, C. eds, forthcoming. *The Promise of Openness*. Leiden: Brill.

Green-Pedersen, C., 2002. New Public Management Reforms of the Danish and Swedish Welfare States. The Role of Different Social Democratic Responses. *Governance*, 15(2), pp. 271–94.

Guy, A., 1991. The Role of Aristotle's *Praxis* Today. *The Journal of Value Inquiry*, 25(3), pp. 287–9.

Haatanen, K., 2000. *Yhteisöllisyyden paradoksit* [The Paradoxes of Communitarism]. Helsinki: Helsingin yliopiston sosiaalipolitiikan laitos 2000:4.

Hadenius, S., 1997. *The Riksdag in Focus. Swedish History in a Parliamentary Perspective*. Stockholm: The Swedish Parliament.

Hakaste, S., 1992. *Yhteiskasvatuksen kehitys 1800–luvun Suomessa. Sekä vastaavia kehityslinjoja naapurimaissa* [The Development of Joint Education in 19th Century Finland. And Corresponding Processes in Neighbouring countries]. Helsingin yliopisto: Kasvatustieteen laitoksen tutkimuksia 133.

Halila, A., 1949. *Suomen kansakoululaitoksen historia vol. 2. Kansakoululaitoksesta piirijakoon* [The History of the Finnish Folk School vol. 2. From the Folk School to School Districts]. Turku: WSOY.

Hall, P., 1993. Policy Paradigms, Social Learning and the State. The case of economic policy making in Britain. *Comparative Politics*, 25(3), pp. 275–96.

Hall, P. and Soskice, D., 2001. *Varieties of Capitalism. The Institutional Foundations of Comparative Advantage*. Oxford: Oxford University Press.

Hammond, J.L. and Hammond, B., 1911. *The Village Labourer*. London: Longmans, Green, and Co.

Hanska, J. and Vainio-Korhonen, K., 2010. *Huoneentaulun maailma. Kasvatus ja koulutus Suomessa keskiajalta 1860–luvulle* [The World of the Wall Board. Education and Childhoon Development in Finland since Medieval times until the 1869s]. Helsinki: Suomalaisen kirjallisuuden seura.

Harrinvirta, M. and Puoskari, P., 2001. Kehysbudjetointi poliittisena päätöksentekkoprosessina [The Framework Budget as a Political Decision Making Process]. *Kansantaloudellinen aikakauskirja*, 97(3), pp. 445–59.

Heckscher, E., 1949. *Sveriges ekonomiska historia från Gustav Vasa vol. 1–2* [Swedish Economic History from Gustav Vasa vols 1–2]. Stockholm: Bonniers.

Heckscher, E., 1957. *Svenskt arbete och liv. Från medeltiden till nutid* [Swedish work and life. From the middle ages to present times]. Stockholm: Bonniers.

Heiskala, R., 1997. *Society as Semiosis. Neostructuralist Theory of Culture and Society*. Research Reports No. 231. Department of Sociology, University of Helsinki.

Held, D., 1996. *Models of Democracy*. Cambridge: Polity Press.

Helin, H and Oulasvirta, L., 2000. Kuntien talouden ja valtionapujärjestelmän kehitys 1990–luvulla [The Development of Municipalities' Economy and State Aid in the 1990s], in *Suomalaisen sosiaalipolitiikan alueellinen rakenne* [The Regional Structure of Finnish Social Policy], edited by H.A. Loikkanen and J. Saari, Juho. Helsinki: Sosiaali- ja terveysturvan keskusliitto, pp. 108–25.

Henriksen, I., 1993. The Transformation of Danish Agriculture 1870–1914, in *The Economic Development of Denmark and Norway since 1870*, edited by K.G. Persson. Aldershot: Edward Elgar, pp. 153–80.

Hentilä, S., 1980. *Veljeyttä yli pohjanlahden* [Brotherhood over the Gulf of Finland]. Helsinki: Gaudeamus.

Hentilä, S., Krötzl, C., and Pulma, P., 2002. *Pohjoismaiden historia* [The History of the Nordic Countries]. Helsinki: Edita.

Hilson, M., 2008. *The Nordic Model. Scandinavia since 1945*. London: Reaktion books.

Hjerppe, R., 1989. *The Finnish Economy 1960–1985. Growth and Structural Change*. Helsinki: Bank of Finland Government Printing Centre.

Honkapohja, S. and Koskela, E., 1999. Finland's Depression. A Tale of Bad Luck and Bad Policies. *Economic Policy*, 14(29), pp. 401–36.

Honkapohja, S., Koskela, E., Leibfritz, W. and Uusitalo, R., 2009. *Economic Prosperity Recaptured. The Finnish Path from Crisis to Rapid Growth.* Cambridge, MA: MIT Press.

Hort, S.E.O., 2003. Back on Track – To the Future? The Making and Remaking of the Swedish Welfare State in the 1990s, in *Changing Patterns of Social Protection.* International Social Security Series vol. 9, edited by N. Gilbert and R.A. Van Voorhis. London: Transaction Publishers, pp. 239–76.

Hort, S.E.O., 2005. After Equality? Normative Innovations from Lindbeck to Svegfors. Towards a Dynamic Conservatism?, in *Normative Foundations of the Welfare State: The Nordic experience,* edited by N. Kildal and S. Kuhnle. London: Routledge, pp. 149–68.

HS [Helsingin Sanomat], (Anon.), 2010. *Kela pompottaa byrokratialla työtöntä yrittäjäpoikaani* [The National Social Insurance Institution Bosses around my Unemployed Entrepreneur Son]. Letter to the Editor, 8 April.

Huber, E. and Stephens, J.D., 2001. *Development and Crisis of the Welfare State. Parties and Policies in Global Markets.* Chicago: University of Chicago Press.

Husserl, E. 1931. *Ideas. General Introduction to Pure Phenomenology.* London: Allen & Unwin.

Hvinden, B., Heikkilä, M. and Kankare, I. 2001. Towards Activation? The Changing Relationship between Social Protection and Employment in Western Europe, in *Nordic Welfare States in the European Context,* edited by M. Kautto, J. Fritzell, B. Hvinden et al. London: Routledge, pp. 137–60.

Hvinden, B. and Johansson, H. eds, 2007. *Citizenship in Nordic Welfare States. Dynamics of Choice, Duties and Participation in a Changing Europe.* London: Routledge.

Isacson, M. and Morell, M., 2006. Jordbruk i industri- och välfärdssamhälle [Agriculture in Industrial and Welfare Society], in *Sverige. En social och ekonomisk historia* [Sweden. A Social and Economic history], edited by S. Hedenborg and M. Morell. Lund: Studentlitteratur, pp. 197–230.

Isling, Å., 1980. *Kampen för och mot en demokratisk skola. 1. Samhällsstruktur och skolorganisation* [The Struggle For and Against a Democratic School. 1. Social Structure and School Organisation]. Stockholm: Sober förlags AB.

Isosaari, J., 1973. *Suomen koululaitoksen rakenne ja kehitys* [The Structure and Development of the Finnish Education System]. Helsinki: Otava.

Iversen, M.J. and Andersen, S., 2008. Co-operative Liberalism. Denmark from 1857 to 2007, in *Creating Nordic Capitalism. The Business History of a Competitive Periphery,* edited by S. Fellman, M.J. Iversen, H. Sjögren and L. Thue. Basingstoke: Palgrave/Macmillan, pp. 265–334.

Iversen, T., 2005. *Capitalism, Democracy and Welfare.* Cambridge: Cambridge University Press.

Jensen, P.H., 2008. Public Expenditures. Is the welfare state manageable? in *Crisis, Miracles, and Beyond. Negotiated Adaptation of the Danish Welfare State,* edited by E. Albæk, L.C. Eliason, A.S. Nørgaard and H.M. Schwarz. Aarhus: Aarhus University Press, pp. 115–45.

Jessop, B., 2002. *The Future of the Capitalist State.* Cambridge: Cambridge University Press.

Joas, H., 1996. *The Creativity of Action.* Cambridge: Polity Press.

Johansen, H., 1979. *Dansk social historie 4. En Samfundsorganisation i opbrud 1700–1870* [Danish Social history vol. 4. A Societal Organisation in Transformation 1700–1870]. Copenhagen: Gyldendal.

Johansson, H., 2001. Activation Policies in the Nordic Countries. Social Democratic Universalism Under Pressure. *Journal of European Area Studies,* 9(1), pp. 63–77.

Jønsson, H.V., Onasch, E., Pellander, S. and Wickström, M. eds, 2013. *Migrations and Welfare States. Policies, Discourses and Institutions.* Nordic Centre of Excellence NordWel Studies in Historical Welfare State Research 3. Helsinki: NordWel.

Julkunen, R., 2001. *Suunnanmuutos. 1990–luvun sosiaalipoliittinen reformi Suomessa* [Change of Direction. The Finnish Social Policy Reform of the 1990s]. Tampere: Vastapaino.

Julkunen, R., 2008. *Uuden työn paradoksit. Keskusteluja 2000–luvun työprosess(e) ista* [The Paradoxes of New Work. Discussions on 21st Century Work Processes].Tampere: Vastapaino.

Julkunen, R., 2009. Perustulo [Basic Income], in *Ajatuksen voima. Ideat hyvinvointivaltion uudistamisessa* [The Power of Thought. Ideas and Welfare State Change], edited by J. Kananen and J. Saari. Jyväskylä: Minerva.

Jutikkala, E., 1958. *Suomen talonpojan historia.* Helsinki: Suomen kirjallisuuden seura.

Jutikkala, E., 1965. *Pohjoismaisen yhteiskunnan historiallisia juuria* [Historical Roots of Nordic Society]. Porvoo: WSOY.

Jutikkala, E., 1982. Omavaraiseen maatalouteen [Towards Self-sustaining Agriculture], in *Suomen taloushistoria vol. 2* [The Economic History of Finland], edited by J. Ahvenainen, E. Pihkala and V. Rasila. Helsinki: Tammi, pp. 204–21.

Kallinikos, J., 2006. *The Consequences of Information. Institutional Implications of Technological Changes.* Northampton, MA: Edward Elgar.

Kananen, J., 2008. Kilpailukyky ja tuottavuus 2000–luvun sosiaalipolitiikassa [Competitiveness and Productivity in 21st-Century Social Policy]. *Yhteiskuntapolitiikka,* 73(3), pp. 239–49.

Kananen, J., 2012a. International Ideas versus National Traditions: Nordic Economic and Public Policy as Proposed by the OECD. *Journal of Political Power,* 5(3), pp. 455–73.

Kananen, J., 2012b. Nordic Paths from Welfare to Workfare: Danish, Swedish and Finnish Labour Market Reforms in Comparison. *Local Economy,* 27(5–6), pp. 558–7.

Kananen, P., 1985. *Asunnottoman yksinäisen miehen asumisen ja avuntarpeen ongelma. Päihdehuollon tukiasumisprojektin loppuraportti* [The Problem of the Lone Homeless Man. Final Report of the Housing Support Project for Substance Abusers]. Helsinki: Sosiaalihallitus.

Kangas, O., 1988. *Politik och ekonomi i pensionsförsäkringen. Det finska pensionssystemet i ett jämförande perspektiv* [Politics and Economics of Old Age Insurance. The Finnish Pension System in Comparative Perspective]. Stockholm: Institutet för socialforskning.

Kangas, O. and Palme, J. eds, 2005. *Social Policy and Economic Development in the Nordic Countries*. London/Basingstoke: Palgrave/Macmillan.

Kangas, R., 2006. *Yhteiskunta* [Society]. Helsinki: Tutkijaliitto.

Kantola, A., 2002. *Markkinakuri ja managerivalta. Poliittinen hallinta Suomen 1990–luvun talouskriisissä* [Market Discipline and Managerial Power. Political Governance During the Finnish Economic Crisis of the 1990s]. Helsinki: Loki-kirjat.

Kantola, A. and Kananen, J. 2013. Seize the Moment. Financial Crisis and the Making of the Finnish Competition State. *New Political Economy*, DOI:10.10 80/13563467.2012.753044.

Karisto, A., Haapola, I. and Takala, P., 1998. *Matkalla nykyaikaan. Elintason, elämäntavan ja sosiaalipolitiikan muutos Suomessa* [On the Way towards the Present. Changing Living Standards, Lifestyles and Social Policy in Finland]. Juva: WSOY.

Kaspersen, L.B., 2005. The Origin, Development, Consolidation and Transformation of the Danish Welfare State, in *Normative Foundations of the Welfare State. The Nordic Experience*, edited by N. Kildal and S. Kuhnle. London: Routledge, pp. 52–72.

Kautto, M., 2000. *Two of a Kind? Economic Crisis, Policy Responses and Welfare during the 1990s in Sweden and Finland*. (SOU 2000: 83) Stockholm: Regeringskansliet.

Kautto, M., Fritzell, J., Hvinden, B., et al. eds, 2001. *Nordic Welfare States in the European Context*. London: Routledge.

Kekkonen, U., 1952. *Onko maallamme malttia vaurastua?* [Does our Country Have the Patience to Prosper?]. Helsinki: Otava.

Keskitalo, E., 2007. Individualising Welfare Provision. The Integrated Approach of the Finnish Activation Reform, in *Citizenship in Nordic Welfare States. Dynamics of Choice, Duties Participation in a Changing Europe*, edited by B. Hvinden and H. Johansson. London: Routledge, pp. 67–79.

Keskitalo, E., 2008. *Balancing Social Citizenship and New Paternalism. Finnish Activation Policy and Street-level Practice in a Comparative Perspective*. STAKES Research Report 177. Helsinki: STAKES.

Kettunen, P., 2003. Yhteiskunta [Society], in *Käsitteet liikkeessä* [Concepts in Motion], edited by M. Hyvärinen, J. Kurunmäki, K. Palonen, et al. Tampere: Vastapaino, pp. 167–212.

Kettunen, P., 2004. The Notion of Nordic Model as a Framework for Comparative Knowledge, in *Research on the Study of the Nordic Welfare State*, edited by

J. Marjanen, H. Stenius and J. Vauhkonen. Renvall Institute Publications 16. Helsinki: University of Helsinki, pp. 125–39.

Kettunen, P., 2006. The Power of International Comparison. A Perspective on the Making and Challenging of the Nordic Welfare State, in *The Nordic Model of Welfare. A Historical Reappraisal*, edited by N.F. Christiansen, K. Petersen, N. Edling and P. Haave. Copenhagen: Museum Tusculanum Press, pp. 31–66.

Kettunen, P., 2008. *Globalisaatio ja kansallinen me* [Globalisation and the National us]. Tampere: Vastapaino.

Kettunen, P., 2011. The Transnational Construction of National Challenges: The Ambiguous Nordic Model of Welfare and Competitiveness, in *Beyond Welfare State Models: Transnational Historical Perspectives on Social Policy*, edited by P. Kettunen and K. Petersen. Cheltenham: Edward Elgar, pp. 16–40.

Kettunen, P. and Petersen, K. eds, 2011. *Beyond Welfare State Models: Transnational Historical Perspectives on Social Policy*. Cheltenham: Edward Elgar.

Kildal, N. and Kuhnle, S. eds, 2005. *Normative Foundations of the Welfare State. The Nordic Experience*. London: Routledge.

Knudsen, T. and Rothstein, B., 1994. State Building in Scandinavia. *Comparative Politics*, 26(2), pp. 203–20.

Kolstrup, S., 2010. Fattiglovgivningen fra 1803 til 1891 [Poverty Law from 1803 until 1891], in *Dansk velfærdhistorie. Frem mod socialhjælpsstaten. Bind I Perioden 1536–1898* [Danish Welfare History. Towards a Social Assistance State. Vol. I Period 1536–1898], edited by J.H. Petersen, K. Petersen and N.F. Christiansen. Odense: Syddansk universitetsforlag, pp. 159–98.

Korpi, W., 1981. *Den demokratiska klasskampen. Svensk politik i jämförande perspektiv* [The Democratic Class Struggle. Swedish Policy in a Comparative Perspective]. Stockholm: Tidens Förlag.

Korpi, W., 1992. *Halkar Sverige efter. Sveriges ekonomiska tillväxt 1820–1990 i jämförande belysning* [Is Sweden Lagging Behind. A Comparative Study of Swedish Economic Growth 1820–1990. Stockholm: Carlssons.

Korpi, W. and Palme, J., 1998. The Paradox of Redistribution and Strategies of Equality. Welfare State Institutions, Inequality and Poverty in Western Countries. *American Sociological Review*, 63(5), pp. 661–87.

Kosonen, P., 1998. *Pohjoismaiset mallit murroksessa* [Nordic Models in Transition]. Tampere: Vastapaino.

Kröger, T., 1997. *Hyvinvointikunnan aika. Kunta hyvinvointivaltion sosiaalipalvelujen rakentajana* [The Era of the Welfare Municipality. The Municipality as the Developer of Social Services]. Tampere: Acta Universitatis Tamperensis 561.

Kruchov, C., 1985. Socialdemokratiet og folkeskolen [Social Democracy and the Folk School], in *Bidrag til den danske skoles historie 1898–1984, vol. 4* [Contributions to Danish School History, 1898–1984, vol. 4], edited by C. Kruchov, K. Larsen and G. Persson. Copenhagen: Unge paedagoger, pp. 127–59.

Krugman, P. 2013. *End This Depression Now!* New York: W.W. Norton & Company.

Kuhn, T. 1966. *The Structure of Scientific Revolutions*. Chicago: Chicago University Press.

Kuhnle, S. ed., 2000. *Survival of the European Welfare State*. London: Routledge.

Kuhnle, S. and Alestalo, M., 2000. Introduction. Growth, Adjustment and Survival of European Welfare States, in *Survival of the European Welfare State*, edited by S. Kuhnle. London: Routledge, pp. 3–18.

Kuhnle, S. and Sander, A., 2010. The Emergence of the Western Welfare State, in *The Oxford Handbook of the Welfare State*, edited by F.G. Castles, S. Leibfried, J. Lewis, H. Obinger and C. Pierson. Oxford: Oxford University Press, pp. 61–80.

Kuikka, M.T., 1992. *Suomalaisen koulutuksen vaiheet* [The Phases in Finnish Education]. Helsinki: Otava.

Kurunmäki, J., 2000. *Representation, Nation and Time. The Political Rhetoric of the 1866 Parliamentary Reform in Sweden*. Jyväskylä: University of Jyväskylä.

Kuusela, J., 2007. *Vaikuttavuutta, tuottavuutta vai molempia* [Efficiency, Productivity or Both]. Sosiaali- ja tervesysministeriön hallinnonalan tuottavuusohjelmatyöryhmän loppuraportti (Sosiaali- ja terveysministeriön selvityksiä 2007: 67). Helsinki: Ministry of Social Affairs and Health.

Kuusi, P., 1964. *Social Policy for the Sixties. A Plan for Finland*. Helsinki: Finnish Social Policy Association.

Kvist, J., 2003. Scandinavian Activation Strategies in the 1990s. Recasting Social Citizenship and the Scandinavian Welfare Model. *Revue Francaise des Affaires Sociales*, 13(4), pp. 223–49.

Kvist, J. and Greve, B., 2011. Has the Nordic Welfare Model been Transformed? *Social Policy and Administration*, 45(2), pp. 146–60.

Kvist, J. and Pedersen, L., 2007. Danish Activation Policies. *National Institute Economic Review*, (202), pp. 99–112.

Larsen, C.A. and Andersen, J.G., 2009. How Economic Ideas Changed the Danish Welfare State: The Case of Neo-liberal Ideas and Highly Organised Social Democratic Interests. *Governance*, 22(2), pp. 239–61.

Larsen, J., 1984 [1899]. *Bidrag til den danske Folkskoles Historie 1536–1784* [Contributions to a History of the Danish Folk School 1536–1784]. Copenhagen: Det Schuhbetheske forlag.

Layard, R., Nickell, S. and Jackman, R., 1991. *Unemployment. Macroecomic Performance and the Labour Market*. Oxford: Oxford University Press.

Lehto, M., 2006. *Pelastusrenkaan paikkaus* [Fixing the Life Ring]. Helsinki: Kunnallisalan kehittämissäätiö. Polemia-sarja nro. 62.

Lijphart, A., 1999. *Patterns of Democracy. Government Forms and Performance in Thirty-Six Countries*. Yale: Yale University Press.

Lindbeck, A., Molander, P., Persson, T., Petersson, O., Sandmo, A., Swedenborg, B. and Thygesen, N., 1994. *Turning Sweden Around*. Cambridge, Massachusetts: The MIT Press.

Lindberg, I. 1999. Välfärdens idéer. Globaliseringen, elitismen och välfärdsstatens framtid [The Ideas of Welfare. Globalisation, Elitism and the Future of the Welfare State]. Stockholm: Atlas.

Lødemel, I., 2001. Discussion. Workfare in the welfare state, in *'An Offer You Can't Refuse'. Workfare in International Perspective*, edited by I. Lødemel and H. Trickey. Bristol: Policy Press, pp. 295–344.

Lødemel, I. and Trickey, H. eds, 2001. *'An Offer You Can't Refuse'. Workfare in International Perspective*. Bristol: Policy Press.

Magnusson, L. 2000. *An Economic History of Sweden*. London: Routledge.

Mahoney, J. and Rueschemeyer, D. eds, 2003. *Comparative Historical Analysis in the Social Sciences*. Cambridge: Cambridge University Press.

Marshall, T.H., 1950. *Citizenship and Social Class, and other Essays*. Cambridge: Cambridge University Press.

Marx, K., 1986. *Karl Marx. A Reader*. Edited by Jon Elster. Cambridge: Cambridge University Press.

Mathiesen, A., 2000. *Nyliberalismen. Og de 'staerke' ledere* [Neo-Liberalism. And the 'Strong' Leaders] (Research Papers from the Department of Social Sciences, no. 3/00). Roskilde: Roskilde University.

McNamara, K.R., 1998. *The Currency of Ideas. Monetary Policy in the European Union*. Ithaca: Cornell University Press.

Meadows, D.H., Meadows, D.L., Randers, J., and Behrens III, William W., 1972. *Limits to Growth*. London: Earth Island Ltd.

Meinander, H., 2006. *Finlands historia* [The History of Finland]. Porvoo: Söderströms/Atlantis.

Miller, P. and Rose, N., 2008. *Governing the Present. Administering Economic, Social and Personal Life*. Oxford: Polity Press.

Milton, P., 1998. *Uppsalamodellen och socialbidragstagarna* [The Uppsala Model and Social Assistance Claimants]. Stockholm: Socialstyrelsen.

Morell, M., 2001. *Det svenska jordbrukets historia. Jordbruket i industrisamhället 1870–1945*. [The History of Swedish Agriculture. Agriculture in Industrial Society 1870–1945.] Borås: Natur och Kultur/Lts förlag.

Mouritzen, P.E., 2008. Danish Local Government, in *Crisis, Miracles, and Beyond. Negotiated Adaptation of the Danish Welfare State*, edited by E. Albæk, L.C. Eliason, A.S. Nørgaard, and H.M. Schwarz. Aarhus: Aaruhus University Press, pp. 201–26.

Muuri, A. and Mandelbacka, K., 2010. Hyvinvointivaltion kannatusperusta [Public Support of the Welfare State], in *Suomalaisten hyvinvointi 2010* [The Welfare of the Finns 2010], edited by M. Vaarama, P. Moisio, and S. Karvonen. Helsinki: Institute for Health and Welfare, pp. 96–111.

Mylly, J., 2006. *Suomen eduskunta 100 vuotta vol. 1. Edustuksellisen kansanvallan läpimurto* [The Parliament of Finland 100 years vol. 1. The Breakthrough of Popular Democracy]. Helsinki: Edita.

Myrdal, A. and Myrdal, G., 1934. *Kris i befolkningsfrågan* [Crisis in the Population Question]. Stockholm: Bonniers.

Myrdal, G., 1973. *Against the Stream. Critical Essays in Economics.* New York: Pantheon Books.

Nannestad, P. and Green-Pedersen, C., 2008. Keeping the Bumblebee Flying. Economic Policy in the Welfare State of Denmark, 1973–1999, in *Crisis, Miracles, and Beyond. Negotiated Adaptation of the Danish Welfare State,* edited by E. Albæk, L.C. Eliason, A.S. Nørgaard and H.M. Schwarz. Aarhus: Aaruhus University Press, pp. 33–74.

Nickell, S., 2001. Has the UK Labour Market Changed? *Bank of England Quarterly Bulletin* (41), pp. 340–51.

Nordström, M., 1987. *Pojkskola, flickskola, samskola. Samundervisningens utveckling i Sverige 1866–1962* [Boys' School, Girls' School, Joint School. The Development of Joint Education in Sweden 1866–1962]. Lund: Lund University Press.

Nussbaum, M., 2000. *Women and Development.* Cambridge: Cambridge University Press.

Nygård, M., 2006. Welfare-Ideological Change in Scandinavia. A Comparative Analysis of Partisan Welfare-Policy Positions in Four Nordic Countries 1970–2003. *Scandinavian Political Studies,* 29(4), pp. 356–85.

Offe, C., Mückenberger, U. and Ostner, I., 1996. A Basic Income Guaranteed by the State. A Need of the Moment in Social Policy, in *Modernity and the State,* edited by C. Offe. Cambridge: Polity Press, pp. 201–21.

Oorschot, W. van and Abrahamson, P., 2003. The Dutch and Danish Miracles Revisited. A Critical Discussion of Activation Policies in Two Small Welfare States. *Social Policy and Administration,* 37(3), pp. 288–304.

Østerud, Ø., 1978. *Agrarian Structure and Peasant Politics in Scandinavia. A Comparative Study of Rural Response to Economic Change.* Oslo: Universitetsforlaget.

Ostergard, U., 1992. Peasants and Danes. The Danish National Identity and Political Culture. *Comparative Studies in Society and History,* 34(1), pp. 3–27.

Pallesen, T. and Pedersen, L.D., 2008. Health Care in Denmark. Adapting to Cost Containment in the 1980s and Expenditure Expansion in the 1990s, in *Crisis, Miracles, and Beyond. Negotiated Adaptation of the Danish Welfare State,* edited by E. Albæk, L.C. Eliason, A.S. Nørgaard and H.M. Schwarz. Aarhus: Aaruhus University Press, pp. 227–50.

Palola, E., Hannikainen-Ingman, K. and Karjalainen, V., 2012. *Nuoret koulutuspudokkaat sosiaalityön asiakkaina. Tapaustutkimus Helsingistä* [Young School Drop-outs as Clients of Social Work. A Case Study of Helsinki]. Helsinki: Terveyden ja hyvinvoinnin laitos.

Parijs, P. Van, 1995. *Real Freedom for All. What (if anything) Can Justify Capitalism?* Oxford: Oxford University Press.

Pekkarinen, J. and Vartiainen, J., 1993. *Suomen talouspolitiikan pitkä linja* [Finnish Economic Policy in the Long Term]. Porvoo: WSOY.

Pesonen, P and Riihinen, O., 2002. *Dynamic Finland. The Political System and the Welfare State.* Studia Fennica, Historica 3. Helsinki: Finnish Literature Society.

Petersen, J.H.,1995. En undersøgelse af nationens velstand [An Inquiry into the Nation's Welfare]. *Nationaløkonomisk Tidskrift*, 133(1), pp. 196–205.

Petersen, J.H. and Petersen, K. eds, 2005. *13 reformer af den danske velfærdsstat* [13 Reforms of the Danish Welfare State]. Odense: Syddansk universitetsforlag.

Petersen, J.H. and Petersen, K., 2010. Indledning [Introduction] in *Dansk velfærdshistorie. Frem mod socialhjælpsstaten. Bind I Perioden 1536–1898* [Danish Welfare History. Towards a Social Assistance State. Vol. I Period 1536–1898], edited by J.H. Petersen, K. Petersen and N.F. Christiansen. Odense: Syddansk universitetsforlag, pp. 9–36.

Petersen, J.H., Petersen, K., and Christiansen, N.F. eds, 2010. *Dansk velfærdshistorie. Frem mod socialhjælpsstaten. Bind I Perioden 1536–1898* [Danish Welfare History. Towards a Social Assistance State. Vol. I Period 1536–1898]. Odense: Syddansk universitetsforlag.

Petersen, K., 2011. National, Nordic and trans-Nordic. Transnational Perspectives on the History of the Nordic Welfare States, in *Beyond Welfare State Models: Transnational Historical Perspectives on Social Policy*, edited by P. Kettunen and K. Petersen. Cheltenham: Edward Elgar, pp. 41–64.

Petersen, K. and Åmark, K., 2006. Old Age Pensions in the Nordic Countries, 1880–2000, in *The Nordic Model of Welfare. A Historical Reappraisal*, edited by N.F. Christiansen, K. Petersen, N. Edling, and P. Haave. Copenhagen: Museum of Tusculanum Press, pp. 145–88.

Phelps, E.S., 1967. Money–Wage Dynamics and Labour Market Equilibrium. *The Journal of Political Economy*, 76(4), pp. 678–711.

Pierson, C., 2004. *Late Industrializers and the Development of the Welfare State*. (Social policy and development programme paper number 16) Geneva: United Nations Research Institute for Social Development (UNRISD).

Pierson, C., 2006. *Beyond the Welfare State. The New Political Economy of Welfare*. Cambridge: Polity Press.

Pierson, P. ed., 2001. *The New Politics of the Welfare State*. Oxford: Oxford University Press.

Pitkänen, K., 1982. Väestönkehitys [Demographic development], in *Suomen taloushistoria vol. 2* [The Economic History of Finland], edited by J. Ahvenainen, E. Pihkala and V. Rasila. Helsinki: Tammi.

Pohjola, M., 1996. *Tehoton pääoma* [Inefficient Capital]. Porvoo: WSOY.

Pohjola, M., 2007. *Työn tuottavuuden kehitys ja siihen vaikuttavat tekijät* [Work Productivity and the Factors Affecting it]. Expert Report Commissioned by the Ministry of Finance 5 March 2007. [online] Available at: http://www.vm.fi/vm/fi/04_julkaisut_ja_asiakirjat/03_muut_asiakirjat/20070315Tyoentu/name.jsp [Accessed 26 April 2013].

Polanyi, K., 1944. *The Great Transformation*. Boston: Gower Beacon Press.

Rabinow, P. ed., 1984. *The Foucault Reader*. New York: Pantheon Books.

Rahkonen, K., 1984. Hakusanoja työstä [Key Words on Work]. *Tiede ja edistys*, 1(84), pp. 16–23.

Rahkonen, K., 2000. Mitä on tapahtumassa sosiaalipolitiikassa ja hyvinvointivaltiolle? Kolmannen tien sosiaalipolitiikasta [What is Happening to Social Policy and the Welfare State? On Third Way Social Policy], in *Sosiaalipolitiikan lukemisto* [A Social Policy Reader], edited by E. Nurminen. Helsinki: Avoin yliopisto, pp. 65–88.

Rainio-Niemi, J., 2009. Yhdistys Heikki Wariksen kaudella 1949–1963 [The Association during the Term of Heikki Waris], in *Työväensuojelusta sosiaalipolitiikkaan. Sosiaalipoliittinen yhdistys 1908–2008* [From Workers' Protection to Social Policy. The Social Policy Association between 1908–2008], edited by R. Jaakkola, S. Kainulainen and K. Rahkonen. Helsinki: Edita, pp. 75–96.

Rasila, V., 1982a. Liberalismin aika [The Era of Liberalism], in *Suomen taloushistoria vol. 2* [The Economic History of Finland], edited by J. Ahvenainen, E. Pihkala, and V. Rasila. Helsinki: Tammi, pp. 13–26.

Rasila, V., 1982b. Väestönkehitys ja sosiaaliset ongelmat [Demographic Development and Social Problems], in *Suomen taloushistoria vol. 2* [The Economic History of Finland], edited by J. Ahvenainen, E. Pihkala and V. Rasila. Helsinki: Tammi, pp. 132–53.

Rasmussen, J., Dickmann, J.S.P., Bjørn, C. and Christensen, J., 1988. 1860–1914, in *Det danske landbrugs historie vol. 3*, edited by C. Bjørn, T. Dahlerup, S.P. Jensen, and E.H. Pedersen. Odense: Landbohistorisk Selskab, pp. 193–431.

Regnér, H., 2000. Ändrade förutsättningar för arbetsmarknadspolitiken? [Changed Preconditions for Labour Market Policy?], in SOU 2000:37. *Välfärdens förutsättningar* [The Conditions of Welfare]. Stockholm: Regeringskansliet.

Rehn, G., 1952. The Problem of Stability. An Analysis and some Policy Proposals, in *Wages Policy under Full Employment*, edited by R. Turvey. London: William Hodge, pp. 30–54.

Richardson, G., 2004. *Svensk utbildningshistoria. Skola och samhälle förr och nu* [Swedish Educational History. School and Society in the Past and the Present]. Lund: Studentlitteratur.

Rokkan, S. and Urwin, D., 1983. *Economy, Territory, Identity. Politics of West European Peripheries*. London: Sage.

Rothstein, B., 1986. *Den socialdemokratiska staten. Reformer och förvaltning inom svensk arbetsmarknads- och skolpolitik* [The Social Democratic State. Reforms and Administration in Swedish Labour Market and Education Policy]. Lund: Studentlitteratur.

Rothstein, B., 1992. *Den korporativa staten. Intresseorganisationer och statsförvaltning i svensk politik* [The Corporatist State. Interest Organisations and State Administration in Swedish Politics]. Stockholm: Norstedts.

Rothstein, B., 2000. The Future of the Universal Welfare State. An Institutional Approach, in *Survival of the European Welfare State*, edited by S. Kuhnle. London: Routledge, pp. 217–33.

Rueda, D., 2007. *Social Democracy Inside Out. Partisanship and Labor Market Policy in Industrialized Democracies*. Oxford: Oxford University Press.

Saarenheimo, J., 2003. Isojako [The Enclosure of Common Fields], in *Suomen maatalouden historia vol. 1. Perinteisen maatalouden aika esihistoriasta 1870–luvulle* [The History of Finnish Agriculture vol. 1. The Era of Traditional Agriculture until the 1870s], edited by V. Rasila, E. Jutikkala and A. Mäkelä-Alitalo. Helsinki: Suomalaisen kirjallisuuden seura, pp. 349–64.

Saari, J., 2006. Sosiaalipolitiikka [Social Policy], in *Suomen malli. Murroksesta menestykseen?* [The Finnish Model. From Transformation to Success?], edited by J. Saari. Helsinki: Helsinki University Press, pp. 227–61.

Sabatier, P.A., 1998. The Advocacy Coalition Framework. Revisions and Relevance for Europe. *Journal of European Public Policy*, 5(1), pp. 98–130.

Salminen, J., 2003. Yksityinen oppikoulu kansalaisyhteiskunnan hankkeena [The Private Secondary School as a Project of Civil Society], in *Koulu ja kansalaisyhteiskunta historiallisessa perspektiivissä* [School and Civil Society in a Historical Perspective], edited by J. Rantala. Helsinki: Hakapaino, pp. 78–93.

Salonen-Soulié, U., 2003. Tanskalainen kannustavuus suomalaisin silmin [Danish Activation through Finnish Eyes], in *Kannustavan sosiaaliturvan haaste* [The Challenge of Incentivizing Social Security], edited by P. Kananen and U. Salonen-Soulié. Reports of the Ministry of Social Affairs and Health, 2003:5. Helsinki: Ministry of Social Affairs and Health, pp. 75–84.

Scharpf, F.W. and Schmidt, V., 2000. Introduction, in *Welfare and Work in the Open Economy. From Vulnerability to Competitiveness*, edited by F.W. Scharpf and V.A. Schmidt. Oxford: Oxford University Press, pp. 1–20.

Schmidt, V., 2002. *The Futures of European Capitalism*. Oxford: Oxford University Press.

Sejersted, F., 2005. *Socialdemokratins tidsålder. Sverige och Norge under 1900–talet* [The Era of Social Democracy. Sweden and Norway during the 20th Century]. Nora: Nya Doxa.

Sen, A., 1999. *Development as Freedom*. Oxford: Oxford University Press.

Sennett, R., 2006. *The Culture of the New Capitalism*. Cambridge: Polity Press.

Sihto, M., 1994. *Aktiivinen työvoimapolitiikka. Kehitys Rehnin–Meidnerin mallista OECD: n strategiaksi* [Active Labour Market Policy. The Development from the Rehn–Meidner Model to the OECD's Strategy]. Tampere: Tampere University Press.

Siipi, J., 1967. *Ryysyrannasta hyvinvointivaltioon* [From a 'Ragshore' to a Welfare State]. Helsinki: Tammi.

Sinko, P. and Vihriälä, V., 2005. Palvelusektorin koko, tuottavuus ja kilpailu. Johdatus aiheeseen ja keskeiset päätelmät [The Size of the Service Sector, its Productivity and Competitiveness. Introduction to the Subject and Central Conclusions], in *Palvelualojen kehitys, tuottavuus ja kilpailu*. Helsinki: Valtioneuvoston kanslia 11/2005.

Sjöberg, O., 2011. Sweden. Ambivalent Adjustment, in *Regulating the Risk of Unemployment. National Adaptations to Post-Industrial Labour Markets in*

Europe, edited by J. Clasen and D. Clegg. Oxford: Oxford University Press, pp. 208–31.

Sjögren, H., 2008. Welfare Capitalism: The Swedish Economy, 1850–2005, in *Creating Nordic Capitalism. The Business History of a Competitive Periphery*, edited by S. Fellman, Susanna, M.J. Iversen, H. Sjögren and L. Thue. Basingstoke: Palgrave/Macmillan, pp. 22–74.

Sjöstrand, W., 1965. *Pedagogikens historia III:2. Utvecklingen in Sverige under tiden 1805–1920* [The History of Pedagogy III:2. The Development in Sweden during the Period 1805–1920]. Lund: Gleerups.

Slater, G., 1907. *The English Peasantry and the Enclosure of Common Fields*. London: Archibald Constable & Co. Ltd.

Soininen, A.M., 1982. Maa- ja metsätalous [Agriculture and Forestry], in *Suomen taloushistoria vol. 2* [The History of the Finnish Economy], edited by J. Ahvenainen, E. Pihkala and V. Rasila. Helsinki: Tammi, pp. 27–51.

Stenius, H., 1980. The Breakthrough of the Principle of Mass Organization in Finland. *Scandinavian Journal of History*, 5(2), pp. 197–217.

Stenius, H., 2010. Nordic Associational Life in European and Inter-Nordic Perspective, in *Nordic Associations in a European Perspective*, edited by R. Alapuro and H. Stenius. Baden-Baden: Nomos, pp. 29–88.

Stenius, H., Österberg, M. and Östling, J. eds, 2011. *Nordic Narratives of the Second World War. National Historiographies Revisited*. Lund: Nordic Academic Press.

Stephens, W.B., 1998. *Education in Britain 1750–1914*. London: Macmillan.

Stiglitz, J., 2010. *The Stiglitz Report. Reforming the International Monetary and Financial Systems in the Wake of the Global Crisis*. New York: The New Press.

Stråth, B., 2005. *Union och demokrati. De förenade riken Sverige och Norge 1814–1905* [Union and Democracy. The Unified Kingdoms of Sweden and Norway 1814–1905]. Nora: Nya Doxa.

Svallfors, S. ed., 2012. *Contested Welfare States. Welfare Attitudes in Europe and Beyond*. Stanford: Stanford University Press.

Swank, D., 2002. *Global Capital, Political Institutions and Policy Change in Developed Welfare States*. Cambridge: Cambridge University Press.

Taylor, C., 1975. *Hegel*. Cambridge: Cambridge University Press.

Taylor, C., 1989. *Sources of the Self. The Making of the Modern Identity*. Cambridge: Harvard University Press.

Taylor-Gooby, P. ed., 2004. *New Risks, New Welfare. The Transformation of the European Welfare State*. Oxford: Oxford University Press.

Taylor-Gooby, P. ed., 2005. *Ideas and Welfare State Reform in Western Europe*. London: Palgrave/Macmillan.

Temmes, M., 1998. Finland and New Public Management. *International Review of Administrative Sciences*, 64(3), pp. 441–56.

Therborn, G., 2004. *Between Sex and Power. Family in the World 1900–2000*. London: Routledge.

Thompson, F.M.L., 1966. The Social Distribution of Landed Property in England since the Sixteenth Century. *The Economic History Review*, 19(3), pp. 505–17.

Timonen, V., 2003. *Restructuring the Welfare State. Globalization and Social Policy Reform in Finland and Sweden*. Cheltenham: Edward Elgar.

Torfing, J., 1999. Workfare with Welfare. Recent Reforms of the Danish Welfare State. *Journal of European Social Policy*, 9(1), pp. 5–28.

Touraine, A., 2002. *Kan vi leva tillsammans? Jämlika och olika* [Can We Live Together? Equal and Different]. Gothenburg: Daidalos.

Tuomaala, S., 2004. *Työtätekevistä käsistä puhtaiksi ja kirjoittaviksi. Suomalaisen oppivelvollisuuskoulun ja maalaislasten kohtaaminen 1921–1939* [From Labouring Hands to Clean and Writing Ones. The Encounter of Compulsory Educational Attendance and Rural Children 1921–1939]. Helsinki: Hakapaino.

Turner, M., 1986. *Enclosures in Britain 1750–1830*. London: Macmillan.

Turner, M., 1980. *English Parliamentary Enclosure. Its Historical Geography and Economic History*. Folkestone: Archon Books.

Turner, M.E., Beckett, J.V. and Afton, B., 2001. *Farm Production in England 1700–1914*. Oxford: Oxford University Press.

Virjo, I., Aho, S. and Koponen, H., 2006. *Passivoiko työttömyysturva?* [Does Unemployment Security Passivate?]. Työpoliittinen tutkimus 303. Helsinki: Työministeriö.

Virrankoski, P., 2001. *Suomen historia vol. 2* [The History of Finland vol. 2]. Helsinki: Suomalaisen kirjallisuden seura.

Voipio, T., 2009. Köyhyyden vähentämisen politiikat. Miten ideat muokkaavat globaalia kehityspolitiikkaa? [The Politics of Reducing Poverty. How Do Ideas Shape Global Development Policy?], in *Ajatuksen voima. Ideat hyvinvointivaltion uudistamisessa* [The Power of Thought. Ideas in Welfare State Reform], edited by J. Kananen and J. Saari. Helsinki: Minerva/SoPhi, pp. 237–364.

Wagner, P., 2001. *Theorising Modernity. Inescapability and Attainability in Social Theory*. London: Sage.

Wallace, H. and Wallace, W., 2000. *Policy-Making in the European Union*. Oxford: Oxford University Press.

Weber, M., 1968. *Economy and Society: An Outline of Interpretative Sociology*. Berkeley: University of California Press.

Wilensky, H., 1975. *The Welfare State and Equality. Structural and Ideological Roots of Public Expenditures*. Berkeley: University of California Press.

Wiman, R., 1982. Maalta kaupunkiin [From the Countryside to Cities], in *Suomen taloushistoria vol. 2* [The Economic History of Finland], edited by J. Ahvenainen, E. Pihkala and V. Rasila. Helsinki: Tammi, pp. 494–505.

Wittgenstein, L., 1981. *Philosophical Investigations*. Oxford: Blackwell.

Wray, R.L., 2012. *Modern Money Theory. A Primer on Macroeconomics for Sovereign Monetary Systems*. London: Palgrave Macmillan.

Wright, G.H. von, 1990. *Explanation and Understanding*. Ithaca: Cornell University Press.

Wright, G.H. von, 1993. *Minervan pöllö* [The Owl of Minerva]. Helsinki: Otava.
Zetterberg, H.L. and Ljungberg, C.J., 1997. *Vårt land. Den svenska socialstaten. Slutrapport från ett forskningsprogram* [Our Country. The Swedish Social State. Final Report of a Research Programme]. Stockholm: City University Press.
Zeuthen, H., 2005. Rettighetsreformerne siden 1990'erne [Reform of Rights since the 1990s], in *13 reformer af den danske velfærdsstat* [13 Reforms of the Danish Welfare State], edited by J.H. Petersen and K. Petersen. Odense: Syddansk universitetsforlag, pp. 203–16.

Parliamentary Acts

Act on Active Labour Market Policy [Lov om en aktiv arbejdsmarkedspolitik] 434/1993. [online] Copenhagen: Folketinget. Available at: https://www.retsinformation.dk/Forms/R0710.aspx?id=69342 [Accessed 26 April 2013].

Act on Active Social Policy [Lov om aktiv socialpolitik] 455/1997. [online] Copenhagen: Folketinget. Available at: https://www.retsinformation.dk/Forms/R0710.aspx?id=85036 [Accessed 26 April 2013].

Act on the Government Development Centre [Laki valtion kehittämiskeskuksesta] 110/1987. [online] Helsinki: Eduskunta. Available at: http://www.finlex.fi/fi/laki/alkup/1987/19870110 [Accessed 26 April 2013].

Act on Municipal Activation [Lov om kommunal aktivering] 498/1993. [online] Copenhagen: Folketinget. Available at: https://www.retsinformation.dk/Forms/R0710.aspx?id=53851 [Accessed 26 April 2013].

Act on Rehabilitative Work [Laki kuntouttavasta työtoiminnasta] 189/2001. [online] Helsinki: Eduskunta. Available at: http://www.finlex.fi/fi/laki/ajantasa/2001/20010189 [Accessed 26 April 2013].

Act on Revising the Act on Active Labour Market Policy [Lov om ændring af lov om en aktiv arbejdsmarkedspolitik] 1085/1994. [online] Copenhagen: Folketinget. Available at: https://www.retsinformation.dk/Forms/R0710.aspx?id=69397 [Accessed 26 April 2013].

Act on Revising the Act on Income Support [Laki toimeentulotuesta annetun lain muuttamisesta] 191/2001. [online] Helsinki: Eduskunta. Available at: http://www.finlex.fi/fi/laki/alkup/2001/20010191 [Accessed 26 April 2013].

Constitution of Denmark. [online] Copenhagen: Folketinget. Available at: https://www.retsinformation.dk/Forms/R0710.aspx?id=45902 [Accessed 26 April 2013].

Income Support Act [Laki toimeentulotuesta] 1412/1997. [online] Helsinki: Eduskunta. Available at: http://www.finlex.fi/fi/laki/ajantasa/1997/19971412 [Accessed 26 April 2013].

Revised Act on Active Social Policy [Bekendtgørelse om lov om aktiv socialpolitik] LBK 1009/2005. [online] Copenhagen: Folketinget. Available at: https://www.retsinformation.dk/Forms/R0710.aspx?id=30304 [Accessed 26 April 2013].

Social Services Act [Socialtjänstlagen] 1980: 620. [online] Stockholm: Riksdagen. Available at: http://www.notisum.se/rnp/sls/lag/19800620.HTM [Accessed 26 April 2013].

Social Services Act [Sosiaalihuoltolaki] 710/1982. [online] Helsinki: Eduskunta. Available at: http://www.finlex.fi/fi/laki/ajantasa/1982/19820710 [Accessed 26 April 2013].

State Enterprise Act [Laki valtion liikelaitoksista] 627/1987. [online] Helsinki: Eduskunta. Available at: http://www.finlex.fi/fi/laki/alkup/1987/19870627 [Accessed 26 April 2013].

Government Bills

Government, Denmark, 2005. *Forslag til Lov om ændring af lov om en aktiv beskæftigelseindsats of lov om aktiv socialpolitik* [Government Bill on Reforming the Act on an Active Employment Initiative and the Act on Active Social Policy]. [online] Available at: https://www.retsinformation.dk/Forms/R0710.aspx?id=100682 [Accessed 26 April 2013].

Government, Finland, 1997. *Hallituksen esitys Eduskunnalle laiksi toimeentulotuesta sekä laiksi sosiaalihuoltolain ja –asetuksen eräiden säännösten kumoamisesta* [Government Bill on an Income Support Act and the Overruling of Certain Paragraphs of the Social Services Act]. (HE 217/1997) [online] Available at: http://www.finlex.fi/fi/esitykset/he/1997/19970217 [Accessed 26 April 2013].

Government, Finland, 2000. *Hallituksen esitys Eduskunnalle laiksi kuntouttavasta työtoiminnasta ja eräiksi siihen liittyviksi laeiksi* [Government Bill on an Act on Rehablilitatve Work and Certain Associated Acts]. (HE 184/2000) [online] Available at: http://www.finlex.fi/fi/esitykset/he/2000/20000184 [Accessed 26 April 2013].

Government, Finland, 2009. *Hallituksen esitys eduskunnalle laeiksi kuntouttavasta työtoiminnasta annetun lain 2 ja 10 §:n, työttömyysturvalain 8 luvun 6 §:n ja toimeentulotuesta annetun lain 10 ja 10 a §:n muuttamisesta* [Government Bill on revising the Act on Rehablilitatve Work and Certain Associated Acts]. (HE 194/2009) [online] Available at: http://www.finlex.fi/fi/esitykset/he/2009/20090194 [Accessed 26 April 2013].

Government, Sweden, 1996. *Ändring i socialtjänstlagen* [Reform of the Social Services Act]. (Prop. 1996/97: 124) Stockholm: Regeringskansliet.

Government, Sweden, 1999. *Förnyad arbetsmarknadspolitik för delaktighet och tillväxt* [Renewed Labour Market Policy for Participation and Growth]. (Prop. 1999/2000: 98) Stockholm: Regeringskansliet.

Government, Sweden, 2006. *Ytterligare reformer inom arbetsmarknadspolitiken, m.m.* [Further Reforms in Labour Market Policy, and Other Issues]. (Prop. 2006/07: 89) Stockholm: Regeringskansliet.

Administrative Documents

EU, 2000. Lisbon European Council 23 and 24 March. *Presidency Conclusions*. Brussels: European Parliament.

Eurostat, 2009. *Unemployment rate by gender*. [online] Available at: www.eurostat. ex.europa.eu [Accessed 13 January 2009].

Committee Report on State Enterprises [Valtion liikelaitoskomitean mietintö], 1985. (1985:2) Helsinki: Government Printing Centre.

Folketinget [Parliament of Denmark], 1997. *Besvarelse af spørgsmål nr. 28 fra Folketingets Socialudvalg vedrørende forslag til lov om aktiv socialpolitik* [Reply to Query no. 28 from the Parliamentary Social Committee on Social Affairs regarding the Proposed Act on Active Social Policy]. (L230 – bilag 34) Socialudvalget. [online] Available at: http://webarkiv.ft.dk/?/Samling/19961/udvbilag/SOU/L230_bilag34.htm [Accessed 26 April 2013].

Government Decree, 1995. *Valtioneuvoston päätös toimeentulotuen yleisistä perusteista annetun valtioneuvoston päätöksen muuttamisesta* [Government Decree on Reforming the Government Decree on the General Conditions of Income Support]. (1676/1995) Available at: http://www.finlex.fi/fi/laki/alkup/1995/19951676 [Accessed 26 April 2013].

Government, Sweden, 1999. *Samverkan för färre bidrag och fler i jobb* [Cooperation for Fewer Benefits and More People in Jobs]. (Ds 1999: 54) Stockholm: Regeringskansliet.

Hallinnon hajauttamiskomitea [Committee on Government Decentralisation]. 1986. (1986:12) Helsinki: Government Printing Centre.

Ministry of Employment [Beskæftigelsesministeriet], 2002. *Regeringen. Flere i arbejde* [The Government. More People in Work]. Copenhagen: Ministry of Employment.

Ministry of Finance [Finansministeriet], 1992. *Rapport om arbejdsmarkedets strukturproblemer*. (Vols I–IV) Copenhagen: Ministry of Finance.

Ministry of Labour [Arbejdsministeriet], 2000. *Effekter af aktiveringsindsatsen* [Effects of the Activation Initiative]. Copenhagen: Ministry of Labour.

OECD, 1994a. *Jobs Study. Facts, Analysis, Strategies*. Paris: OECD.

OECD, 1994b. *White Paper on Growth, Competitiveness and Employment*. Paris: OECD.

OECD, 2000. *Regulatory Reform in Denmark*. OECD Reviews of Regulatory Reform. Paris: OECD.

OECD, 2003. *Finland. A New Consensus for Change*. OECD Reviews of Regulatory Reform. Paris: OECD.

OECD, 2006. *Boosting Jobs and Incomes. Policy Lessons from Reassessing the OECD Jobs Strategy*. Paris: OECD.

OECD, 2007a. *Sweden. Achieving Results for Sustained Growth*. OECD Reviews of Regulatory Reform. Paris: OECD.

OECD, 2007b. *Sweden*. OECD Economic Surveys volume 2007/4 – February 2000. Paris: OECD.

OECD, 2008a. *Employment Outlook.* Paris: OECD.

OECD, 2008b. *Denmark.* OECD Economic Surveys volume 2008/2 – February 2008. Paris: OECD.

OECD, 2008c. *Finland.* OECD Economic Surveys volume 2008/6 – June 2008. Paris: OECD.

OECD, 2009a. *Education at Glance 2009.* OECD Indicators. Paris: OECD.

OECD, 2009b. *Denmark.* OECD Economic Surveys volume 2009/19. Paris: OECD.

OECD, 2010a. *Education at Glance 2010.* OECD Indicators. Paris: OECD.

OECD, 2010b. *PISA 2009 Results. Executive Summary.* Paris: OECD.

OECD, 2010c. *Finland.* OECD Economic Surveys volume 2010/4. Paris: OECD.

OECD, 2011. *Sweden.* OECD Economic Surveys. Paris: OECD.

PeVL, 1997. *Statement by Constitutional Committee of the Parliament on Government Bill on an Income Support Act and the Overruling of Certain Paragraphs of the Social Services Act* [Perustuslakivaliokunnan lausunto 31, Hallituksen esitys laiksi toimeentulotuesta sekä laiksi sosiaalihuoltolain ja –asetuksen eräiden säännösten kumoamisesta]. (31/1997) Available at: http://www.eduskunta.fi/valtiopaivaasiat/he+217/1997 [Accessed 26 April 2013].

Socialkommissionen, 1993. *Reformer. Socialkommissionens samlede forslag* [Reforms. The Complete Proposals of the Social Commission]. Copenhagen: Socialkommissionen.

Statskontoret, 1999. *Staten i omvandling 1999* [The State in Transition 1999]. Statskontorets publikationer. (1999:15) Stockholm: Statskontoret.

Statskontoret, 2000. *Staten i omvandling 2000* [The State in Transition 2000]. Statskontorets publikationer. (2000:15) Stockholm: Statskontoret.

Sveriges Riksbank [Central Bank of Sweden], 2008. *Penningpolitiken i Sverige* [Monetary Policy in Sweden]. Stockholm: Sveriges Riksbank.

TEM, 2008. *Työllisyyskertomus 2007* [Employment Review 2007]. (Työ- ja elinkeinoministeriön julkaisuja, työ ja yrittäjyys 12/2008) Helsinki: Työ- ja elinkeinoministeriö.

VNK [Valtioneuvoston kanslia, Prime Minister's Office], 2004. *Osaava, avautuva ja uudistuva Suomi. Suomi maailmantaloudessa-selvityksen loppuraportti* [Skillful, Opening and Renewing Finland. Final Report of the Inquiry Finland in the Global Economy]. (19/2004) Helsinki: Valtioneuvoston kanslian julkaisusarja.

Velfærdskommissionen, 2005. *Fremtidens velfærd. vores valg* [The Welfare of the Future. Our Choice]. Copenhagen: Welfare Commission.

Index

For Product Safety Concerns and Information please contact our
EU representative GPSR@taylorandfrancis.com Taylor & Francis
Verlag GmbH, Kaufingerstraße 24, 80331 München, Germany.